Russian Minority Politics
in Post-Soviet Latvia and Kyrgyzstan

National and Ethnic Conflict in the 21st Century

Brendan O'Leary, Series Editor

Russian Minority Politics in Post-Soviet Latvia and Kyrgyzstan

The Transformative Power of Informal Networks

Michele E. Commercio

PENN

UNIVERSITY OF PENNSYLVANIA PRESS

PHILADELPHIA

Published by
University of Pennsylvania Press
Philadelphia, Pennsylvania 19104-4112

Printed in the United States of America on acid-free paper

10 9 8 7 6 5 4 3 2 1

Library of Congress Cataloging-in-Publication Data

Commercio, Michele E.
    Russian minority politics in post-Soviet Latvia and Kyrgyzstan : the transformative power of informal networks / Michele E. Commercio.
        p.   cm. — (National and ethnic conflict in the 21st century)
    Includes bibliographical references and index.
    ISBN 978-0-8122-4221-8 (hardcover : alk. paper)
    Russians—Latvia—Politics and government.   2. Russians—Kyrgyzstan—Politics and government.   3. Russians—Latvia—Ethnic identity.   4. Russians—Kyrgyzstan—Ethnic identity.   5. Social networks—Latvia.   6. Social networks—Kyrgyzstan.   7. Nationalism—Latvia.   8. Nationalism—Kyrgyzstan.   9. Latvia—Ethnic relations.   10. Kyrgyzstan—Ethnic relations.   I. Title.
DK504.35.R86C66   2010
305.891'7104796—dc22

                                                        2009043577

Contents

Note on Transliteration

All transliterations of Russian-language sources found in this book are based on the Library of Congress Transliteration system. All translations from Russian-language sources are my own.

Part I

Chapter 1
"What the Hell Kind
of 'Non-Native' Am I?"

To the Kazakh who divides us into "native" and "non-native"

An evil will has made it so more than once already:
Broken fates scattered,
Shaking, dangling, buried around the world
In a foreign land, on a foreign shore. . . .
LEAVE? I DON'T WANT TO, I CAN'T!

So yes, it is not only war that kills
Not only war that grays the hair.
Striking down on the spot, as if with a stray bullet,
The word of lead—"non-native."

For centuries we shared joy and tears,
We tended our gardens and raised our children,
With roots grown into this land together with you—
What the hell kind of "non-native" am I?

Our grandfathers' graves are here, our children were born here,
Here our talents and skills turned into business.
Our fathers were comrades-in-arms in the war.
What the hell kind of "non-native" am I?

My grandson and your granddaughter have been married for a long
   time.
Borshch and *besbarmak* go great together.[1]
But you—for your own—just like clockwork. . . .
What the hell kind of "non-native" am I?

You believe in Allah according to your faith?
Well, He doesn't teach people evil.

I don't know a single verse in the Koran
Where the word "non-native" appears.

You've decided to sow sparks of dissent?
But won't our children have to put out this fire?
Over you hangs a curse
Which will be uttered by your "native" grandson.

This stupid favorite troubles your soul?
But his age is short—he knows this.
Chokan and Abai don't agree with you.[2]
They would recognize me as native.[3]

The use of the phrase "non-native" in this poem about Russian-Kazakh relations suggests that though not characterized by violence, ethnic relations in post-Soviet Kazakhstan can be tense. Like the poem, which serves as a metaphor for this book, the war between Russia and Georgia that broke out in 2008 indicates the continued relevance of ethnic conflict in the post-Soviet region. The war concerned South Ossetia, a separatist region in Georgia that declared its independence in the early 1990s. The confrontation stemmed, in part, from the fact that South Ossetians have long declared a collective desire to live among "their own," or with North Ossetians who reside across the border within the Russian Federation. While Russia may be willing to accommodate this request, Georgia is committed to the preservation of its territorial integrity. Although Russia recognizes South Ossetia's independence, the international community considers the region an integral part of Georgia. This book is about ethnic relations between Russians and non-Russians in certain Central Asian and Baltic states. While some Russians in these states want to live among "their own" and thus migrate to Russia, others have no desire to abandon what they view as their homeland and therefore simply coexist or attempt to organize themselves on a political basis.

The Meaning of *To the Kazakh who divides us into "native" and "non-native"*

Though the poem entitled *To the Kazakh who divides us into "native" and "non-native"* refers to Russians in post-Soviet Kazakhstan, it depicts the plight of Russians in many post-Soviet states including Kyrgyzstan and Latvia. Svetlana Nazarova, a middle-aged Russian woman who lives in Almaty and edits a local journal, wrote the poem in 1997—Kazakhstan's officially designated "year of ethnic harmony." Three years later, Nazarova stood in front of a large group of people who had come together to celebrate Russian culture. Before she recited her poem, the poet explained that despite the fact that she and her family had lived in Kazakhstan for generations and considered Kazakhstan their homeland, since the Soviet Union's demise, Kazakhs had come to regard them as non-native.

The poem is an artistic attempt to express this irony and in so doing unite Russians who are less content in post-Soviet Kazakhstan than they were in Soviet Kazakhstan. Nazarova achieved her objective. Several Russians who were touched by the sentiment of her eloquent yet simultaneously germane poetry surrounded Nazarova at the end of the evening to receive an autographed copy of the poem. During an interview I had the pleasure of conducting a few weeks later, the poet described her view of the Russian minority question as follows: the status of Russians in Kazakhstan deteriorated once the country declared itself independent because this historic change in status gave Kazakhs the freedom to declare Russians colonizers and carriers of imperial policy and to create a state of and for the indigenous population.[4] In other words, independence gave Kazakhs the freedom to "nationalize" their state, or to build a state of and for ethnic Kazakhs.

The widely held perception among Russians that Kazakhs consider them non-native has a decisive impact on their attitudes, preferences, and behavior. This book offers a systematic comparative analysis of the initial stage of post-communist transition—1991 to 2005—and its effects on Russian minority populations in two newly independent states: Kyrgyzstan and Latvia. Keeping in mind causal mechanisms embedded in long-term historical processes, the analysis focuses on the role played by formal and informal institutions in the formation of Russian attitudes, preferences, and behavior in these states. I argue in general that informal institutions have a stronger influence on Russian minority politics than formal institutions, and in particular that the absence or presence of dense interpersonal informal networks explains different responses of Russians in Kyrgyzstan and Latvia to various forms of discrimination. The emphasis I place on informal institutions contributes to a growing body of research that suggests that many rules of the game structuring political life are established, communicated, and followed outside official boundaries.[5] Informal institutions can therefore be considered an integral element of a complex constellation of variables that shapes outcomes related to minority politics. This collection of variables in the Kyrgyz and Latvian cases is simultaneously rooted in history and connected to level of economic development.

The approximately twenty-five million Russians who lived outside

Russia proper but within the former Soviet Union suddenly acquired minority status when Lenin's geopolitical creation collapsed in 1991. The federation's disintegration forced these Russians to cope with various implications of minority status in new conditions characterized by dramatic political, economic, and social upheaval. The Russian minority problem raises compelling questions regarding nationalism and ethnic conflict, such as what factors encourage peaceful coexistence in potentially unstable multiethnic states, and how do those factors influence post-communist development? At the same time, the Kyrgyz and Latvian cases raise an important question concerning minority responses to a range of post communist challenges: Why is there more out-migration and less political mobilization among Russians in Kyrgyzstan, a state that implements accommodating policies, and less out-migration and more political mobilization among Russians in Latvia, a state that implements antagonistic policies? In probing these questions I take into account contrasting historical legacies of state socialism, perceptions of existing socioeconomic opportunity, and future expectations of socioeconomic mobility.

Because the ethnic conflict literature emphasizes drastic responses that minorities have to grievances such as violence, boundary reconfiguration, and assimilation, it overlooks critical moderate responses like out-migration and political mobilization. For example, a highly regarded taxonomy of methods to regulate ethnic conflict consists of four ways to eliminate differences—genocide, forced mass-population transfers, partition and/or secession, integration and/or assimilation—and four ways to manage differences—hegemonic control, arbitration, federalism, and consociationalism.[6] Yet tense Russian-titular relations have failed to generate any of these extreme outcomes.[7] Instead, there is a real but relatively narrow range of variation within generally moderate Russian responses to post-communist challenges that includes different levels of out-migration and political mobilization.

Frustrated minorities do adopt less confrontational measures to redress grievances. The puzzle of Russian minority politics concerns moderate responses, such as "exit" or voluntary out-migration and "voice" or political mobilization, to what Russians perceive as highly dissatisfying circumstances.[8] The existence of widespread grievances among Russians in post-Soviet states regarding their political, economic, and cultural status vis-à-vis the relevant titular nation indicates that the status quo is being challenged. That challenge, however, manifests itself in ways that are apparent only when we explore temperate strategies such as out-migration and political mobilization. And there is significant variation in terms of the degree to which Russians in these states exercise these options: while the level of Russian exit from Kyrgyzstan is higher than it is from Latvia, the level of Russian voice in Kyrgyzstan is lower than it is in Latvia.

Variation in Levels of Exit and Voice

Possible hypotheses regarding this variation include arguments about level of development, inclusive versus exclusive institutions, and regime type. Explanations found in the comparative political economy literature suggest that variation in levels of exit corresponds to variation in levels of economic development. Given that Kyrgyzstan is far less developed than Latvia, these arguments would predict a higher level of Russian exit from the Central Asian state than from the Baltic state. Although this is in fact the case, the effect of informal institutions must be taken into account in order to comprehend precisely how economics play out. The Kyrgyz and Latvian cases suggest the following: (1) both formal *and* informal institutions determine access to the economy; (2) degree of access to the public *and* private sectors of an economy influences perceptions of prospects; and (3) when minority access to the public sector is denied, level of economic development is critical because the more developed a private sector is, the more likely a minority with access to it will consider commercial activity a viable alternative to a battle with the core nation for influence in the political arena.

Institutional explanations are inclined to focus on formal rather than informal institutions. Arguments in this literature claim, for example, that inclusive institutions facilitate political participation while exclusionary institutions foster alienation from the political system. Given that minority policies implemented in Kyrgyzstan are inclusive while those implemented in Latvia are exclusive, these arguments would predict a higher level of Russian voice in Kyrgyzstan than in Latvia. The fact that Russians in the Baltic states are far more politically active than their counterparts in the Central Asian states indicates that something other than formal institutions impacts Russian voice in the post-Soviet region.

Regime type explanations also address variation in levels of exit and voice. Regime type might affect exit in the sense that all else being equal, rational, self-interested individuals will choose to migrate from an authoritarian state rather than a democratic state. And this is the case here: the level of Russian exit from the more authoritarian state, Kyrgyzstan, is higher than it is from Latvia. Data presented in Chapter 6, however, show that regime type is not a motivation for migration from either state. Furthermore, in the course of interviews I conducted with representatives from six organizations working on behalf of Russians in Kyrgyzstan and ten working on behalf of Russians in Latvia, regime type did not arise as a factor contributing to exit. Another regime type hypothesis is that levels of voice are higher in democracies than in non-democracies because people are afraid to demonstrate in authoritarian societies. Yet the "Tulip Revolution" that occurred in Kyrgyzstan in 2005 and the antigovernment protests that broke out in Burma in 2007 render this hypothesis questionable. In both cases people took to the streets despite the fact that they confronted fairly authoritarian governments.

The story this book tells is much more interesting than these arguments suggest. The Kyrgyz and Latvian cases illustrate that the absence or presence of strong informal networks explains variation in levels of exit and voice among Russians in post-Soviet states: connectedness to or isolation from such networks affects Russian access to the public and private sectors of the economy. That access (or the lack thereof) influences Russian perceptions of socioeconomic prospects, which then drive decisions regarding exit and voice. The conclusion of this analysis—that informal institutions are more influential than formal institutions—highlights the need to move beyond straightforward analyses of formal politics. In some cases, informal politics matter most.

The Significance of Informal Networks

Every Russian minority population in the post-Soviet region confronts a particular opportunity structure, or set of institutions that governs power relations between ethnic groups.[9] In the process of governing such relationships, these institutions generate perceptions of socioeconomic prospects that then determine choices made by members of the minority in question. Opportunity structures are made up of formal policies that affect citizenship, language, and public sector employment, as well as informal personnel practices that privilege the ethnic majority in the labor market. In some cases, a minority inherits dense informal networks that are based on socially shared unwritten rules designed to resist efforts made by elites to exclude the minority from power. These networks create economic opportunities that would otherwise not exist because of various nationalization efforts, and thus permit alteration of the respective opportunity structure.

Institutions are formal organizations and informal rules and procedures that structure behavior and therefore enable or privilege some actors and constrain or disadvantage other actors.[10] But formal institutions differ from informal institutions. The former are "rules and procedures that are created, communicated, and enforced through channels widely accepted as official," while the latter are "socially shared rules, usually unwritten, that are created, communicated, and enforced outside of officially sanctioned channels."[11] Legislatures, political parties, ministries, courts, bureaucracies, and labor unions are examples of formal institutions. Constitutions, laws, and policies fall into the same category because they flow through officially sanctioned channels. Clientelism, patrimonialism, clan-based norms, and corruption are examples of informal institutions. Personnel practices that favor one group and in the process undermine the mobility of other groups are also informal institutions because they are based on socially shared rules that are communicated by example rather than enforced by officially sanctioned channels.

Though the networks that Russians in some republics inherited when the Soviet Union collapsed are technically informal organizations rather than informal institutions, they operate on the basis of unwritten rules that aim to resist attempts made by elites to exclude Russians from power and can therefore be considered institutions.[12] The core rule is straightforward: Russians must "take care of their own" in an environment of discrimination that greatly restricts the labor market for those outside the titular nation. These informal networks, which encourage collective action because they provide trust, resources, communication, and opportunities in an atmosphere of shortage, resemble Soviet *blat*. Alena Ledeneva considers *blat* "a reaction of ordinary people to the structural constraints of the socialist system of distribution—a series of practices which enabled the Soviet system to function and made it tolerable."[13] The use of networks by Russians in certain post-Soviet states is a reaction of ordinary individuals to structural constraints imposed by nationalization policies and/or practices designed to curb their ability to prosper. Dense interpersonal networks render nationalization tolerable for most Russians in such states. Connections played a critical role in the second wave of business development in post-Soviet Russia, which was "formed by the representatives of the upper echelons of the Soviet bureaucracy or the nomenclatura, [and] was profound. . . . The dissolution of the Communist party and attempts to reduce the influence of the former nomenclatura do not mean that such a strong and well connected apparatus has disappeared."[14] In fact, Ledeneva argues that individuals well connected to the system, particularly those running the Komsomol, had in the immediate aftermath of the federation's demise much better starting conditions than other individuals. Chapter 4 illustrates that this is the case in Latvia as well: just as in post-Soviet Russia, networks in post-Soviet Latvia continue to play a central role in the business community. A comparison of the Kyrgyz and Latvian cases indicates that variation in network strength affects interethnic relations.

This variation is best understood within the context of the degree to which formal and informal institutional outcomes converge.[15] Figure 1.1 diagrams the role of informal networks in Russian minority politics in independent Kyrgyzstan and Latvia. Institutional outcomes converge

Figure 1.1.   The role of informal networks in Russian minority politics.

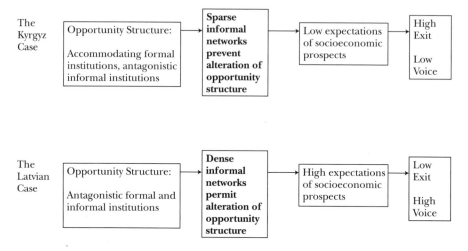

when following an informal set of rules generates a substantively similar result to what strict and exclusive observance of a formal set of rules would produce. Such convergence generates complementary institutions. Institutional outcomes diverge when following an informal set of rules generates a substantively different result from what strict and exclusive observance of a formal set of rules would produce. Such divergence produces competing institutions.

While elites in Kyrgyzstan and Latvia aim to promote the interests of the respective core nation in order to ensure core nation "ownership" of the state, Figure 1.1 indicates that they pursue this goal differently. Although Kyrgyz elites design formal institutions to promote Kyrgyz interests, they make sure these institutions simultaneously take Russian interests into consideration. This results in formal policies that accommodate Russians. In contrast, Latvian elites design formal institutions to promote the interests of Latvians at the expense of Russians. This generates formal policies that antagonize Russians.

Institutions that provide differential access to resources and thus dictate who gets what from the economy are a critical part of the Russian minority story. Both formal and informal institutions can influence minority access to the economy because they have distributional consequences. For example, informal personnel practices favoring ethnic Kyrgyz restrict Russian access to Kyrgyzstan's public sector. This means that Russians derive little benefit from state assets, meager as they are. While the country's stagnant economy presents few opportunities in general, sparse informal networks hinder Russian entry into the slowly emerging but still undeveloped private sector. In contrast, language and citizenship policies as well as personnel practices favoring Latvians restrict Russian access to Latvia's public sector. As a result, Russians realize little benefit from state assets. The country's developed economy, however, presents private sector opportunities to well-connected Russians. Dense informal networks facilitate Russian entry into the flourishing private sector. Figure 1.1 shows that whether or not Russians inherited strong interpersonal informal networks determines their ability to alter the opportunity structure created by elites in the aftermath of the Soviet Union's demise.

In the Kyrgyz case, competing informal institutions diminish the potential merits of accommodating formal institutions. Formal policies are designed to placate Russians, but the interaction of those policies with informal personnel practices blocks any intended accommodation. Because they contradict the intended effect of formal policies, widespread informal personnel practices that privilege ethnic Kyrgyz are competing informal institutions. Adding insult to injury, Russians did not inherit networks that might facilitate collective action on their behalf. So although formal policies are designed to protect Russian interests, informal nationalization practices and sparse informal networks constrain Russian conduct.

Though the Kyrgyz opportunity structure appears permissive because it is characterized by accommodating policies, it is actually confining because it is also characterized by informal personnel practices that lessen the potential merits of accommodating policies. But the key variable here is sparse informal networks, which hinder collective action and thus impede the minority's ability to alter its situation. A confining opportunity structure that provides Russians with minimal access to the public and private sectors generates negative expectations of socioeconomic prospects among Russians. These expectations have crystallized into a collective preference for exit over voice.

The Latvian case is more nuanced. Complementary informal institutions reinforce the intended effect of formal institutions: informal personnel practices and formal policies privilege Latvians at the expense of Russians. However, Russians inherited dense networks that facilitate participation in the economic and political spheres of society, and thus contradict the intended impact of these policies and practices. Russians have tapped into informal networks that emerged from the reconstruction of formal Soviet institutions to dodge nationalization policies and practices, and this allows them to reconfigure their opportunity structure. Within the context of a developed economy, these networks have enabled Russians to establish business firms as well as political parties and nongovernmental organizations that represent their interests. This has generated positive perceptions of socioeconomic prospects.

Although the Latvian opportunity structure is confining because it is characterized by antagonistic policies and practices that privilege the majority, being connected to dense informal networks permits Russians to reconfigure its boundaries. These networks contradict the intended effect of nationalization policies and informal practices, which is to obstruct Russian mobility, and provide Russians with unrestricted access to the private sector. This access generates positive expectations of socio-economic opportunity, which have crystallized into a collective preference for voice over exit.

Discovering the Informal

This study is based on qualitative data obtained from a paired comparison of two cases selected on the basis of the most-different design method.[16] The Kyrgyz and Latvian cases differ in terms of two critical independent variables: level of economic development and type of nationalization strategy.[17] World Bank data discussed in Chapter 6 establish Kyrgyzstan's economy as considerably less developed than Latvia's economy, and a comparative analysis of formal policies governing majority-minority ethnic relations including those related to citizenship, language, and public-sector employment presented in Chapter 4 reveals that Kyrgyz nationalization is accommodating while Latvian nationalization is antagonistic.

By the same token, the cases share similar background characteristics that were held constant as possible explanatory factors were explored. Both the Kyrgyz and Latvian Soviet Socialist Republics (SSR) maintained union status, which bequeathed to post-Soviet elites almost all of the trappings of statehood necessary for the implementation of nationalization projects. As Rogers Brubaker has said, "the successor units already existed as internal quasi-nation-states, with fixed territories, names, legislatures, administrative staffs, cultural and political elites."[18] Moreover, during the Soviet era Moscow imposed collectivization, industrialization, and central planning policies in the union republics that continue to affect Russian-titular relations in the post-Soviet republics. The Kyrgyz and Latvian republics were similar in terms of demography as well: at the time of the Soviet Union's collapse, the titular nation comprised 52 percent of the Kyrgyz SSR's population and 52 percent of the Latvian SSR's population, while Russians comprised between 21 and 35 percent of each republic's total population.[19]

In order to uncover sources of varied minority politics in these cases, I interpreted opinions Russians have about their individual and collective situations via textual analysis of a large collection of interviews I conducted between September 1999 and December 2000, and between June and August 2005.[20] The book is based on an original data set of 425 interviews with non-elite Russian respondents in Bishkek (the capital of Kyrgyzstan), Riga (the capital of Latvia), and Almaty (the former capital of Kazakhstan), plus numerous interviews with representatives of local Russians in each city. The Almaty data form the foundation of Chapter 7, where I assess the Kazakh case in order to develop a theory of ethnic system transition. I interviewed Russians as opposed to "Russian-speakers" because the former were accustomed to majority status for seven decades. Although the Soviet Union contained many nationalities, Russians were the numerically, politically, and culturally dominant group since the federation was founded in 1922. By 1989 they constituted 51 percent of the union's total population; Ukrainians, the next largest group, constituted 15 percent of the total population.[21] Moreover, Russian was the lingua franca throughout Soviet territory, and Russians dominated all-union institutions in most of the republics. The transfer of power to the core nation that accompanied the union's disintegration rendered Russians a numerical, political, and cultural minority within most successor states. Russians in these states therefore acquired an unprecedented subordinate status vis-à-vis the respective titular nation.

Unlike many scholars, I do not define the twenty-five million Russians residing in non-Russian republics at the time of the federation's demise in broad terms emphasizing the language component of identity. Sweeping terms like "Russian-speakers" and "Russified settler communities" blur acute historical and cultural differences that distinguish Russians from other Russian-speaking groups.[22] While Russians, Ukrainians, and Belarusians may speak Russian, each group has its own homeland, native language, culture, and history. As Walker Connor points out, "'Mother Russia' evokes one type of response from a Russian and something quite different from a Ukrainian."[23] The inclusion of the many groups that speak Russian into a conglomerate collective identity precludes a study based solely on the ethnic group that suffered the most dramatic transformation in status when the Soviet Union collapsed. This book is thus based on interviews with individuals who identify as Russian, rather than Russian-speaking Ukrainian or Russian-speaking Belarusian.

I conducted research in capital cities for two reasons. First, headquarters of political parties and nongovernmental organizations that represent Russians as well as associations that facilitate Russian out-migration are located in capital cities. Sometimes these entities maintain affiliate branches outside the capital, but this is not always the case. Second, Russians in post-Soviet states tend to be concentrated in capital cities. Bishkek is Kyrgyzstan's most Russian city: Russians constitute 33 percent of the capital's total population.[24] Though more dispersed than Kyrgyz-stan's Russian population, Latvia's Russian population is concentrated in three cities, including the capital: Russians constitute 55 percent of Daugavpils's population, 51 percent of Rezekne's population, and 44 percent of Riga's population.[25] Kazakhstan's Russian population is also dispersed: Russians reside in all fourteen administrative regions. However, they are most heavily concentrated in five oblasts and two cities, constituting over 40 percent of the East Kazakhstan, Northern Kazakh-stan, Pavlodar, Karaganda, and Kostanai oblast populations, and over 40 percent of the Astana and Almaty city populations.[26]

I triangulated interview data in an attempt to address the inevitable problem of questionable and/or unreliable responses. This means that I interviewed three groups of Russians in each city. The first group was potential migrants, or Russians who at the time of the interview were planning to move to Russia. While I cannot confirm that these Russians actually left, the point is that they were in the process of figuring out the logistics of migration when the interviews took place.[27] The second group was likely permanent residents, or Russians who at the time of the interview planned to remain in their current city of residence. Lastly, the third group was representatives of local Russians affiliated with political parties or nongovernmental organizations that defend the rights of Russians.[28] Data from interviews with potential migrants and likely permanent residents informed questions I later posed to representatives of each Russian minority population. Answers to these questions served as a check on responses from interviews with additional potential migrants and likely permanent residents. Elites confirmed trends in potential migrant and likely permanent resident data, while potential migrants and likely permanent residents confirmed trends in elite data. I interviewed respondents in their native language without the assistance of an interpreter in parks, private homes, offices, or my apartment. With one exception interviews were open-ended, tape-recorded, and transcribed by local Russians. Potential migrants in Riga, however, completed a written survey because bureaucratic restrictions prevented oral interviews at the Latvian Ministry of Interior Immigration Police.

Though a post hoc check of each sample ensured variation in typical categories such as age, gender, education, and occupation, I generated potential migrant and likely permanent resident samples differently.[29] Repeated visits to the organization responsible at the time for processing paperwork that alleviates bureaucratic hassles migrants encounter en route to Russia produced each potential migrant sample. Potential migrants in Bishkek visited the Federal Migration Services of Russia, which is a Russian government agency with branches in Armenia, Kyrgyzstan, Latvia, Tajikistan, and Turkmenistan. Potential migrants in

Riga visited either the Federal Migration Services of Russia or the Latvian Ministry of Interior Immigration Police, but bureaucratic restrictions blocked access to the former so I conducted interviews at the latter. Finally, potential migrants in Almaty visited a private institution called the Public Foundation for Migration.[30] I went to each organization three times a week and approached every possible Russian with an interview request until I obtained a large set of interviews containing similar responses. Because I was an anonymous entity to whom they could tell their personal story without repercussion, potential migrants rarely turned down my request for an interview.

It was a challenge to generate a heterogeneous sample of Russian likely permanent residents because this group does not gather at a particular place to accomplish a particular task. Moreover, when I started my fieldwork entrepreneurs were just beginning to establish market research firms and they frequently confronted bureaucratic restrictions regarding survey subject matter. I therefore utilized the "snowball" method of selection to interview members of a population that is difficult to locate because it is so spread out.[31] Referrals from initial interviews with Russians I knew fairly well eventually created an extensive network of contacts. Most initial respondents put me in touch with a few Russians they thought might be willing to discuss the Russian minority problem; Russians who were willing to talk about the issue provided contact information for additional Russians. This method gradually produced samples of Russian likely permanent residents of Bishkek, Riga, and Almaty that vary in standard categories like age, gender, education, and occupation.

While the interview data are dispersed throughout the book, they dominate the second half. The first part of the book establishes a framework for understanding the parameters of the opportunity structures Russians respond to in post-Soviet states. Chapter 2 presents various approaches to understanding Russian minority politics in Soviet successor states and, in so doing, emphasizes the need to consider the significance of informal networks as a key explanatory variable. Chapter 3 discusses certain aspects of the socialist legacy with powerful implications for the Russian minority question such as federalism, nationalities policy, demographics, and the success or failure of locally initiated affirmative action polices. Chapter 4 considers the role informal networks play in the reconfiguration of opportunity structures that arose in the wake of the Soviet Union's collapse.

The second part of the book analyzes Russian perceptions of and responses to opportunity structures in post-Soviet Kyrgyzstan and Latvia. Chapter 5 illustrates that although Russians in both states view themselves as victims of discrimination, Russians in the Baltic state envision a brighter future for themselves than do Russians in the Central Asian state. The conventional wisdom argues that this is because the former picture a prosperous future connected to Latvia's membership in the European Union, while the latter cannot even dream of such opulence because membership in such an elite club is not an option.[32] In fact, Russians in Latvia envision a brighter future for themselves than do Russians in Kyrgyzstan because the former have utilized informal networks to organize on an economic and political basis, while the latter lack the tools required to achieve this objective. Chapter 6 analyzes Russian responses, including exit and voice, to perceptions of socioeconomic prospects that stem directly from the opportunity structure they confront on a daily basis. Chapter 7 develops a theory of ethnic system transition based on the Kyrgyz, Kazakh, and Latvian cases, which states that a minority can move from a subordinate to a satisfactory position vis-à-vis the majority if (1) elites dominate the public sector, and (2) the state in question has a developed economy.

Chapter 2
Informal Networks, Exit, and Voice

To the Kazakh who divides us into "native" and "non-native"

So yes, it is not only war that kills
Not only war that grays the hair.
Striking down on the spot, as if with a stray bullet,
The word of lead—"non-native"
　　　　　　　—Svetlana Nazarova, *Ne ostavliaite na potom. . . .*

This stanza from Nazarova's poem suggests that a label as emotionally laden as "non-native" speaks volumes to Russians in post-Soviet states other than the Russian Federation. The union's disintegration had a devastating effect on Russians not only because it conferred minority status on them vis-à-vis the respective titular nation, but also because it thrust them into newly independent states dominated by elites determined to promote "their own" through nationalization policies and/or practices. In discussing various approaches to understanding Russian minority politics in Soviet successor states, this chapter highlights the need to recognize the importance of informal networks as a critical explanatory variable. A brief discussion of the difference between nationalization and nation-building will clarify the intended meaning of the phrase in Nazarova's poem "it is not only war that kills."

Ethnic Differentiation Versus Ethnic Integration

Nationalization differs from nation-building, which is a process that transforms a traditional entity into a modern state by uniting a diverse population into a nation or an integrated community based on a shared national identity. Efficient processes of communication are critical for the foundation of a coherent integrated society.[1] What is happening in the post-Soviet states explored here has nothing to do with nation-building: these states are not traditional entities on the path to modern statehood. Instead they are fairly developed—though arguably misdeveloped—states in the midst of transition. Moreover, elites in these states do not seek to transform the multiethnic societies over which they preside into integrated nations based on a shared identity; they are not engaged in nation-building, or "building group cohesion and group loyalty for purposes of international representation and domestic planning."[2] On the contrary, post-Soviet elites are engaged in nationalization, which is founded on the principle of *ethnic differentiation* rather than *ethnic integration.*

The nation-building literature also fails to explain political development in Soviet successor states because it either considers ethnicity a phenomenon that vanishes with the advent of modernity or ignores the role of ethnicity in this process entirely. Walker Connor criticizes nation-building scholars for overlooking the importance of ethnicity in any state's development, whether democratic, authoritarian, federal, unitary, Asian, African, or European.[3] He highlights problems associated with ethnic diversity, such as "the importance of ethnic consciousness as a barrier to the political integration of the multiethnic state."[4] Developments in Kyrgyzstan and Latvia suggest that ethnic diversity has a strong impact on a state's political trajectory. Elites in both states politicize ethnicity in order to promote the respective titular nation, and this emphasis on ethnic differences furthers nationalization.

According to Rogers Brubaker, nationalizing states "are conceived by their dominant elites as nation-states, of and for particular ethnocultural nations, yet as 'incomplete' or 'unrealized' nation-states, as insufficiently 'national' in a variety of senses."[5] To resolve this problem elites take measures "to promote the language, culture, demographic preponderance, economic flourishing, or political hegemony of the core ethnocultural nation."[6] All post-Soviet states can be characterized as nationalizing because they seek, albeit to varying degrees, to promote the core nation through formal policies and/or informal practices. The one caveat to this statement, which I discuss in Chapter 7, is that once elites consolidate the political hegemony of the core nation, their determination to promote the economic flourishing of that nation begins to wane. While the foundation of most post-Soviet nationalization projects is a cluster of formal policies that privilege the titular nation in as many areas as possible, informal practices with the same function reinforce those policies. Nationalization cannot be properly understood unless the nature and impact of such practices are seriously considered. The Kyrgyz and Latvian cases support Brubaker's prediction that "the everyday experience of successor state Russians," including anti-Russian attitudes and practices, will be more important than formal policies in stimulating Russian exit from post-Soviet states.[7]

Brubaker analyzes the relationship between the politics of three entities: a Russian diaspora, the post-Soviet state in which that diaspora resides, and Russia. He argues that we cannot grasp the consequences of the Soviet Union's collapse without taking into account distinct and mutually antagonistic nationalisms of a national minority, the nationalizing state in which its members reside, and its external homeland. Brubaker's assertion that the antagonistic nationalisms of a national minority and the nationalizing state in which its members reside influence the preferences and behavior of the minority in question is apt, but his emphasis on the external homeland to which the minority belongs is overstated. Russia has made noise on a sporadic basis about the treatment of its compatriots in the "near abroad" but has done very little to alleviate grievances.[8] Russia's decision to avoid meddling in domestic affairs concerning its compatriots in the near abroad is reflected in the interviews cited throughout this book, which suggest that nationalization policies and practices as well as local economic conditions have a *far* greater impact on minority perceptions than Russia's foreign policy. Because Brubaker's work is largely theoretical, he calls for "a more nuanced, differentiated approach that would take systematic account of the varied and multiform conditions facing successor state Russians and their varied and multiform responses, including migration, to those conditions."[9] My analysis begins where Brubaker's analysis ends.

Post-Soviet nationalization strategies are characterized in terms of how formal policies governing majority-minority ethnic relations affect members of a specific Russian minority population. These projects are based on a cluster of policies related to demography, the composition of the citizenry, the primary language of instruction in government and institutes of education, and the legal designation of various languages. The distinction between language of interethnic communication, official language, and state language renders an understanding of linguistic subtleties that characterize types of nationalization projects adopted by post-Soviet elites possible.

Each union republic adopted legislation in the late 1980s designating the titular language the sole state language of the republic. But at that time, the notion of a state language was alien to Soviet citizens because the federation lacked a formal state language. Lenin ensured the absence of a formal state language when his fear of Russian chauvinism drove him to eliminate a provision of tsarist law requiring the mandatory use of Russian in state offices.[10] Though Russian was the union's lingua franca, it was not legally codified as the state language. Russians thus found themselves in an unfamiliar situation when union republic elites adopted legislation that not only identified a state language but also designated the titular language the state language.

This change in policy threatened Russians' identity and status despite the fact that the new legislation defined Russian as the language of inter-ethnic communication. The phrase "language of interethnic communication" merely acknowledged the obvious: Russian was, and would continue to be, the region's sole common language. Moreover, the language laws were a psychological affront to Russian identity and status because they gave symbolic significance to languages most Russians did not speak.[11] The practical effect of the legislation, which established the mandatory use of the state language in most workplaces, was to render Russians' job security tenuous. Russians therefore considered the new language laws a rejection of their language and a grave economic threat.

Most representatives of Russian minority populations in post-Soviet states seek to elevate the legal status of Russian from language of inter-ethnic communication to official language. They appear cognizant of the fact that elites are reluctant to define Russian as a second state language because this would equalize the status and public use of Russian and the respective titular language. Representatives of local Russians realize that equalization contradicts the fundamental premise of nationalization, which is that ethnic differences matter. As a result, most representatives seek a compromise. The legal distinction between a state and an official language is slight: the former is the dominant means of communication in all spheres of society, while the latter can be used on an equal basis with the state language in certain spheres of society such as government. Nevertheless, evidence indicates that the distinction is of practical and symbolic importance to Russians in the post-Soviet region. Representatives of Russian minority populations hope to achieve two objectives by promoting Russian as an official language. The symbolic task is to secure legal recognition of the fact that Russian is spoken to some degree by the overwhelming majority of successor-state residents and thus remains a vital means of communication; the practical task is to secure for Russians the right to use their native language in as many public interactions as possible.

One reason Kyrgyz nationalization is classified as accommodating is that post-Soviet language policy is characterized by a delicate balance between the promotion of Kyrgyz and the preservation of Russian: Kyrgyz is the state language and Russian is the official language. In part, Latvian nationalization is classified as antagonistic because post-Soviet language policy is characterized by a deliberate attempt to eliminate the legal use of Russian in the public sphere: Latvian is the state language and Russian is a foreign language equal in status to Chinese or Arabic.

Few post-Soviet nationalization projects are particularly accommodating or antagonistic; elites in most states adopt projects that fall somewhere in between these types. Three factors influence the direction of a particular nationalization strategy: (1) national security concerns, (2) economic considerations, and (3) the socioeconomic status of the core nation vis-à-vis the respective Russian population. The more dependent a post-Soviet state is on Russia for national security needs and on Soviet infrastructure and the skills of its local Russian population for economic prosperity, the more likely it is to implement accommodating nationalization; the less dependent a post-Soviet state is on these factors, the more likely it is to implement antagonistic nationalization. The socioeconomic status of the core nation vis-à-vis the respective Russian population, a factor that stems from the extent to which Russians dominated state and party organs during the Soviet era, influences the degree to which nationalization privileges the former group at the expense of the latter group. Chapter 4 elaborates on the connection between these variables and the type of nationalization implemented in Kyrgyzstan and Latvia.

Russians in post-Soviet states respond to a widespread sense of perceived ethnic discrimination that is a direct result of nationalization. By perceived ethnic discrimination I mean instances and/or patterns of discrimination that Russians believe exist; whether they actually exist is of little importance. Consider Brubaker's comment on the significance of perception: "To ask whether such policies, practices, and so on are 'really' nationalizing makes little sense. For present purposes, a nationalizing state (or nationalizing practice, policy, or event) is not one whose representatives, authors, or agents understand and articulate it as such, *but rather one that is perceived as such* in the field of a national minority or the external national homeland."[12] Despite the fact that they face different types of nationalization projects, Russians in Kyrgyzstan and Latvia view themselves as victims of systemic discrimination based on ethnicity. Russians in both states feel that their ethnic identity compromises their ability to put bread on the table. While we might expect antagonistic nationalization to produce a widespread sense of perceived discrimination among Russians, the fact that accommodating nationalization generates the same sentiment is surprising. The key to explaining this counterintuitive finding lies in the source of perceived inequity. In Latvia, where elites implement antagonistic policies, perceptions of inequuity are a result of formal policies and informal personnel practices; in Kyrgyzstan, where elites implement accommodating policies, these notions stem solely from informal personnel practices.

The fact that Russian exit is a more prevalent response to accommodating nationalization than to antagonistic nationalization is ironic. But motivations for Russian out-migration from Kyrgyzstan have nothing to do with accommodating policies. Instead they have everything to do with informal personnel practices and sparse informal networks, both of which restrict access to resources. The Latvian case is different. While formal policies and informal practices spur the low level of Russian exit we do see, Russian connectedness to dense informal networks diminishes adverse effects of these policies and practices and thus stunts out-migration. Coordinated activity in the private sector spawns positive perceptions of opportunity, which generally outweigh objectionable consequences of nationalization. The ability to survive, and in some cases thrive, despite nationalization policies and practices designed to restrict mobility encourages Russians to remain in Latvia.

Approaches to the Study of Russian Minority Politics

Scholars tend to study Russian minority politics in post-Soviet states in terms of national identity. For example, David Laitin claims that in response to challenges posed by post-Soviet nationalization, Russian-speakers in Estonia and Latvia are likely to embrace linguistic assimilation while Russian-speakers in Kazakhstan and Ukraine are likely to adopt a new Russian-speaker identity.[13] Neil Melvin argues that the poorly developed character of Russian ethnicity during the pre-Soviet and Soviet eras contributes to a weak sense of identity among Russians in independent Estonia, Latvia, Ukraine, Kazakhstan, and Moldova. According to Melvin, this "ill-defined nature of Russian ethnicity" deprives Russians in successor states of a base for political mobilization.[14] Similarly, Jeff Chinn and Robert Kaiser find that since Russians in union republics did not view themselves as a minority during the Soviet era, they failed to form minority communities in independent states during the post-Soviet era.[15] They reason that this lack of a minority identity renders political mobilization exceedingly difficult for Russians. And Bhavna Dave argues that various factors, including "the internal fragmentation within the so-called community of Russian-speakers," contribute to the lack of ethnic conflict in Kazakhstan.[16] She suggests that this group is plagued by "the contradictory legacy of the imperial, national, and regional elements" of its identity.[17]

This book bucks the trend because it addresses Russian responses to post-communist challenges other than national identity formation such as exit, voice, and what I call coexistence. Albert Hirschman's original conceptualization of responses employees and customers have to a particular firm includes three possibilities: exit, voice, and loyalty.[18] Dissatisfied members of a particular group or organization choose to exercise exit or voice. The former is an attempt to escape disquieting conditions through flight (in the context of ethnic conflict we call this migration), while the latter is an attempt to alter such conditions internally through resistance (in the context of ethnic conflict we call this political mobilization). Loyalty is a response adopted by individuals who are satisfied enough with the group or organization in question to accept its rules of the game. Depending on the extent of the satisfaction, in the context of ethnic conflict, loyalty can facilitate assimilation.

The difference between loyalty and coexistence is a question of degree: people who coexist are less satisfied than people who are loyal to the entity in question. Coexistence can be interpreted as a step toward loyalty as it refers to a response adopted by individuals who do not flee or resist either because they deem these choices too costly and/or risky or because they possess the means to alleviate grievances to an extent that renders membership in the group or organization tolerable. Because it does not imply full acceptance of the rules of the game, coexistence is unlikely to facilitate assimilation and can more easily morph into exit or voice than loyalty. We see coexistence rather than loyalty among Russians in Kyrgyzstan, Kazakhstan, and Latvia who do not exercise exit or voice. In contrast to other scholars, including David Laitin, I offer evidence of continued Russian resistance to assimilation even in post-Soviet states like Latvia that have not experienced a major outflow of Russians.

This book explores the effect of formal and informal institutions on divergent preferences of Russian minorities within multiethnic states and thus problematizes inclinations. In considering preferences, goals, and strategies unknown and thus something to be explained, I adopt a historical institutionalist approach to the Russian minority problem. Historical institutionalism avoids broad assumptions about self-interested behavior and views preference formation as problematic rather than given.[19] The preference for exit, voice, or coexistence must be analyzed within the context of institutional evolution during the Soviet and early post-Soviet periods. While historical institutionalism argues that in the process of constraining and refracting politics institutions shape preferences, it underscores the fact that institutions are never the *sole* cause of outcomes. Since formal and informal institutions have critical resource distribution consequences in the sense that they determine the degree to which Russians in post-Soviet states have access to the public and private sectors of an economy, they comprise the foundation of the opportunity structure that influences perceptions of socioeconomic prospects.

Historical institutionalists differ from rational choice institutionalists in terms of their interpretation of the institutions they study: are they "distributive switchboards" that serve to highlight the uneven distribution of resources as the former claim, or "sites of cooperation" where problems of collective action are resolved as the latter claim?[20] A comprehensive analysis of the Russian minority problem suggests that this dichotomy is misleading. In fact, institutions can function as distributive switchboards *or* sites of cooperation depending on the context. Jack Knight's emphasis on the discriminating benefits of institutions or the distributional consequences of institutions helps disentangle this point.[21] Consider informal nationalization practices affecting public sector employment: in the Kyrgyz and Latvian cases, these practices serve as distributive switchboards because they reserve access to public sector employment for members of the titular nation and deny such access to Russians. These practices have obvious distributional consequences. At the same time, the Baltic case illustrates that informal networks can function as sites of cooperation. Interpersonal networks inherited from the Soviet era enabled Russians in Latvia to establish a weighty presence in the private sector, where they continue to resolve problems of collective action. This book illustrates that in response to institutional obstacles that exclude Russians from the public sector, Russians in Kyrgyzstan choose exit because they lack mechanisms for cooperation while Russians in Latvia choose voice because they have tools that facilitate coordinated activity.

The Birth of Informal Networks

My explanation for varied Russian minority politics is path dependent because it considers institutions "products of specific historical episodes or turning points that result in configurations that then set constraints on subsequent developments."[22] The pertinent historical episode is the collapse of the Soviet Union, which allowed for the emergence of nationalization policies and practices. The federation's disintegration also generated the dissolution of most state and party organs. This enabled the birth of informal networks. These networks, made up of individuals who were closely associated with formal Soviet institutions, play a crucial role in post-Soviet societies because they provide access to valuable resources. The degree to which Russians are connected to this kind of network profoundly influences their perceptions and preferences. Thus, institutions serve as constraints on and resources for actors engaged in post-communist battles over economic, political, and cultural assets, and in this capacity have a direct effect on ethnic relations.

Institutions emerge within a particular historical context. Scholars from various fields acknowledge the importance of historical legacies in political, economic, social, and cultural evolution. While the literature on post-communist transformation is informed by the general notion that legacies of state socialism matter, it tends to treat such legacies in monolithic terms.[23] Grzegorz Ekiert and Stephen E. Hanson's analysis of how communist rule affects capitalism and democracy in Central and Eastern Europe is an exception precisely because it accentuates the need to take issues of space and time into account in order to identify *distinct* legacies of state socialism.[24] In the following pages I present a contextualized regional comparison of preferences and behaviors exhibited by Russian minority populations, which demonstrates that legacies of state socialism must be differentiated in order to comprehend diverse outcomes related to exit and voice.

There is an important distinction between legacies of Leninism and legacies of state socialism. The former refer to institutions of Leninism found in all communist countries, while the latter refer to institutional variation and idiosyncratic social relations and cultural patterns that rendered a communist country or region somehow unique.[25] The feature of state socialism that most strongly influences Russian perceptions of post-Soviet nationalization in Kyrgyzstan and Latvia is the degree to which the respective Russian population dominated state and party organs at the end of the 1980s. While the party, Komsomol, and KGB or variations of these institutions were found in all communist countries, Leninist ideology did not determine varied degrees of Russian institutional dominance in the republics during the Soviet era. Yet this variation was an intrinsic element of the system that influenced diverse patterns of social relations in the Central Asian and Baltic republics. For reasons discussed in the next chapter, throughout the post–World War II era Baltic Russians were part of and Central Asian Russians were ousted from dense political networks embedded in the party, Komsomol, and KGB.

The Latvian case supports Ekiert and Hanson's argument that certain manifestations of state socialism have had *positive* effects on post-communist transformation. Russian dominance of state and party organs in the Latvian SSR facilitated coordinated activity in the early post-Soviet era that enabled Russians to engage Latvia's business sector and thus participate in the market economy. At the same time, the Kyrgyz case highlights *negative* legacies of state socialism that cannot be ignored. Titular dominance of state and party organs in the Kyrgyz SSR hindered coordinated activity among Russians in the early post-Soviet era and continues to render their ability to work in the country's emerging business sector exceedingly difficult.

The extent to which Russians inherited dense informal networks also influences the degree to which they mobilize politically. In both the Baltic and Central Asian regions, formal party, Komsomol, and KGB networks were transformed into informal networks with the Soviet

Union's demise. In the early post-Soviet era, these informal networks facilitated the creation of political parties and nongovernmental organizations that represent Latvia's Russian population. But in the Kyrgyz SSR Russians were ousted from party, Komsomol, and KGB networks and were thus isolated from the informal networks that arose as the Soviet Union collapsed. Russians in post-Soviet Kyrgyzstan have difficulty establishing effective associations capable of representing their interests because they lack the informal networks that Russians in post-Soviet Latvia possess. The next chapter addresses historical conditions that either connected Russians to or isolated Russians from party, Komsomol, and KGB networks during the Soviet era.

Chapter 3
Soviet Socialist Legacies and Post-Soviet Nationalization

To the Kazakh who divides us into "native" and non-native"

Our grandfathers' graves are here, our children were born here,
Here our talents and skills turned into business.
Our fathers were comrades-in-arms in the war.
What the hell kind of "non-native" am I?
          —Svetlana Nazarova, *Ne ostavliaite na potom.* . . .

Given the 1916 rebellion against Russian colonization and Moscow's subsequent determination to Russify Kazakh culture, the implied assertion of friendly Russian-Kazakh relations in this stanza of Nazarova's poem is questionable.[1] On top of that, independence rendered Russian-titular relations in all Soviet successor states, including Kazakhstan, potentially conflictual. A key premise of this book is that legacies of state socialism shape various post-Soviet political phenomena such as the emergence of nationalization projects in general, the development of distinct types of nationalization projects in particular, and, most important, whether or not Russians inherited dense informal networks.

Certain aspects of the Soviet legacy such as federalism, nationalities policy, demographics, and the success or failure of locally initiated affirmative action policies have powerful implications for the Russian minority question. Federalism and nationalities policy shed light on the origins of post-Soviet nationalization. The territorial division of the Soviet Union based on nationality provided elites with the necessary tools to implement nationalization projects in the aftermath of the USSR's demise. While *korenizatsiya*, or nativization, created long-term enthusiasm for the development of local languages and traditions, Russification generated resentment toward Russians that provided legitimacy for nationalization policies and practices. In addition, demographic trends and the success or failure of locally initiated affirmative action polices in the Central Asian and Baltic regions determined the degree to which Russians dominated various state and party organs; in other words, the results of these affirmative action policies governed the socioeconomic status of Russians. And, as stated previously, the socioeconomic status of the core nation compared to Russians contributed to decisions made by elites to adopt accommodating or antagonistic nationalization.

Soviet Federalism: A Source of Post-Soviet National Self-Determination

The foundation of Soviet federalism was a set of union republics that served as territorial homelands for different nationalities. Although these republics were an integral part of the union and did not function as independent units, they possessed important elements of statehood. Elites presiding over union republics were well equipped to implement nationalization projects when the Soviet Union collapsed because they were able to manipulate such manifestations of statehood to their advantage.

Various characteristics of the federal system enshrined in the 1924 constitution facilitated the development of post-Soviet nationalization. Scholars have argued for decades that the union's structure provided certain groups with attributes of formal statehood that allowed elites to pursue the interests of their own nation. For example, in the 1970s Teresa Rakowska-Harmstone claimed that Soviet federalism "proved important in the ability of major nationalities . . . to withstand powerful pressures toward assimilation . . . [and] affords numerous opportunities for evading central directives and promoting local interests."[2] In the 1980s, Gail Lapidus acknowledged that the federation provided "an organizational context, a political legitimacy, and a cultural impetus for the assertion of group interests, values, and demands and even served to shape group identities."[3] In the early 1990s, Philip G. Roeder made a similar argument regarding the role of federal institutions in fueling ethnic mobilization: "Institutions that were designed to expand Moscow's control over ethnic groups . . . have taken on a new life. Autonomous homelands provide essential resources for the collective mobilization of ethnic communities, and both federal institutions and indigenous cadres shape ethnic agendas."[4] And in the mid-1990s, Rogers Brubaker suggested that the purpose of the union republics was "to serve as the institutional vehicles for national self-determination."[5]

Moscow was compelled to create a territorial-administrative system capable of accommodating a large multiethnic state. Contentious debate generated a decision to adopt a federal system based on the principle of national-territory autonomy.[6] In pursuit of socialist equality and the eventual union of denationalized peoples, the Bolsheviks created administrative territories based on the nationality principle. However, they were deeply troubled by the question of whether groups like tribes and clans should be classified as nations. Ethnographers, geographers, and statisticians assisted Bolshevik leaders in determining which groups should in fact be identified as nations.[7] Moscow then carved up the map on the basis of ethnographic, economic, and administrative/political principles in order to give each designated nation a homeland.

But these homelands were not created equally. The hierarchical federation was composed of fifteen union republics that reigned supreme in terms of status, as well as dozens of subordinate units including autonomous republics, oblasts, and *okrugs*. The constitution granted union republics the right to secede from the federation and extended considerable administrative and cultural autonomy to the titular nation of each union republic. These privileges were not extended to other units. Union republics also possessed formal attributes of sovereignty such as indigenous elites and republic-level political, economic, and cultural institutions, which gradually afforded elites a sense of republic ownership.

The politics of the immediate post-Soviet era suggest that Rakowska-Harmstone, Lapidus, Roeder, and Brubaker were right: federalism did facilitate national self-determination. Not only were elites equipped to transform union republics into independent states, but they also had at their disposal institutional and psychological tools required to implement extensive nationalization projects. Not surprisingly, independence heightened the sense of republic ownership elites had acquired during the Soviet era. Moreover, elites who wished to nationalize the state over which they presided were able to mobilize popular support based on the plausible claim that Moscow had, at some point, persecuted the respective titular nation. This made it easy for elites to frame nationalization projects as remedial and therefore justifiable.

Soviet Nationalities Policy: Inconsistent But Beneficial to Post-Soviet Elites

Federalism was one of two responses to the nationalities question. The acquisition of vast territory encompassing one-sixth of the earth's land surface as well as numerous ethnic, linguistic, and religious groups presented the Bolsheviks with a unique circumstance: "Article 70 of the 1977 Soviet Constitution defined the USSR as 'an integral federal multinational state.' While some 90 percent of all contemporary countries are also multinational, there are few states so ethnically complex. The 1989 Soviet census listed more than 100 national groups."[8] Moscow's management of one hundred plus nationalities for over seventy years influences ethnic relations in post-Soviet states today. However, the center's policy toward the nationalities was inconsistent. Initially Moscow implemented *korenizatsiya*, which was designed to promote non-Russian peoples and develop non-Russian languages and cultures. Ultimately, *korenizatsiya* provided post-Soviet elites with valuable cultural resources that formed the basis of individual nationalization projects. After Lenin died Moscow implemented Russification, which entailed the promotion of Russian personnel and the development of Russian culture and traditions. This was, of course, at the expense of indigenous personnel, cultures, and traditions. Russification eventually generated anti-Russian sentiment that elites channeled into support for nationalization projects in the aftermath of the Soviet Union's demise.

Lenin's approach to the nationalities question was based on the assumption that Russian chauvinism represented a grave threat to the multiethnic Union of Soviet Socialist Republics. The founder of the union considered non-Russian nationalism a logical consequence of the negative experience minorities had as second-class citizens in tsarist Russia, which he referred to as a prison of nations. To counteract Russian chauvinism, Lenin implemented *korenizatsiya*, an accommodating policy based on ethnic pluralism, cultural development, and socioeconomic equalization. *Korenizatsiya* thrived during the 1920s and early 1930s: "Despite its strong admixture of political expediency, the Bolshevik attitude toward nationality problems had a more positive side in the 1920s. During most of that decade the Communist Party leadership attempted to chart a course that curbed Russian chauvinism and treated non-Russian national groups more fairly than had been the case in the late tsarist era."[9] Political and cultural equality were core components of *korenizatsiya*, which encouraged the training and promotion of indigenous personnel, the development and use of native languages, and the celebration of local cultures. While Lenin did consider the merging of nations a historically determined and inevitable process, *korenizatsiya* supported the flourishing (*ratsvet*), rather than merging (*sliyanie*), of nations. His dialectic approach was based on the premise that "permitting, indeed encouraging for a time the national language and other overt characteristics of the various national groups would lead the groups toward fusion."[10] But Lenin also believed that socioeconomic equality was a prerequisite for the *sliyanie* of nations, and this conviction explains his decision to implement a policy geared toward the development of deprived regions and nations. In the end, "the policy of socio-economic equalization among regions and peoples increasingly came to be the key operational principle behind the Leninist solution, as it lends itself to quantifiable policy measures and observable implementation."[11]

In contrast, Lenin's successor viewed non-Russian nationalism as a grave threat to the stability of the union. Stalin embraced Russification, a policy that promoted Russian personnel and demanded official use of the Russian language throughout Soviet territory. He worked arduously to advance assimilation, which he defined as the fusion of all nations into the Russian nation. The treatment of non-Russians deteriorated considerably under Stalin's dictatorship: "After the early 1930s, when *korenizatsiia* reached its height, Stalin's drive for industrialization and personal autocracy made sensitivity to ethnic interests a thing of the past. Under his dictatorship, the state's treatment of non-Russian peoples reached an absolute nadir as their national Communist leaders were imprisoned or executed, their national writers and artists persecuted, and several small nationalities deported from their homelands."[12] Stalin relied on various forms of terror including violent political purges, artificially created famine, and deportation to eliminate groups he considered "nationalist." He also Russified local languages and widened the public sphere of communication in which the use of Russian was required. A 1938 policy designating Russian an obligatory subject in non-Russian schools rendered Russian the most common language in urban locales. In the aftermath of World War II, Stalin launched a campaign to promote the Russian nation, which he characterized as the "elder brother" committed to the development and civilization of non-Russians, to new heights: "In later stages of his life, Stalin became more explicit about the primacy of the Russians. His well known toast in the Kremlin at the end of World War II singled them out as the most heroic of the Soviet peoples. The 'anti-cosmopolitan' and anti-Western campaigns of the 1940s, along with absurd claims of Russian superiority, flowed from this commitment to elevate the Russians above all others."[13]

If Lenin encouraged the flourishing of nations and Stalin encouraged the merging of nations, Khrushchev promoted the simultaneous flourishing and drawing together (*sblizhenie*) of nations. In theory, *sblizhenie* was supposed to eventually generate *sliyanie*. Khrushchev adopted a fairly moderate stance toward the nationalities question that was neither as accommodating as Lenin's position nor as brutal as Stalin's position. Indeed, certain policies were favorable to non-Russians. For example, Khrushchev eliminated a number of central all-union industrial ministries and created over one hundred regional economic councils in an effort to decentralize economic decision-making power. This gave elites in the republics increased jurisdiction over local economic issues. Other policies, however, were unfavorable to non-Russians. For example, in the late 1950s Khrushchev implemented education reforms that privileged Russian as the language of instruction in native schools, and exempted Russians from learning native languages. These policies "paved the way for the promotion of Russian language teaching. . . . Whereas almost half of the non-Russian population claimed a knowledge of Russian by the 1979 census, only 3.5 per cent of Russians could claim a similar knowledge of another Soviet language."[14] Khrushchev ultimately settled on a compromised understanding of the nationalities question whereby non-Russian nationalities would flourish, gradually come together, and eventually merge into one nation.[15] It was Khrushchev's successor who boldly asserted that the nationalities question had been solved.

The claim that decades of socialism had finally created a "Soviet People" constituted the essence of Brezhnev's approach to the nationalities question. During his tenure in office, "a discursive frame established and enforced by the Soviet regime boldly proclaimed that the USSR had 'solved' its nationalities problems and had produced 'a new historical community—the Soviet people' (*Sovetskii narod*)."[16] Brezhnev's decision to abandon Lenin's commitment to socioeconomic equality was particularly injurious and offensive to non-Russians. The alleged existence of a *Sovetskii narod* weakened the logic behind the need to pursue socioeconomic equalization, and by the end of the 1970s the regime had stopped promoting such equality: "After Leonid Brezhnev, in his speech of December 1972 commemorating the fiftieth anniversary of the USSR, declared that 'the problem of the equalization of development of the national republics has been resolved, on the whole,' the word 'equalization' disappeared from published plan documents."[17]

Because the concept of a *Sovetskii narod* was based on the notion of a single geopolitical space, single economic system, single language, and single culture, Brezhnev implemented assimilation policies in an effort to legitimize acceptance of this formulation. Not only did he increase the number of hours Russian was taught in schools throughout the Soviet Union, but he also adopted a constitution that identified the important role of the state in the *sliyanie* of nations: "The state helps enhance the social homogeneity of society, namely . . . the all-round development and drawing together of all the nations and nationalities of the USSR."[18] At the same time, governance during the Brezhnev era was based on a system of patronage that rewarded elites who maintained order within their respective republic, fulfilled or surpassed economic quotas, and respected central authority. Brezhnev granted elites significant autonomy, *including the power to make key personnel appointments,* if they met these requirements. This system generated widespread corruption and facilitated the implementation of affirmative action policies that privileged Central Asians.

Fraud was particularly rampant in Central Asia, home to the now notorious cotton scandal. Uzbekistan's niche in the Soviet economy was that of primary cotton producer. In the mid-1970s, the first secretary of the Uzbek Communist Party and his cronies began to overreport cotton production in order to accrue profit from state revenues. The first secretary, Sharaf Rashidov, managed a conspiratorial pyramid made up of farmers, *kolkhoz* (collective farm) managers, transport sector workers, and party and state officials who benefited from the distortion of production figures. Brezhnev's successor, Andropov, investigated the scheme but it was Gorbachev who put an end to the scandal with an intense anticorruption campaign that purged the region's party leadership.[19]

Both Andropov (general secretary from 1982 to 1984) and his successor, Chernenko (general secretary from 1984 to 1985), ruled for brief periods of time. Gorbachev became general secretary of the Communist Party of the Soviet Union in March 1985. Unlike his predecessors, Gorbachev lacked a coherent approach to the nationalities question and tended to make ad hoc decisions related to the issue. But he did implement certain policies, such as glasnost', which created a permissive environment that unintentionally placed the nationalities question at the top of the leadership's agenda. In fact, "the *glasnost'* political opening gave rise to an explosion of challenging acts across multiple sectors of society."[20] These challenges revealed that the nationalities question had *not* been solved. Conflicts like the Armenian-Azeri dispute over Nagorno-Karabakh suggested that non-Russians were eager to right historical wrongs. Emboldened by the tolerant atmosphere of the late 1980s, non-Russians began to express pent-up grievances that ultimately formed the basis of demands for independence from the Soviet Union.

Although Soviet nationalities policy became obsolete with the demise of the union and the emergence of fifteen newly independent states, its legacy continues to shape developments within those states. The brief support for the flourishing of indigenous personnel, languages, and cultures came to an end once Stalin consolidated power. Savvy post-Soviet elites tapped into resentment among non-Russians that stemmed from decades of Russification to garner popular support for the implementation of nationalization projects. But there were important differences in how Moscow Russified the two regions considered in this book. First, the antireligion component of Russification was somewhat stronger in Central Asia than in the Baltics because Moscow considered Islam a potent force around which indigenous populations might unite in opposition to the regime. Second, Russification was far more lenient in Central Asia than in the Baltics because Moscow faced strong nationalist sentiment that threatened the integrity of the union in the Estonian, Latvian, and Lithuanian SSRs. Most critical to this analysis is the fact that Moscow tolerated efforts to implement local *korenizatsiya* in Central Asia. The center's willingness to look the other way facilitated the removal of Russians from key positions within those republics.

Russification of the Central Asian Republics

The history of Soviet rule in Central Asia has been appropriately described as "a series of attempts to transform the region."[21] Prior to World War II, the regime sought to revolutionize the region through the collectivization of agriculture, settlement of nomads, Russification of local languages, and containment of Islam. Moscow implemented collectivization and settlement policies with brutality in the late 1920s via the expropriation of land, mass arrests, and deportation. Though unsuccessful, Kyrgyz and Kazakh nomads resisted the regime's determination to force them to abandon their way of life. Approximately two million Kazakhs either perished or fled during the violent campaign to collectivize agriculture and settle nomads.[22]

With the brief exception of World War II when the drive to Russify Central Asia ceased temporarily, Moscow implemented Russification policies on a steady basis. In terms of language, the goal was to Russify local languages and promote asymmetric bilingualism. Moscow imposed a mandatory change in alphabet from Arabic to Latin in 1926 and a mandatory change in alphabet from Latin to Cyrillic in 1940. The shift to Cyrillic denied future generations access to both writings of previous generations and Arabic literature from neighboring countries. In addition, the regime inserted a plethora of Russian words into the Central Asian languages to reduce their purity: "The penetration of Russian words was encouraged in everything to do with ideology, administration (*vilayat* becomes *oblast* in the local languages from the 1930s), science, and even technology (*poyezd*, 'train,' *samoliot*, 'aircraft')."[23] Moscow also imposed Russian-language instruction in schools and institutes of higher education and restricted the number of non-Russian-language schools within each republic. During the early Soviet period three of Bishkek's sixty-nine schools used Kyrgyz as the main language of instruction, and after the 1930s Moscow refused to open new Kyrgyz-language schools.[24]

Russification in Muslim regions of the Soviet Union like Central Asia contained a fierce anti-Islam component. There was a brief era of tolerance toward religion during the civil war when the Bolsheviks needed allies, but this lenience vanished by the late 1920s. The regime initiated a brutal *hujum* or onslaught against Islam in 1927 and waged its war with varying degrees of intensity through the late 1980s.[25] Moscow banned Islamic law, destroyed Sharia courts, shut down mosques and madrasas, persecuted clergy, confiscated property of the *waqf*, and eradicated official Muslim activity in the fields of education and law. By 1930 the regime had closed over 80 percent of the union's mosques and rendered at least 90 percent of its Muslim leaders officially inactive.[26]

The threat of a second world war—and the awareness of the immense manpower and popular support required to win such a war—led Moscow to adopt a two-pronged approach to Islam based on suppression and co-optation. As a result,

> practicing Muslims, rather than only being the victims of communist repression, coexisted with and at times benefited from the Soviet bureaucracy. This is not to say that the Soviet leaders did not employ coercion in their early attempts to consolidate authority in Central Asia . . . [but] after the brutality of the 1920s and 1930s, Moscow began what ultimately would prove a remarkably successful assimilation of the region's Islamic elite into the patronage-based system of Soviet rule.[27]

Initiatives to co-opt influential Muslim leaders, such as the creation of an institutional forum for Islam, coexisted with repression for the remainder of the Soviet era. In 1943 Stalin established SADUM (the Central Asian Spiritual Directorate of Muslims), which regulated the registration of mosques, appointed clerics to lead congregations, controlled religious education, and dictated the content of sermons. "Approved" clergy functioned within SADUM as long as they remained subservient to the regime.[28] Moscow's long-term containment strategy involved the simultaneous co-optation of religious leaders and recognition of Islam through official channels, as well as the suppression of unsanctioned religious practice.[29] Muslim elites followed the rules of the game if they wished to climb state and party ladders: "Elites who desired career advancement in the state and party organs were instructed to separate their belief in Islam from their political ideology, because Islam was associated with both cultural backwardness and disloyalty to the Soviet regime."[30] And as Mark Saroyan suggests, Muslim religious boards including SADUM were led by clerics who were not only "fundamentalist" in their determination to bring Muslims back to the scriptural bases of the religion but also "accommodationist" in their determination to promote a version of Islam that supported political participation and loyal citizenship.[31]

Stalin increased the number of functioning mosques during World War II in order to mobilize Central Asians against the Germans, but

Khrushchev initiated a second attack on Islam with the abrupt closure of 25 percent of the region's mosques.[32] He also launched an attack against the clergy, put existing antireligion laws into practice, and intensified penalties for religious offenses.[33] Although Brezhnev was comparatively lenient and even permitted theology students to study in certain countries like Libya, Syria, Egypt, and Jordan, he did not alter the substance of the state's policy toward Islam.

Gorbachev initiated the final Soviet *hujum* in 1985. Because the last Soviet premier considered Islam reactionary and thus an impediment to reform, he declared it incompatible with socialism and sent party ideologues to rural Central Asia to promote atheism, control the spread of Islam, and arrest Islamic leaders who defied the regime. The *hujum* came to an end in 1988. Gorbachev adopted a relaxed policy toward religion at this time because the defeat of the conservative faction of the Politburo opened the door to further reform, he came to the realization that ideological reform had to accompany economic reform if the latter were to succeed, and he felt pressure from below to extend glasnost' to the spiritual domain of society.[34] The implementation of a relatively lenient policy generated a resurgence of Islam as Central Asian elites recognized Muslim holidays, reestablished the *waqf*, reopened mosques and madrasas, and increased the volume of publications related to Islam. Yet the Islamic revival manifested itself differently in each republic. Today it appears in Uzbekistan and Tajikistan as a renewed interest in urban Transoxiana culture and distinguished representatives of the Islamic tradition, and in Kyrgyzstan and Kazakhstan as "an assertion of local (Kazakh or Kyrgyz) identity against the Russians, who had come to dominate local cultural life."[35]

Although Moscow restricted official Islam, it had little control over unofficial or "parallel" Islam. In fact, many Central Asians observed Muslim customs, holidays, and rites of passage on a regular basis in private settings throughout the Soviet era.[36] Adeeb Khalid argues that connections based on kinship, which were necessary for navigating the economy of shortages, allowed Islam to survive: "The practice of Islam and Islamic ritual beyond the purview of the officially recognized religious directorates—the so-called unofficial Islam—existed in this realm of community-based solidarity networks that penetrated even state and Party institutions."[37] In particular, it was a challenge for the regime to contain Islam in rural areas where religious figures easily blended into life on the *kolkhoz*. Unofficial clergy sought refuge on the collective farm where they worked as farmers, mechanics, or tractor drivers, and obtained protection from members of the *kolkhoz* who valued their services. In contrast to official clergy who studied in SADUM-monitored madrasas, unofficial clergy obtained knowledge of Islam from their fathers and grandfathers and were thus difficult to identify:

> The parallel mullahs were protected by their solidarity groups, who employed them to officiate at rites such as for burials and weddings. Children came to them discreetly, outside of official school time, to learn the basic catechism. These mullahs had a few dozen religious books that had been handed down from their fathers and grand fathers. . . . Their knowledge of Arabic and Persian in the Arabic script was minimal, but they were able to pass on an oral knowledge, and especially the practices of Islam.[38]

In light of parallel Islam's survival, it is safe to conclude that the regime's settlement policies were more successful than its religious containment policies. Slavic settlement diversified Central Asia considerably. In the early 1900s, Russian and Ukrainian peasants migrated to the region in search of farmland. The tsar's decision to confiscate and then redistribute land inhabited by Kyrgyz and Kara-Kyrgyz to emancipated Slavic peasants was an attempt to settle the frontier and eliminate the "too many peasants too little land" problem that arose in the aftermath of the abolition of serfdom.[39] Government incentives encouraged massive Slavic in-migration to Central Asia: by 1911 the steppe population was 40 percent Russian;[40] by 1916 there were 530 Cossack and Russian peasant settlements in the region;[41] and by 1917 there were roughly 1.6 million Russian settlers in Central Asia.[42]

The first wave of Soviet-era Russian migration occurred during the late 1920s and early 1930s. The regime faced an acute problem in Central Asia that it did not confront in the modernized Baltic region: it was unable to persuade local inhabitants to shift their loyalty from traditional to Soviet elites. Indeed, "after nearly ten years of Soviet rule Central Asian traditional elites (religious, tribal, and communal) still commanded 'respect,' 'influence,' and 'authority' among the natives; the Soviet regime did not."[43] In response, Moscow sent Russians to Central Asia as leaders of social transformation and carriers of Soviet ideology, culture, and authority. The goal was to transform the region in order to render it amenable to communist rule:

> Instead of diminishing, the weight of European, and especially Slavic, personnel in the political and administrative apparatuses (particularly in the most authoritative and security-sensitive positions) of the Central Asian republics inexorably grew. The jurisdiction of Republican agencies was severely delimited, and their dependence on central decision-making bodies was commensurately increased. Local patterns of economic and cultural activity were tied in ever more forcefully with centrally prescribed molds. At the same time, the influx of Slavic settlers to the Central Asian countryside, and of European and especially Russian technical personnel

to local cities, was not only permitted to continue as under Tsarist rule but was perceptibly accelerated.[44]

Migrants weakened opposition to central rule, founded and managed political, cultural, and academic institutes, and encouraged collectivization and industrialization.

The first and second Five-Year Plans were devoted to restoring industry to pre-revolution levels, increasing electric power production, and building a cotton textile industry.[45] Russians settled in urban areas where they built and staffed industrial enterprises, but they also settled in rural areas where they became an integral part of the agricultural labor force.[46] Poor farmland, a large agricultural population, and high birthrates stimulated rural out-migration from Russia during the late 1920s:

> The Russians have mixed with nationalities largely because traditional Russian areas have experienced the most rural out-migration. This has occurred since the nineteenth century, but particularly after the late 1920s, when rural depopulation began to accelerate. The Russian regions possessed a surplus agricultural population, experienced rapid natural increase until fairly recently, and had at their disposal relatively poor agricultural land resources. These factors resulted in low agricultural wages, which stimulated much out-migration.[47]

Peasants in search of farmland as well as over 190,000 exiled *kulaks*[48] from Russia contributed to the growth of a rural Slavic workforce in the region.[49] An ethnic division of agricultural labor in which Central Asians held unskilled jobs and Slavic migrants held skilled jobs developed quickly.[50]

The second Soviet-era wave of Russian migration to Central Asia was linked to Stalin's decision to accelerate the development of industry in the region. Rapid industrialization began during the war and continued through the 1960s. Not only did the government relocate hundreds of industrial enterprises from European to Central Asian republics for security reasons, but it also built several new industrial enterprises in the eastern region. Within the context of an indigenous labor shortage, industrialization created a demand for workers that stimulated a flood of skilled Russians. During the first four decades of Soviet rule, Central Asia witnessed an influx of Slavs "coming in response to political necessity or, often, offers of lucrative jobs which the unskilled indigenous population could not or would not fill."[51] Two factors contributed to an indigenous labor shortage: (1) the concentration of industry in urban areas, which were unappealing to traditional nomads, and (2) Central Asians' lack of industrial training and experience.[52] Many migrants were "yesterday's peasants," eager to acquire new skills that would enable them to enter the industrial workforce and "change their lives forever."[53] In-migration increased the size of Russian populations in local cities considerably: by 1979 Russians made up the majority of the Kyrgyz and Kazakh republics' urban population.[54]

The Virgin Lands Program generated the final wave of Soviet-era Russian migration. One reason elites in the Kazakh SSR opposed the program was that they predicted—accurately—a concomitant influx of Russians. The nature of the program, which aimed "to create a new breadbasket out of the allegedly underutilized lands of southern Siberia and Kazakhstan," meant that most settlement was rural.[55] Between 1950 and 1970, Moscow sent approximately 1.5 million Slavs to the region to cultivate new farmland.[56] Although Moscow did not subject the Baltics to anything as drastic as the Virgin Lands Program, it did impose settlement, collectivization, and industrialization policies on the three small republics.

Russification of the Baltic Republics

The following quotation captures the oppressive nature of Soviet Russification in the Baltic republics:

> The Kremlin treated Estonia, Latvia, and Lithuania more like colonies than quasi-independent states. It killed or deported suspected oppositionists; decided how the local economy would be organized and what it would produce for the USSR; and proceeded with an intensive campaign of Russification that included not only language training and indoctrination but waves of non-Baltic immigrants who tried to make Russian not just the lingua franca but the dominant tongue.[57]

The first effort to Russify the Baltics was launched in the late nineteenth century, when the tsar attempted to alleviate his distrust of the Baltic Germans who controlled the provinces through settlement policies.[58] In addition to Russian peasants who were sent to the provinces as a result of the tsar's mandate, "tens of thousands of impoverished Russian peasants" were attracted to the coast's new factories and docks.[59] Several decrees supplemented demographic Russification. One designated Russian rather than German or Latvian the language of legal and academic settings, while another aimed to increase the power of the Russian Orthodox Church by requiring the religious conversion of partners of mixed marriages.[60] Despite these efforts, the overall impact of Russification on Latvians at this time was marginal: Latvians learned German because it was necessary and Russian because it was required, but they did not assimilate into German or Russian culture.[61]

These attempts did, however, strengthen Latvian contempt for Russian rule and "probably did much in a crucial period in Latvian nation-building to ensure that enmity towards a Russian-dominated state became a feature of the nationalist struggle."[62] The composition of Riga's population contributed to this animosity. In 1867 Latvians comprised 24 percent of the city's population, Germans 43 percent, and Russians 25 percent.[63] Moreover, by the early 1900s Russians, Germans, and Jews overshadowed Latvians in the political and economic spheres of society: while Russians and Germans dominated politics, Jews and Germans dominated commerce and the professions. And although agriculture was traditionally a Latvian occupation, Germans, Russians, and Poles owned or leased about 60 percent of arable land at the time.[64]

The period between the two world wars brought independent statehood to Latvians. During this time Latvia was an internationally recognized sovereign state, a member of the League of Nations, and a flourishing democracy until a 1934 coup brought dictator Karlis Ulmanis to power. The 1939 Molotov-Ribbentrop Pact between the Third Reich and the Soviet Union brought interwar independence, which was a critical period of Latvia's political development, to an abrupt end. Various groups of Slavs settled in Latvia once Moscow had occupied the region. According to one account, "soldiers and prisoners together contributed 7,000–8,000 annually to the growth of Latvia's non-titular population" throughout the Soviet era.[65] The republic's all-union industrial enterprises attracted specialists, managers, and workers because they offered jobs as well as political ties with industrial counterparts in Moscow. Furthermore, thousands of Russians and *latovichi* (heavily Russified Latvians who migrated from Latvia to Russia prior to the interwar period) arrived to fill positions within the Communist Party of Latvia, which was "minuscule" in 1945 and in desperate need of party functionaries.[66] After the war, "tens of thousands" of *latovichi* returned because the state requested their service or because they sought higher living standards and professional opportunity.[67] The arrival of Russian and *latovichi* personnel resulted in "an ethnic hierarchy, with Russians or Russified *latovichi* ruling over the indigenous Latvians."[68] Slavs continued to migrate to the republic throughout the Soviet period.

Many migrants worked in the industrial sector of the economy. Baltic industry became Russian industry, in part, because of this: "It was an industry based on Russian investment and Russian labor, managed by Russians according to goals set by Russians, importing a large part of the raw materials from Russia and exporting most of its products. The whole show was called 'Baltic' industrial growth because the Soviets decided to run it on Baltic soil."[69] Because these were the most modernized republics in the early postwar era, Stalin developed industry intensely in the Baltics. Nineteenth-century industrialization had already altered the region. Expanded cities housed major industrial centers and strategic ports, while the physical infrastructure of the republics— apartment complexes, schools, roads, and factories—survived World War II relatively intact. All of this provided a solid base for further industrialization. Despite the fact that the Latvian SSR lacked a raw material or energy base, Moscow rapidly transformed its agricultural economy into an industrial economy.

Although central planners had difficulty managing Latvia's agriculture sector because interwar reforms had increased the number of individual farms considerably, by 1950 less than 5 percent of those farms remained.[70] Officials relied on *kulak* deportation and its powerful psychological effects to force collectivization on reluctant farmers. By 1960 agricultural output barely reached its 1940 level, while industrial output had increased tenfold, metal-building and machine-working sixtyfold, and chemical industry fiftyfold.[71] Latvia became a center for heavy industry over the course of two five-year plans. By 1980 the republic's total industrial production was eight times higher than it was in 1955.[72]

A central objective of Russification was to spread the mandatory use of Russian in as many spheres of communication as possible. As a result of the asymmetric bilingualism that Moscow's promotion of Russian fostered, Latvians gradually lost control over the public use of their language as it slipped from its previous position of dominance. In Latvia "both institutional and migrational pressures continued to facilitate the spread of the Russian language, challenging the dominance of the native language and culture."[73] The presence of bilingual schools in regions with few Russians encouraged Latvians to study in Russian.[74] Moreover, the republic's Russian-dominated Communist Party implemented policies that curtailed the use of Latvian. Prior to the Gorbachev era, Russian-language schools required two hours of Latvian language study, while Latvian-language schools required at least twice as many hours of Russian language study; and Russian high school students took final exams in their native language, while Latvian high school students took final exams in Russian.[75] Russification created an environment in which knowledge of Russian was required and knowledge of Latvian was optional. When the Soviet Union collapsed, only 23 percent of the republic's non-Latvian population was proficient in Latvian.[76]

Demographic Trends and Locally Initiated *Korenizatsiya*: Working for Baltic Russians and Against Central Asian Russians

Demographic trends and the success or failure of locally initiated *korenizatsiya* affected the socioeconomic status of Russians vis-à-vis the respec-

Table 3.1. Changes in the Kyrgyz SSR Population

	1939	1959	1970	1979	1989	1999
Kyrgyz Share of Total Population	52%	40%	44%	48%	52%	65%
Russian Share of Total Population	21%	30%	29%	26%	21.5%	13.5%

Source: *Kyrgyzskaia gosudarstvennost' statistika vekov* (Bishkek: Natsional'ny statisticheskii komitet Kyrgyzskoi Respubliki, 2003), 49.

tive titular nation in every Soviet republic. Both phenomena forced Russians into a disadvantageous position in the Central Asian republics and kept them in an advantageous position in the Baltic republics. Russian out-migration from Central Asia began in the 1970s, continued through the 1980s, and intensified during the 1990s. This trend was most prevalent in the Uzbek, Tajik, and Turkmen SSRs where comparatively few Russians resided, but it was considerable even in the Kyrgyz and Kazakh SSRs where many Russians resided.[77] Two factors related to diminished economic opportunity in general and restricted Slavic mobility in particular caused Russian out-migration to commence. First, Brezhnev's decision to abandon the commitment to regional equalization resulted in rapid deterioration of economic conditions in the region. Second, during the 1960s Central Asians began to compete with Russians for coveted positions within formal institutions. Not only were Central Asian populations growing rapidly as a result of naturally high birthrates, but members of these populations were increasingly educated and propelled into high-status positions via locally initiated *korenizatsiya*. This resulted in a gradual erosion of Russian institutional dominance. The cumulative effect of these factors was to make Russians "feel increasingly unwelcome in the region."[78] Russian out-migration in the 1970s and 1980s reflected "a widespread feeling among Russians that they had become victims of Soviet nationality policy in the non-Russian republics."[79] Table 3.1 illustrates that between 1959 and 1989 the Kyrgyz share of the Kyrgyz SSR's total population increased while the Russian share decreased.

Rapid population growth made Central Asia "the fastest growing region" of the Soviet Union. Between 1959 and 1989 the Tajik population increased by 202 percent, the Uzbek population by 177 percent, the Turkmen population by 171 percent, the Kazakh population by 125 percent, and the Kyrgyz population by 161 percent; the Russian population increased by 27 percent.[80] Furthermore, Central Asians were increasingly educated and thus increasingly competitive in the education and labor markets. Between 1959 and 1970, the proportion of individual Central Asians with higher education doubled and in many cases almost tripled.[81] Trends in education suggested that "far from remaining a tradition-bound, isolated rural community, the younger generation of Central Asians clearly aspires toward greater levels of participation in modernized sectors of society."[82] Indeed, the percent of each Central Asian population among scientific workers in the five republics increased from a 6.4–16.9 percent range in 1947 to a 29.8–50.8 percent range in 1973.[83] In sheer numbers, Slavic scientific and technical personnel doubled between 1960 and 1975, while Central Asian scientific and technical personnel quadrupled.[84]

In the 1960s elites reacted to decades of Russification with the implementation of *korenizatsiya* policies favoring Central Asians: "A kind of 'affirmative action' policy in the republics resulted in large numbers of non-Russians entering higher education and taking important positions in the republics, to the point that Russians and other nonindigenous peoples complained that they were being discriminated against."[85] Central Asian *korenizatsiya* involved the indigenization of elite positions within economic and political institutions, as well as the indigenization of university student bodies:

> As indigenes became more socially mobilized, they increasingly competed with Russians for dominance in Central Asia. Indigenes were successful in gaining greater control over the local power structures, although the region as a whole remained economically dependent on Moscow and linguistic russification continued to be promoted by the center. From their elite positions at the local and republican scales, titular elites used *korenizatsiya* to gain a competitive advantage over outsiders, including Russians.[86]

As their power increased, elites "packed republic political, economic, and cultural institutions with their relatives, friends, political allies, and other colleagues from their home regions."[87] Moscow's surprisingly lenient reaction to this development was based on the fact that local elites maintained order within their respective republic, fulfilled and in some cases surpassed economic quotas, and yielded to Moscow's authority. Moreover, unlike the Baltic region, the center was not threatened by local nationalities in this region because it had never experienced independent, internationally recognized statehood. As a result, Moscow was not compelled to extend privileges to Russians in order to keep Central Asians in the fold.

The replacement of Slavic personnel with indigenous personnel greatly restricted Russian mobility. Within this context, Nancy Lubin's conclusion regarding labor relations in the Uzbek SSR applies to the other republics as well: although Russians continued to occupy certain key positions, Central Asians increasingly occupied high-level party, administrative, and managerial positions in every sector of the economy.[88] By 1989 the percent of each republic's urban Russian population that occupied party and government positions was 0.3 percent in Kyrgyzstan, Kazakhstan, and Uzbekistan, 0.5 percent in Turkmenistan, and 0.7 percent in Tajikistan.[89] In short, Russians were in a disadvantageous socioeconomic position vis-à-vis Central Asians when the Soviet Union collapsed.

The situation was different in the Baltic republics, where Russians were in an advantageous socioeconomic position when the Soviet Union disintegrated. World War II losses, deportations, out-migration in anticipation of renewed Soviet rule, and rapid postwar industrialization created a plethora of job vacancies in the Latvian SSR, which stimulated Russian in-migration.[90] An estimated 535,000 Slavs, most of whom were Russian, migrated to Latvia between 1945 and 1955.[91] While Moscow aimed to dilute indigenous populations and strengthen pro-Soviet sentiment in the region through settlement policies, most migrants did not require incentive to relocate. A high standard of living and economic opportunity "sucked in workers, especially those young and unmarried, from all over the Union."[92] Migrants preferred Riga to other industrialized cities because it was the region's most powerful magnet for foreign capital and Western technology.

The initial Soviet-era wave of Russian settlement in Latvia occurred just after World War II, but in-migration continued through the late 1980s. It was primarily in-migration that caused the republic's Russian population to almost quadruple between 1935 and 1989 and the Latvian population to decrease from 77 to 52 percent during the same period (see Table 3.2). The rate of Slavic in-migration to the Latvian SSR during the postwar era was unprecedented: "Proportionally, Latvia has experienced the highest rate of immigration among all the states of Europe and the republics of the USSR. An all-Soviet comparison of population increase due to migration also shows Latvia to be far ahead of all republics of the USSR."[93] One factor distinguishing the Latvian and Estonian SSRs is the fact that as late as the 1970s and early 1980s, when migration to other SSRs had slowed or reversed, in-migration accounted for roughly two-thirds of the population growth in both the Latvian and Estonian SSRs.[94] Economic and political opportunity continued to attract workers, managers, specialists, party personnel, and military retirees.[95] Between 1951 and 1989, in-migration exceeded out-migration almost every year in Latvia; Russians, Belarusians, and Ukrainians comprised the immigrant population.[96] Equally low Russian and Latvian birthrates combined with continuous in-migration eventually rendered Latvians a bare majority within their homeland.[97] Table 3.2 illustrates

Table 3.2. Changes in the Latvian SSR Population

	1935	1959	1970	1979	1989	2000
Latvian Share of Total Population	77%	62%	57%	54%	52%	58%
Russian Share of Total Population	9%	27%	30%	33%	34%	30%

Source: *Results of the 2000 Population and Housing Census in Latvia* (Riga: Central Statistical Bureau of Latvia, 2002), 121.

that between 1935 and 1989 the Latvian share of the republic's total population decreased while the Russian share increased.

Russians maintained a prestigious socioeconomic status within the Latvian SSR, where they dominated industry, technology, information and computer services, and the managerial class. Riga's factories and cosmopolitan atmosphere attracted unskilled Russian labor and highly educated Russians, who by 1989 represented 62 percent of Latvia's industrial workforce and, in combination with Russian Jews, held 58 percent of the republic's scientific jobs and 51 percent of information and computer service jobs.[98] By 1989 Slavs dominated every economic sector except agriculture.[99]

Their occupation of responsible political posts enabled Slavic migrants to exercise a disproportionate voice in the republic's future.[100] After the 1959 political purge, which I discuss below, Russians dominated the Latvian Communist Party. By 1970 Russians and non-Latvians comprised 54 percent of the republic's party membership, while Latvians comprised 46 percent.[101] Russian dominance of the republic's political and economic sectors had a devastating effect on Latvians: "As the Latvians recovered from the destruction of the war they learned that their new status as citizens of a Soviet socialist republic included severely diminished control by the Latvian *tauta* [nation] over the affairs of the republic, as symbolized by the proportion of non-Latvians (especially Russians) in the LKP [Latvian Communist Party] and in all domains of socioeconomic life."[102]

In order to eliminate these injustices, local elites tried during Khrushchev's de-Stalinization campaign to implement policies that favored Latvians. The existence of open opposition to Russification testifies to the fact that "even compliant party members in Latvia felt squeezed by the growing demographic and linguistic weight of the Russian presence."[103] Between 1957 and 1959, prominent party officials prioritized local interests in an attempt to expand the use of Latvian in party affairs and education, compel Russians to learn Latvian, reduce the rate of Slavic in-migration, promote Latvian personnel, and increase economic autonomy. But because the region had known and appreciated independent, internationally recognized statehood Moscow had no tolerance for this behavior. As a result, the center not only extended privileges to Russians in order to keep local nationalities in the fold, but also cracked down on attempts to implement local *korenizatsiya*. Khrushchev responded ruthlessly to open opposition to Russification in 1959—he exiled the movement's leader, Eduards Berklavs, to eastern Russia, promoted Berklavs's opponent to first party secretary, purged two thousand party functionaries, and sent a fresh crop of Russians and *latovichi* to fill party vacancies created by the purge. Continued in-migration consolidated a regime dominated by Russians. In 1989 Russians occupied 46 percent of the republic's state and party positions, Latvians occupied 34 percent, and Belarusians, Ukrainians, and Poles occupied 16 percent.[104] The administration thus "remained in the hands of Russian Latvians [*latovichi*] with a significant admixture of Russians and other non-Latvians" throughout the Soviet era.[105]

Augusts Voss oversaw Latvia during the Brezhnev era, which was a prosperous time for the republic. Agriculture and the communications and electronics industries developed, consumption patterns returned to prewar levels, inflation remained low, incomes rose, and the standard of living improved. By 1970 Latvia's per capita income surpassed the Soviet average per capita income by 43 percent; following Estonia, its per capita income was second of the fifteen union republics; average rural incomes were approaching average urban incomes; and industrial production was almost five times higher than it had been in 1955.[106]

But economic prosperity failed to compensate for the adverse effect of Russification on Latvians, and random unsuccessful acts of protest occurred throughout the Soviet era. For example, in 1972 a group of Latvians wrote a letter, which was leaked to the West, criticizing both continued Russian in-migration and the Russified nature of the republic's party in terms of ethnic composition and the inability of party leaders to speak Latvian. Complementing a long line of nationalists who began to shape Latvian national consciousness in the 1800s when Germans dominated the area, this kind of activity contributed to Moscow's distrust of Latvians. Suspicion of locals who had tasted the sweetness of independent statehood as well as the strategic importance of a region that served as a buffer between the East and West motivated Moscow to suppress locally initiated *korenizatsiya*. And this meant, in short, that Russians dominated the republic's institutions.

The Impact of Socialist Legacies on Post-Soviet Nationalization

Central Asian and Baltic reactions to the impending collapse of the Soviet Union were indicative of the type of nationalization project elites within each region would adopt. Gorbachev's appointment paved the way for an era of liberalization that permitted, for the first time in Soviet history, the public expression of grievances. While Central Asians aired few complaints and accepted independence with reluctance, Balts embraced Gorbachev's invitation to voice discontent and fought aggressively for the right to independent statehood.

Although anti-Soviet demonstrations occurred in Latvia before Gorbachev's reform efforts had crystallized, Latvian nationalism made its debut in 1988 at the founding of the Popular Front. This movement called for the recognition of Latvia as a sovereign territory with one state language and offered a program "based on liberal nationalism and the priority of the Latvian nation."[107] The Front maintained an estimated 250,000 members, the overwhelming majority of whom were Latvian, and mobilized impressive numbers of individuals on a repeated basis.[108] A movement known as Interfront (or the International Front), dedicated to protecting the interests of local Russians, emerged in reaction to the Popular Front's increasing strength and the designation of Latvian as the republic's state language.[109] The overwhelming majority of Interfront's members were Russian conservative party members, workers, retired military officers, and managers of the military-industrial complex. Because the movement was unable to gain the momentum necessary for longevity, it faded into history after the 1990 parliamentary elections. Ironically, the Popular Front owed its victory in these elections to Latvian *and* non-Latvian voters. Many Russians supported the Front's emphasis on "the territorial and political character of the struggle with Moscow," as well as the Front's promise "that all ethnic groups would be guaranteed equal rights when independence had been achieved."[110] The Supreme Soviet voted for the reestablishment of Latvia's independence shortly after the elections.

Gorbachev's struggle with conservative party functionaries in Moscow culminated in an all-union referendum on the future of the Soviet Union that posed the following question: Do you consider necessary the preservation of the Union of Soviet Socialist Republics as a renewed federation of equal sovereign republics, in which the rights and freedoms of an individual of any nationality will be guaranteed?[111] Rather than support an effort to maintain a union, Latvia held its own referendum in March 1991 on the question of independence. Seventy-four percent of the electorate voted for independence from the Soviet Union.[112] Widespread support for independence motivated leaders of the Latvian SSR to declare the republic an independent state during the August 1991 coup attempt in Moscow. Russia's first president, Boris Yeltsin, recognized Latvia's independence later that month.

In contrast, the Central Asian republics were uninterested in independence: "In examining Central Asia's response to Gorbachev's challenge and to the disintegration of the USSR one is struck by the relative slowness of the Central Asian republics to declare independence."[113] The political movements that emerged in this region were far less influential than those that arose in the Baltic republics. Elites in Central Asia supported the union's preservation because they presided over republics that were financially dependent on the center, sought to maintain positions guaranteed only by the existing system, and did not face popular pressure to jump on the independence bandwagon: "Because of the economic weakness and political instability of the region, members of the Central Asian leadership to the very end were the most persistent champions of keeping the Soviet Union intact."[114]

Each Central Asian republic held a referendum on the question of the preservation of the Soviet Union or a reconstituted union. The Kyrgyz referendum contained a supplementary question to Gorbachev's question: Do you agree that the Republic of Kyrgyzstan should be in the renewed Union as a sovereign republic (state) with equal rights? Ninety-three percent of eligible voters went to the polls, and over 94 percent supported the preservation of a renewed union of equal sovereign republics.[115] While the Latvian SSR voted for independence from the Soviet Union, the Kyrgyz SSR voted for continuation of the union. Determined to maintain some type of formal union, the first secretary of the Kazakh Communist Party, Nursultan Nazarbaev, participated in talks with representatives of Russia, Belarus, and Ukraine regarding a new community of states. These discussions gave birth to the Commonwealth of Independent States, an organization that every post-Soviet state except Latvia, Lithuania, Estonia, and Georgia joined in December 1991.[116]

In retrospect, it is not surprising that Latvia adopted antagonistic nationalization while Kyrgyzstan adopted accommodating nationalization. Each nationalization project was a logical continuation of the path the respective republic took toward independence. Latvia was eager for independence and the opportunity to divest itself of everything related to Russia, while Kyrgyzstan accepted independence reluctantly and sought to preserve close ties with Russia. But certain aspects of the socialist legacy further clarify why these republics reacted so differently to the notion of independence and why they implemented dissimilar types of nationalization. Soviet federalism and Soviet nationalities policy explain the source of varied reactions to the notion of independence, as well as the emergence of post-Soviet nationalization projects. Federalism gave post-Soviet elites the institutional and psychological tools required to implement such projects, while *korenizatsiya* and Russification gave elites valuable resources to draw upon such as distinct languages and customs, as well as anti-Russian resentment.

Other aspects of the socialist legacy shed light on the appearance of diverse nationalization projects. Continued Russian in-migration combined with low Baltic birthrates generated a large Russian population that dominated state and party organs within Latvia. In an effort to stem this trend, elites attempted to implement affirmative action policies that favored members of the titular nation. But the center cracked down. Latvia never recovered from the 1959 political purge Moscow conducted in response to these efforts. Both Russian institutional dominance and the failure of locally initiated *korenizatsiya* discouraged Russian out-migration. By the time the Soviet Union collapsed, Russians were in an advantageous socioeconomic position vis-à-vis Latvians and thus posed a threat to the future of the Latvian nation. This encouraged post-Soviet elites to implement antagonistic nationalization designed to further the interests of the Latvian nation at the expense of the Russian nation.

In contrast, Russian in-migration to Central Asia had ceased by the 1960s. At this point, opportunity was reserved for Central Asians as a result of high Central Asian birthrates, educated indigenous populations, general economic downturn, and locally initiated *korenizatsiya*. Russian exclusion from state and party organs and rising competition from Central Asians, who were given preferential treatment in the education and labor markets, encouraged Russian out-migration. When the Soviet Union collapsed, Russians were in a disadvantageous socioeconomic position vis-à-vis the Kyrgyz and thus did not pose a threat to the future of the Kyrgyz nation. This encouraged post-Soviet elites to implement accommodating nationalization designed to further the interests of the Kyrgyz nation and protect the interests of the Russian nation.

When the Soviet Union became obsolete Russians in Kyrgyzstan were isolated from preexisting formal institutions, while Russians in Latvia were connected to such institutions. Within this context, it is worth highlighting research Rasma Karklins conducted on Germans who migrated from the Baltic and Central Asian republics to West Germany in the late 1970s. Interviews with these immigrants reveal a perception among Baltic Germans that Baltic nations were losing power in relation to European nations, and a perception among Central Asian Germans that Central Asian nations were gaining power in relation to European nations.[117] Karklins rightly identifies demographic factors as one cause of this difference in perception, but she overlooks Russian dominance of Baltic institutions and Central Asian dominance of Central Asian institutions as an additional explanatory factor. Despite different responses to the Soviet Union's demise, there was a shared sense among elites in both regions that independence presented a unique opportunity to redefine the meanings and boundaries of nations and national identities. Freedom from the Soviet Union and this sense of entitlement produced a spectrum of nationalizing states. The next chapter analyzes the subtleties of Kyrgyz and Latvian nationalization.

Chapter 4
Opportunity Structures and the Role of Informal Networks in Their Reconfiguration

To the Kazakh who divides us into "native" and "non-native"

My grandson and your granddaughter have been married for a long time.
Borshch and *besbarmak* go great together.
But you—for your own—just like clockwork. . . .
What the hell kind of "non-native" am I?
         —Svetlana Nazarova, *Ne ostavliaite na potom.* . . .

The third line of this stanza from Nazarova's poem, "But you—for your own—just like clockwork," refers to the Kazakhs' determination to promote their own via nationalization policies and practices but applies to the core nation's decision to do the same in other post-Soviet states as well. Gorbachev's reforms facilitated a permissive environment that encouraged the Soviet Union's disintegration to emerge as a distinct possibility in the imaginations of union republic elites. As representatives of various nations began to voice demands for autonomy within or independence from the federation, elites in non-Russian republics began to envision nationalization projects designed to promote the respective titular nation. Once they declared their republics independent sovereign states, elites in Kyrgyzstan and Latvia immediately implemented citizenship policies that signaled the inclusive or exclusive nature of their respective nationalization project. This chapter analyzes the accommodating nature of Kyrgyz nationalization and the antagonistic nature of Latvian nationalization, and illustrates how the presence of dense informal networks permits the reconfiguration of an elite-created opportunity structure while the absence of such networks prohibits such an alteration.

The collapse of the Soviet Union created a historic opportunity for elites to nationalize the newly independent state over which they presided through the legislative process. A comparison of the Central Asian and Baltic cases reveals that elites do not necessarily implement similar types of nationalization policies. In addition to particular aspects of the Soviet socialist legacy discussed in Chapter 3, two contemporary factors I mentioned earlier influenced the type of formal nationalization policies elites adopted in the post-Soviet era: national security concerns and economic considerations.

The implementation of anything but accommodating nationalization policies was risky for Kyrgyz elites because Kyrgyzstan depends on Russia for its national security and maintains an economy that depends on both the all-union infrastructure and the local Russian labor force. Kyrgyzstan and Russia are members of various regional security regimes including the Collective Security Treaty (CST; established in 1992) and the Shanghai Cooperation Organization (SCO; established in 1996 as the Shanghai Five and renamed when Uzbekistan became a member in 2001). The CST and SCO existed primarily on paper until terrorist incursions into Kyrgyzstan and U.S. involvement in Central Asia after September 11 prompted elites to invest in the development of these organizations. China conducts joint antiterrorism exercises with Kyrgyzstan, and although Russian border guards had gone home by the end of 1999, Russia continues to train Kyrgyz officers for service on the border and to provide Kyrgyzstan with military and security equipment.[1] In 2001 Russia and Kyrgyzstan signed a bilateral treaty providing for political cooperation as well as joint military planning, strategic assessment, and operations; in 2003 Russia established an air base on Kyrgyz territory.[2]

Two factors render the Kyrgyz economy highly dependent on close ties with former Soviet republics including Russia. First, like the Kyrgyz SSR, independent Kyrgyzstan has limited trading partner options. Prior to independence, 98 percent of the republic's exports were sent to and 75 percent of its imports came from other union republics.[3] With the exception of gold and water, the latter a highly valued commodity in the region, Kyrgyzstan is not abundantly rich in natural resources. Primary export commodities include gold, electricity, cotton, and tobacco. The country's most important trading partners remain members of the Eurasian Economic Community, such as Russia, Belarus, Kazakhstan, Tajikistan, and Uzbekistan. Uzbekistan supplies much needed natural gas, while Russia and Kazakhstan provide critical markets for Kyrgyz goods as well as trade routes to other markets.[4] Kyrgyzstan's relations with these countries are critical to its economic survival. Stanislav Zhukov argues that the Central Asian economies in general "exist only through their inclusion in the international division of labor. If cut off from the channels of international trade, they would immediately atrophy and wither away."[5] Moreover, as assistance from the West proves too little and/or too ineffective, Kyrgyzstan is focusing on Russia and Kazakhstan as potential foreign investors.[6] The second factor rendering the Kyrgyz economy highly dependent on close ties with former Soviet republics is the fact that Kyrgyz industry relies on highly skilled specialists, who tend to be Russian. The ethnic division of labor in the republic during the Soviet era was characterized by a Russian-dominated industrial sector and a Kyrgyz-dominated agricultural sector. Close military relations with Russia and a dependence on both regional trade partners and highly skilled specialists made the implementation of formal policies that might antagonize local Russians in the post-Soviet era dicey.

In contrast, Latvian elites were able to implement antagonistic nationalization policies because Latvia does not rely on Russia to protect its borders and is independent of all-union infrastructure. Some scholars argue that Latvia's approach to the Russian minority question is related to its historically hostile relationship with Russia. For example, Graham Smith asserts the following: "For the nationalizing elites of Estonia and Latvia, statehood is about reclaiming a central role for the homeland-nation after five decades of what is unambiguously interpreted as subjugation by 'the Soviet empire.'"[7] Memories of tragedies such as the occupation, deportations, and massive purge of indigenous communists certainly inspired antagonistic nationalization. Other scholars, such as Juris Dreifelds, argue that Russian in-migration and Russification generated a "fear of minoritization," which motivated the aggressive nature of Latvian nationalization.[8] Latvians were in fact a bare majority in their own republic in 1989, when they constituted 52 percent of the total population and Russians constituted 34 percent. But the Kyrgyz also constituted 52 percent of their republic's total population at the time, while minorities including Russians (22 percent) and Uzbeks (13 percent) constituted 35 percent. While this factor certainly inspired aggressive nationalization, the implementation of antagonistic policies was possible because Latvia does not rely on Russia to protect its borders and is economically oriented toward the West. In other words, Latvia can afford to alienate Russia.

An unambiguous constituent of Europe, post-Soviet Latvia has strong military and economic ties with the West. By 1994 Latvia had expelled Russian troops from its territory; in 1999 it joined the World Trade Organization; and in 2004 it joined the North Atlantic Treaty Organization (NATO) and the European Union (EU). NATO membership means that Latvia relies on the West rather than on Russia for its national security. European economic integration allows factory directors, for example, to turn to Europe when post-Soviet states fail to place production orders or send critical raw materials. And Latvia has reoriented the direction of its trade activity from the Commonwealth of Independent States (CIS) toward Europe: in 1995 trade with the EU represented 44 percent of Latvia's total export activity; by 2003 it represented 62 percent. In 1995 trade with the CIS represented 34 percent of Latvia's total export activity; by 2003 it represented 10 percent. While the level of import activity from the EU remained constant during these years, in 1995 trade with the CIS represented 28 percent of Latvia's total import activity; by 2003 it represented 15 percent.[9]

In sum, national security concerns and economic considerations influenced the type of formal nationalization policies implemented by elites in both post-Soviet states. However, aspects of the Soviet legacy such as center responses to locally initiated *korenizatsiya* as well as demographic trends determined the socioeconomic status of the core nation vis-à-vis local Russians, which shaped the degree to which each nationalization project privileges the titular nation at the expense of Russians. From this perspective, it is not surprising that Kyrgyz elites tended toward moderation while Latvian elites tended toward excess when they crafted their respective nationalization policies.

Inclusion in the Political Community: Kyrgyz Citizenship Policy

The core of any nationalization project is a decision regarding the composition of the citizen body, or demos, which resolves important questions about the problem of inclusion such as "What persons have a rightful claim to be included in the demos?" "Who must be included in a properly constituted demos, and who may or may not be excluded from it?"[10] Like their counterparts in every post-Soviet state except Estonia and Latvia, elites in newly independent Kyrgyzstan resolved these issues with the adoption of a "zero-option" policy, which granted all legal residents of a republic automatic citizenship of the successor state. The policy thus renders all permanent residents of the Kyrgyz SSR members of the newly created Kyrgyz demos. President Askar Akayev's decision to prohibit dual citizenship was part of a broad strategy to consolidate loyalty to an inclusive demos.[11]

Since all residents of the Soviet Union were citizens of the union as opposed to individual republics, the Kyrgyz SSR adopted a law on citizenship in 1990 establishing citizenship of the Kyrgyz SSR. The policy defines a citizen of the Kyrgyz SSR as a citizen of the Soviet Union who at the time of the law's implementation resided in the Kyrgyz SSR; a citizen of the Soviet Union who at the time of the law's implementation resided beyond the borders of the Kyrgyz SSR but would apply for citizenship of the Kyrgyz SSR in three years; and an individual who acquired citizenship of the Kyrgyz SSR in accordance with current legislation.[12]

The collapse of the Soviet Union did not alter the all-encompassing nature of this policy. Independent Kyrgyzstan constructed a citizenship regime based on the automatic inclusion of all citizens of the Kyrgyz SSR in the newly constituted demos. The 1993 law on citizenship defines citizens as "individuals who were citizens of the Kyrgyz Republic on the day of the adoption of the Declaration of State Sovereignty of the Kyrgyz Republic (December 15, 1990), and who did not submit an application for affiliation with citizenship of another state."[13] The equality embedded within this legislation renders Russians legally entitled to the same rights and privileges and beholden to the same responsibilities as Kyrgyz.[14] This notion of equality sharply distinguishes Kyrgyzstan's citizenship regime from Latvia's citizenship regime.

Exclusion from the Political Community: Latvian Citizenship Policy

Newly independent Latvia adopted an exclusive citizenship regime that created a demos based on ethnicity. The first step was taken in 1991, when the government passed a ruling restricting the post-Soviet demos to individuals (and their descendants) who were citizens of Latvia on 17 June 1940—the date of the Red Army invasion. Because large numbers of Russians came to the Baltic republics during the postwar period, most Russian residents of Latvia in 1991 were *not* citizens of Latvia in 1940 and were thus excluded from the post-Soviet demos. The need to compensate for historical injustices that are related to the occupation and subsequent arrival of illegal migrants justifies this ruling:

> As a result of the prolonged and unlawful, in terms of international relations, annexation of the territory of Latvia, a large number of citizens of the USSR settled as residents, and their entry and stay were not approved by a single agreement between the Latvian Republic and the USSR.
>
> With the aim to liquidate in Latvia the consequences of the occupation and annexation on the part of the USSR, and to restore for citizens of the Latvian Republic their legal rights, the Supreme Council of the Latvian Republic rules . . .[15]

Three aspects of this policy generated a society composed of citizens of Latvia, noncitizens or "aliens," and citizens of Russia.[16] First, only individuals who were citizens of Latvia on 17 June 1940 and their descendants became citizens of post-Soviet Latvia automatically. Second, while some individuals who did not obtain citizenship automatically can acquire it through registration, the majority must naturalize if they wish to join the demos.[17] Third, certain individuals are permanently banned from the demos including people who fought against independence, the creation of a democracy, or existing state authority; served in Soviet military and/or security forces; and came to Latvia after the occupation to serve in the party or Komsomol.

A 1994 law on citizenship establishes additional exclusionary parameters.[18] For example, new naturalization regulations further restrict access to the demos. The 1991 ruling allowed individuals to naturalize after July 1992 if they were at least sixteen years old, had mastered the state language, relinquished any former citizenship they might have had, knew the constitution, and took an oath of loyalty. The 1994 policy also requires applicants to reside in Latvia for five years and to know the history of Latvia as well as the state anthem.[19] More important, the law establishes a "window" system that as of January 1996 limits the number of people eligible to naturalize annually and thus slows the expansion of a multiethnic demos. Finally, the policy calls for the creation of a commission to test the state-language skills of naturalization applicants.[20]

Europe did not fail to notice the increasingly exclusive quality of Latvia's citizenship regime. Pressure from the EU to ease naturalization requirements stimulated a referendum on the citizenship question in 1998. According to the president of Latvia at the time, Guntis Ulmanis, "Countries of the European Community advised us to adopt amendments to the law on citizenship. The results of the referendum testify to the fact that the advice was heard."[21] Two of the seventeen possible changes to the law that were submitted to parliament were submitted to voters. Referendum results indicate that less than 50 percent of the electorate supported the adoption of amendments.[22] Nevertheless, the results prompted the government to abolish the window system and naturalization applications are now considered in order of submission.[23] The government also expanded the civic rights of children. According to the 1994 policy, children born in Latvia to a set of noncitizen parents are required to naturalize.[24] The amended law recognizes children born in Latvia after 21 August 1991 as citizens who may register for citizenship before the age of fifteen; if they wish to join the demos thereafter they must submit documentation confirming education in a Latvian-language school or fluency in the state language.

Though it abolished the window system and expanded the civic rights of children, the referendum did not eliminate the many restrictions that apply to noncitizens.[25] For example, noncitizens are deprived of electoral rights, banned from certain professions, and forced to jump legal and financial hurdles if they wish to travel abroad. Moreover, during the privatization period the average citizen received almost three times as many vouchers as the average noncitizen. While citizens and noncitizens received one voucher for every year of residence in Latvia, citizens received an extra fifteen vouchers. The government also subtracted time worked in upper-level party or KGB positions from years of residence, which diminished the number of vouchers noncitizens received because Russians dominated these posts.[26] By March 1998, citizens had received 86 percent of state-issued vouchers.[27]

Although the Cabinet of Ministers has reduced the naturalization fee from 30 to 20 Lat and has identified categories of applicants eligible for a discount or payment exemption, Latvia's citizenship policy has created a demos based on ethnicity and in the process generated a second-class society composed primarily of Russians.[28] While 67 percent of noncitizens are Russian, less than 1 percent is Latvian; while 74 percent of citizens are Latvian, 19 percent is Russian.[29] Table 4.1 compares Kyrgyzstan's inclusive citizenship policy to Latvia's exclusive citizenship policy.

Embracing the Russian Language: Kyrgyz Language Policy

Citizenship and language policies affect access to public sector employment because they have distributional consequences that privilege or discriminate depending on the group in question. As in the realm of citizenship policy, in the realm of language policy Kyrgyzstan has adopted a far more conciliatory approach toward Russians than has Latvia. Since 1989, elites have struck a delicate balance between the promotion of the state language and the protection of Russian. Though they have ensured the mandatory use of Kyrgyz in certain spheres of communication, they remain cognizant of the fact that many urban Kyrgyz are more comfortable with Russian and thus tend to use Russian rather than Kyrgyz whenever possible. A newspaper article written by a Kazakh sheds light on this issue, which remains salient in Kyrgyzstan and Kazakhstan. The author states the following: "Not only Russians, but also Kazakhs worry about the fate of their children owing to weak knowledge of the [Kazakh] language . . . the fate of Russian-speaking Kazakhs troubles me, as a Kazakh, and also [the fate of] mixed families who received higher education in Russia or Northern Kazakhstan but speak Kazakh poorly."[30] According to the last census, almost 50 percent of Kyrgyz fifteen years or older residing throughout the country speak Russian; 84 percent of Kyrgyz fifteen years or older residing in Bishkek speak Russian.[31] Elites also recognize the fact that less than 3 percent of Russians

Table 4.1. Inclusive and Exclusive Citizenship Policies

Kyrgyz Policy	*Latvian Policy*
1990 Law on Citizenship • Establishes citizenship of the Kyrgyz SSR • Declares every citizen of the Kyrgyz SSR a citizen of the Union of Soviet Socialist Republics • Prohibits dual citizenship	1991 Government Ruling on Citizenship • Grants citizens of the first Latvian Republic automatic citizenship of newly independent Latvia • Establishes who is permanently excluded from the citizenry, who may acquire citizenship through registration, and who may obtain citizenship through naturalization
1993 Law on Citizenship • Declares all citizens of the Kyrgyz SSR automatic citizens of the newly independent Kyrgyz Republic • Prohibits dual citizenship	1994 Law on Citizenship • Expands category of individuals who cannot become citizens • Establishes window system • Mandates creation of a commission to test state-language skills of naturalization applicants
	1998 Amended Law on Citizenship • Abolishes window system • Recognizes children born in Latvia after 1991 as citizens of Latvia
	2001 Regulation 234: Cabinet of Ministers • Reduces naturalization fee • Enumerates categories of people eligible for lower fee or payment exemption

who are fifteen years or older speak the state language.[32] As a result, Kyrgyz language policy has become increasingly accommodative toward Russian-speakers.

Almost all union republics launched their respective nationalization projects prior to the collapse of the Soviet Union with a law establishing the titular language as the republic's state language. In 1989 the Kyrgyz Supreme Soviet passed a law designating Kyrgyz the state language. Two additional stipulations promote Kyrgyz. First, managers and employees of a wide range of institutions must be proficient in Kyrgyz: "Managers and all other employees of organs of state power and administration, public and cooperative organizations, law enforcement bodies, national education, public health, culture, transport, trade, everyday services, and communal households, in functions which involve association with citizens, must use the state language to an extent which secures the fulfillment of their official duties."[33] Second, Kyrgyz is the working language of government: "The state language is the working language of organs of state power and administration in the Kyrgyz SSR. It is used in office paperwork, at meetings, and at conferences, while a translation into Russian for those people who are not fluent in the state language is provided."[34] These stipulations expand the spheres of communication in which the use of Kyrgyz is required. However, as indicated above, the policy simultaneously mandates Russian translations of government-related documents, meetings, and conferences. This early piece of legislation also designates Russian as the language of interethnic communication: "The Kyrgyz SSR secures the free functioning of the Russian language as the language of interethnic communication for the peoples of the Soviet Union, and does not oppress the right of citizens of other nationalities to use their native language."[35]

Like many post-Soviet constitutions, the Kyrgyz constitution has been amended several times. Versions passed prior to 2000 confirm Kyrgyz as the state language, guarantee the preservation, development, and functioning of Russian, and prohibit the infringement of rights and freedoms based on ignorance of the state language.[36] The 2003, 2006, and 2007 versions confirm Kyrgyz as the state language, define Russian as the official language, and prohibit the infringement of rights and freedoms based on ignorance of the state language or the official language. In an attempt to balance the promotion of Kyrgyz and the preservation of Russian in the political realm, the constitution stipulates that the president must speak the state language fluently but does not demand the same of deputies of parliament.[37]

President Akayev began to pursue a more flexible language policy in 1994 when he signed a decree stating that motivations for Russian out-migration include poor economic conditions, a lack of proportional representation in government, Kyrgyz nationalism, and various language problems. The decree marks the birth of his campaign to reduce the rate of Russian exit, which by the mid-1990s had engendered a fairly severe brain drain. This piece of legislation permits the public use of Russian in geographic areas and economic sectors dominated by Russian-speakers, as well as in economic sectors that require use of an international language for continued progress: ". . . in territorial and industrial groups in which the majority is comprised of Russian-speaking citizens of the Kyrgyz Republic, and also in those spheres of activity where the achievement of progress is linked with the use of the Russian language (public health and technical science, for example), the official language [to be used on an equal basis with Kyrgyz] is Russian."[38] The government also delayed the introduction of a mandate requiring the publication of official documents in Kyrgyz as of 1 January 2005.[39]

Although it is unlikely that this mandate will ever be enforced given the limited language proficiency among urban Kyrgyz, the next chapter shows that rumors regarding the impending transformation continue to generate anxiety among Russians.

Deputies of parliament blocked Akayev's initiatives to expand the public sphere of communication in which the use of Russian is accepted until 2000. For example, a proposed constitutional amendment designating Russian the official language fell to the wayside in 1998.[40] On one occasion, individuals who opposed granting Russian any status other than language of interethnic communication threatened to resort to violence. A newspaper article entitled "They Condemned Dooronbeka Sadyrbaeva to Death" claimed that parliament received a letter from an organization called Independence demanding that the legislature block deputies, such as Sadyrbaeva, who support a change in the legal status of Russian. The letter stated that if Russian were designated an official language, outside forces would detonate parliament to punish enemies of the Kyrgyz people.[41] Despite the intensity surrounding the issue, Akayev continued to push for an expanded realm of communication in which the use of Russian is permitted.

In accordance with the broad goals of Kyrgyz nationalization, the president worked simultaneously to develop and promote the state language. In 1998 the government founded the National Commission for the State Language to transform Kyrgyz into a functioning state language. According to the only Russian member of the commission at the time, the nomadic origins of the Kyrgyz language render such a transformation problematic: "Kyrgyz is a language of an ancient nomadic culture which developed in an epic age as a supple, rich, and beautiful language. Today Kyrgyz is experiencing completely natural difficulties in the fields of science, technology, law, and politics."[42] As a result, the commission is developing a contemporary vocabulary. In 1999 the government ordered samples of official documents written in Kyrgyz so the commission could begin to modernize the language.[43] That same year, the government passed a law on civil service requiring public servants to know the state language "to the extent necessary for the fulfillment of their employment duties."[44]

Akayev's determination to preserve the Russian language in an official capacity finally paid off. The following excerpt from a speech he delivered to parliament a month before the adoption of a new language law conveys the former president's comprehension of the importance of the Russian language in Kyrgyzstan:

> Today we must pay attention to their [Russians'] problems and make maximum efforts in order to prove that the slogan "Kyrgyzstan—our common

home" is not empty words, that it is the genuine will of the Kyrgyz people to live in harmony and friendship, working side by side with our brothers—Russians, Ukrainians, Bellorussians, and Germans, representatives of other peoples who are an integral part of the people of Kyrgyzstan. The thread linking national diversity was, and is the Russian language—a language which is itself an inexhaustible fountain, and one of the most valued spiritual and material resources of the people of Kyrgyzstan.[45]

Russian became Kyrgyzstan's official language in May 2000. According to the law on the official language, which does not affect the designation of Kyrgyz as the state language, Russian is to be used on an equal basis with the state language "in the spheres of state administration, legislation, and legal proceedings of the Kyrgyz Republic, and also in other spheres of public life."[46] Moreover, the speaker and members of parliament, the government, and guests have the right to address parliament and government sessions in Russian. In addition, simultaneous Kyrgyz-Russian and Russian-Kyrgyz translations of speeches delivered during parliament and government sessions must be provided.[47]

Three aspects of the policy further accommodate local Russians. First, the law confirms that the state will protect and create conditions for the functioning and development of Russian. Second and more important in terms of daily life, the policy grants citizens the right to appeal to organs of state and local administration in Russian and requires those agencies to accept documents submitted in Russian. This is vital to Russian-speakers because numerous transactions, from paying phone bills to filing complaints, are conducted in government offices. Finally, the law designates Russian a required subject in all schools including state institutions of higher education.[48]

Education policy also aims to balance the promotion of Kyrgyz with the preservation of Russian. While the 1989 law on the state language designates Kyrgyz the main teaching language, it also guarantees a choice of language of instruction.[49] Subsequent policies promote Kyrgyz but ensure the preservation of Russian. For example, the law on education establishes that although the primary language of instruction is Kyrgyz, teaching may be conducted in any language. Moreover, citizens are guaranteed a choice of language of instruction in all state institutions, and students are required to study three languages: the state language, Russian, and a foreign language.[50] A second law on the state language, which was passed in 2004, appears to take a tougher stance on Russian because it eliminates the guarantee of a choice of language of instruction. But this is a reflection of the need to consider the appearance of private schools, where students still have that choice.[51] The 2004 legislation states that Kyrgyz is the main language of instruction in institutes of education financed by local budgets, and that along with the official and other languages of instruction the teaching in and study of the state language will be provided.[52]

This does not mean, however, that elites are willing to sacrifice the preservation and use of their native language. Shortly after signing the law on the official language, the government launched a program to develop and expand the use of Kyrgyz between 2000 and 2010. This program requires the publication of official documentation in the state language and specifies three tasks designed to increase the obligatory use of Kyrgyz in political, administrative, and professional spheres: (1) develop measures for managing documentation in the state language in all government ministries, departments, institutions, committees, and education establishments; (2) define minimal state-language proficiency requirements that managers and workers at all levels will be required to meet; and (3) develop a system of periodic language testing for managers of state organs and administrative and self-governing bodies, as well as for employees who work with the public.[53] The very need for such a policy indicates resistance among the Kyrgyz themselves to use the state language on a regular basis.

The 2004 law on the state language discussed above reiterates Russian's status as official language and establishes the government's decision to create conditions to support the use of Kyrgyz and finance programs for the study and development of Kyrgyz.[54] The working language of the state is Kyrgyz: only individuals fluent in the language can occupy high-level positions like president, prime minister, chair of parliament, and chair of the Constitutional Court; public servants must know Kyrgyz well enough to carry out their duties; and paperwork must be in Kyrgyz in organs of state power and local administration.[55] At the same time, the law is more lenient than the 1989 legislation in terms of the state's relationship to Russian. Not only does it state that the republic "guarantees representatives of all nationalities . . . protection of their native language and the creation of conditions for their study and development . . . and forbids the oppression of rights and freedoms of citizens based on lack of knowledge of the state or official language," but it also eliminates the article found in the first law on the state language requiring managers and employees of a wide range of institutions to be proficient in Kyrgyz.[56] Instead, the 2004 legislation (1) states that in certain regions, districts, cities, and villages paperwork can be in the state *and* official languages; (2) requires all documentation of a scientific/technical or accounting/financial nature coming from enterprises, organizations, and institutions of the republic to be in the state *and* official languages; and (3) obliges managers of all state institutions to create conditions for their employees to master the state language. In contrast to their counterparts in Latvia, elites in Kyrgyzstan are dedicated to the preservation of Russian as the country's official language.

Eliminating the Russian Language: Latvian Language Policy

Like the Kyrgyz SSR, the Latvian SSR passed legislation in 1989 declaring the titular language the state language and defining Russian as "the most widely used language in the Latvian SSR, and one of the languages of interethnic communication."[57] But the Soviet Union's demise enabled elites to nationalize their newly independent state as they wished, and elites in Latvia have approached the question of how the promotion of a non-Russian language affects Russian-speakers far less sympathetically than have their counterparts in Kyrgyzstan. Latvia's language policy is characterized by an explicit commitment to promote the state language, has become increasingly adverse in terms of its impact on Russian-speakers, and aims to eliminate de jure and de facto use of Russian despite the fact that 67 percent of the country's Latvian population speaks Russian.[58] By 2005 elites had classified Russian as a foreign language, increased the number of spheres of communication in which the use of Latvian is required, and implemented a policy compelling schools for national minorities to teach 60 percent of all classroom hours in Latvian.

The country's second language law, which was adopted in 1992, altered the direction of its linguistic regime dramatically. This policy marks the beginning of a process to eliminate de jure and to as great an extent as possible de facto use of Russian. It not only retracts the language of interethnic communication status and therefore deprives Russian of legal status, but it also permits an appeal to state agencies in Russian *only* if the request is accompanied by a notarized translation in the state language.[59] The ubiquitous presence of official documentation in society and the cost of notarized translations render this highly problematic for Russian-speakers. Finally, unlike the first language law, this policy does not ensure the development of non-Latvian cultures in their native languages.[60]

The 1992 legislation diminishes the use of Russian and expands the use of Latvian in many ways. For example, state employees are obligated to use Latvian, and state agencies must publish documentation in the state language and may accept documents in languages other than Latvian only if they are accompanied by a notarized translation. Furthermore, state agencies may respond to inquiries in a language other than Latvian only after an initial response is given in the state language.[61] These stipulations effectively render Latvian *the* language of the state.

The law also calls for the creation of a State Language Center, an Inspection Board, and a Language Commission to ensure policy implementation. The State Language Center, which was founded in 1992, employs approximately seventeen inspectors who drop by public and private organizations including offices, restaurants, and retail stores to (1) check the language of record keeping, public information, and product labeling; (2) test the state-language skills of employees; and (3) eavesdrop on conversations to confirm that employees speak with each other and with their customers in Latvian. Fines are issued for violations. Given that less than 3 percent of Latvians do not speak their native language, it is not surprising that most of the people who have been fined since 1992 are Russian.[62]

The government's decision to adopt a radical language law in 1999 marks the apex of linguistic nationalization. This policy widens the sphere of communication in which Latvian is required and discontinues the legal use of Russian in the public realm.[63] The law promises to preserve, protect, and develop Latvian as well as the cultural-historical heritage of the Latvian nation; to ensure the right to use Latvian; and to promote the integration of national minorities into society while observing their right to use their native languages.[64] With the exception of the last clause, these stipulations aim to expand the mandatory use of the state language in all fields of communication.

Four aspects of the policy adversely affect Russian-speakers. First, Latvian is *the* language of public and private organizations.[65] Any transaction conducted in Russian within such an organization is technically illegal. Second, employees of public and private organizations must use the state language when their activities affect the public interest. Third, documents submitted to a public organization must be in the state language unless they concern urgent calls for assistance; documents submitted in a foreign language must be accompanied by a notarized translation in the state language. Most symbolic is the fact that all languages used in Latvia except the state language and Livonian (a Finnic rather than Baltic language) are considered foreign.

Strict regulations accompany this policy. In the early 1990s the government created a system of language testing based on three levels of proficiency. The fact that state officials grade language tests is not surprising, but the fact that they are generally Latvian does matter. An individual's level of proficiency in the state language dictates which professions are accessible regardless of his experience and qualifications. In 1999 elites doubled the number of language proficiency categories—now there are six—and as a result employers often require an updated language certificate.[66] Proficiency was initially categorized as beginning, intermediate, or advanced; now there is a subdegree for each group. Beginning categories restrict an individual to unskilled manual labor; intermediate categories allow an individual to work in the service sector as well as in technical and accounting fields; the lower level of the advanced category permits an individual to manage an organization or work as a specialist, medical worker, social worker, or teacher; only the higher level of the advanced category allows an individual to work in state agencies and corresponding subdivisions or with documents and administrative record keeping. The advanced levels demand native fluency.

Education laws also illuminate the antagonistic nature of Latvia's nationalization program. The constitution guarantees everyone the right to an education but does not address the question of language of instruction.[67] Policies regulating the language of instruction used in academic institutions have become increasingly hostile to Russian-speakers. Although the 1989 law on languages guarantees the right to receive secondary education in Latvian or Russian and secures Latvian and Russian instruction in vocational, professional, and higher education institutes according to specialties needed in Latvia, subsequent policies are designed to ensure that the state language becomes the only language used in academic settings.[68]

The government announced its intention to phase out education conducted in any language other than Latvian in 1991: "In institutes of higher-education financed by the state, beginning with the second year of study the primary language of instruction is Latvian. . . . In schools for national minorities in which the language of instruction is not Latvian, in classes 1–9 not less than 2, and in classes 10–12 not less than 3 of the liberal arts subjects must be taught, for the most part, in the state language."[69] The first law on education guarantees residents the right to study in the state language. Although students have the right to study in their native language and the state is responsible for the realization of this right, they must pass exams in Latvian in order to graduate high school.[70] Similarly, the 1992 law on languages promises "teaching in the state language and other languages" in vocational and professional schools according to specialties needed in Latvia, but specifies that beginning with the second year of study the primary language of instruction will be Latvian in institutes of higher education financed by the state.[71] Exams are administered in the state language in all institutes of higher education.[72]

It is the 1998 law on education, however, that bans Russian-speaking students from state institutions: "In state institutions of education and in self-governing institutions of education the language of instruction is the state language."[73] While students are permitted to study in other languages in private institutions, it is important to note that private institutions have the authority to determine payment and are thus more expensive than public institutions, which lack such jurisdiction.[74] Moreover, students who fail to learn Latvian independently encounter obstacles in the future owing to regulations that keep individuals who do not master the language out of a variety of professions. According to the 1998 policy, professional exams are administered in the state language, work must be written and defended in that language in order to receive an academic or scientific degree, and vocational training financed by state and municipal budgets is conducted in the state language.[75] Until recently students could study in other languages in state institutions with national minority programs, but an amendment to the law on education curtails the use of Russian in these schools.[76]

Unlike their counterparts in Kyrgyzstan, elites in Latvia actively pursue "societal integration." While the government's formal program does address the need to protect minority rights, it simultaneously identifies widespread proficiency in Latvian as the means to achieve integration: "A common language, in the linguistic sense, is necessary for the successful integration of society, and for the formation and understanding of a common system of values. The state language is the symbol of the state, and the instrument of societal integration."[77] This clause is followed by a stipulation that emphasizes respect for a minority's right to preserve its language and culture as a basis of identity. In terms of education, the program aims to ensure that all residents master the state language so that they may use it as a means of communication. This clause is followed by a stipulation regarding the need for programs of national minority education "which support the goals [of the societal integration program] and further the preservation of the identities of national minorities, and their integration into the society of Latvia."[78] Nevertheless, the implementation of a highly controversial education policy in 2004, which I discuss in Chapter 6, indicates that the state intends to cultivate a society based on one language. Table 4.2 compares Kyrgyzstan's tolerant language policy to Latvia's rigid language policy.

Informal Nationalization Practices

Latvian is a profession.

When they see the cut of your eyes they may turn you down, they may pay such a low salary that the thought to work there will not occur.

While elites in Kyrgyzstan embrace the formal aspect of nationalization to less of an extent than do their counterparts in Latvia, this is not the

Table 4.2. Tolerant and Rigid Language Policies

Kyrgyz Policy	*Latvian Policy*
1989 Law on the State Language • Declares Kyrgyz the state language of the Kyrgyz SSR • Declares Russian the language of interethnic communication in the Kyrgyz SSR	1989 Law on the State Language • Declares Latvian the state language of the Latvian SSR • Declares Russian the language of interethnic communication in the Latvian SSR
1992 Law on Education • Declares Kyrgyz the main language of education • Permits teaching in any language and guarantees a choice of language of instruction in all state institutions • Requires students to study the state language and Russian	1992 Law on Languages • Compels employees of state agencies to use Latvian exclusively • Establishes language police system • Terminates Russian's "language of interethnic communication" status • Grants right to appeal to state agencies in Russian only if the request is submitted with a notarized translation
1994 Presidential Decree on Migration • Extends introduction of official documents in the state language to 2005 • Allows public use of Russian in economic sectors where Russian-speakers dominate and in scientific realms where the use of Russian is conducive to progress	1998 Law on Education • Designates Latvian the language of instruction in all state institutions • Demands that professional exams be administered in Latvian, work be written and defended in Latvian in order to receive a degree, and vocational training financed by the state be conducted in Latvian
2000 Law on the Official Language • Designates Russian as the official language of the Kyrgyz Republic • Confirms Kyrgyz as the state language	1999 Law on the State Language • Establishes Latvian as the language of public and private institutions • Requires employees of these institutions to use Latvian • Doubles the number of state-language proficiency categories and dictates which professions are accessible based on an individual's official categorization • Designates all languages except Latvian and Livonian foreign
2004 Law on the State Language • Declares Kyrgyz the main language of instruction in educational institutions financed by local budgets • States that along with the official language (Russian) and other languages of instruction (such as Uzbek), the teaching in and study of the state language (Kyrgyz) will be provided in public institutions	2004 Amendment to the 1998 Law on Education • Declares that 60 percent of classroom hours must be taught in Latvian in schools for national minorities

case when it comes to the informal aspect of nationalization. Elites in both countries condone informal personnel practices that privilege the respective titular nation and consequently disadvantage Russians. These practices are an opaque but critical element of nationalization projects that seek to heighten the core nation's sense of "ownership" of the state. A forty-six-year-old Russian woman in Riga who was unable to land a job for seven years because she does not speak Latvian refers to these nontransparent practices in the following quotation: "Is it harder for Russians to find good work? Of course, because they say that this is their country and that we are invaders. It's harder because we're Russian— this is the sole reason- -because we're Russian. If there's a Latvian who is not a specialist and a Russian who is a specialist, they hire the Latvian. It's a question of nationality."[79] Interview data shed light on informal aspects of nationalization, including the use of "administrative discretion to pursue a nationalizing agenda," and indicate that informal personnel practices privileging the core nation are extensive in both states.[80] One twenty-three-year-old Russian man in Bishkek who worked at a variety of institutions before enrolling in graduate school explained it this way:

> Is it more difficult for Russians to find good work? Well, naturally. Here's the situation: they understand the national state as the Kyrgyz state, not as a multinational state, and this is the problem. Few Russians work in the state apparatus; you can count them on your fingers. When they see the cut of your eyes they may turn you down, they may pay such a low salary that the thought to work there will not occur, or they may create such conditions that according to your own wish you leave because of such difficult conditions.[81]

Similar sentiments are echoed in Riga. According to a thirty-seven-year-old male resident of the city who was a salesclerk at the time of the interview:

> In Latvia they divide us on the basis of nationality. First, education— Russian children basically have no future because they are Russian. They are losing their education. It's harder and harder to get an education in their native language. It's possible to get a higher education in Russian but only in private universities, which are not free. You cannot get a higher education in Russian in a state university. In addition, Russians are deprived of electoral rights, and they are not hired in state agencies. It's harder for Russians to find good work. Latvians advance their own. There's even a saying now: Latvian is a profession. Your qualifications are not important if you are Latvian because Latvian is a profession.[82]

An article in *Chas* entitled "Nationality Has Become a Profession" explains the phrase "Latvian is a profession" as follows: "Currently, according to state statistics, 92 percent of officials are Latvian—only 8 percent are non-Latvian. Apparently the official apparatus is acquired by nationality, kinship, nepotism, acquaintances, and recommendations of nationally anxious people. Obviously, a tendency of aggressive exclusion of Russian speakers from many spheres of activity is visible."[83] One researcher at the Russian Academy of Sciences asserts that the practice of excluding Russians from key positions in the state sector intensified when Kyrgyzstan became an independent state:

> Indeed, after the proclamation of independence, politics [i.e., practices] to exclude them [Russians] from governing and management positions, from those spheres in which they predominated earlier—education, public health, culture, services—intensified. Now access to the majority of 'soft' jobs in the state sector (the state apparatus, banks, taxes, customs, law enforcement, judicial organs, and so on) is very difficult. It is here that the strongest discrimination of Russian-speakers appears.[84]

Research substantiates this claim and confirms the existence of a widespread sense of perceived ethnic discrimination among Bishkek and Riga Russians that is rooted in informal personnel practices promoting the core nation. The interviews that form the foundation of this chapter were designed to uncover Russian perceptions about informal practices based on unwritten rules and procedures—in other words, practices that are neither enforced by law nor discussed in employee handbooks.

When asked about their experience as a new minority, Bishkek and Riga Russians emphasize the detrimental impact of informal personnel practices that favor the titular nation and as a result curtail economic opportunity available to Russians. Figure 5.1 in the next chapter shows that the overwhelming majority of Bishkek likely permanent residents (80 percent) and a considerable portion of Riga likely permanent residents (33 percent) refer to the adverse effect of such practices.[85] A forty-four-year-old Bishkek Russian who at the time of the interview was an assistant to a rector at the Slavic University sums up the problem:

> When there's a promotion to management that is based on nationality, ethnicity, this means the end of democracy. When skills and knowledge of the work do not play a decisive role but ancestry does—this is a dead-end situation, and the beginning of the end of democratic reform. And this is what we have now. The number of Russian managers is decreasing. There are very few Russians in parliament; it's not proportional in relation to the makeup of society. Very few representatives of the Russian population are in organs of administrative authority, the militia, customs—so there is an active process of segregation. It's informal, it's not declared, but it's carried out in local organs. Statistics confirm this—if the city of Tokmak has 80 percent Russian-speakers, 100 percent of the militia there is Kyrgyz—there is not one representative of the Russian-speaking population. And this sort of thing always offends people.[86]

Riga Russians express similar views regarding the manner in which informal nationalization practices restrict opportunity. Consider the following quotation from an interview with a forty-five-year-old Russian
schoolteacher: "We used to laugh at the phrase 'certainty in tomorrow,'
but every Soviet citizen had certainty in tomorrow; we knew we'd go to
work the next day. Today certainty doesn't exist. And uncertainty affects
Russians first and foremost because if a Russian and a Latvian lose their
jobs, the Latvian will find a job the next day even if he has lower qualifications than the Russian simply because he's Latvian."[87]

In both cases, informal personnel practices ensure that members of
the respective core nation occupy management positions. And managers dictate hiring procedures. According to a sixty-nine-year-old Bishkek
Russian who at the time of the interview taught history at a university:

> Life's gotten more difficult for everyone, Russians and Kyrgyz, but we feel
> the emigration of the Russian population. Many Russians, especially spe-
> cialists and technicians, have left Kyrgyzstan particularly after the adop-
> tion of the law on the state language. Many people left in connection with
> this, and now there are very few Russian workers in organizations—for the
> most part representatives of the local nationality work in management
> positions. And it is harder for Russians because everywhere Kyrgyz fill
> management positions, and naturally they hire people of their own
> nationality.[88]

Informal personnel practices operate in the same fashion in Latvia. As
one fifty-seven-year-old Russian who worked in building management at
the time of the interview put it, "Things are more difficult for Russians
because nationality does have an influence. If you go for an interview,
you find that managers tend to be Latvian. And who do you think they
hire? They don't hire Russians."[89] Thus, interviews indicate that titular
domination of management is partially responsible for the deterioration
of labor market conditions for Russians. A forty-four-year-old Russian
engineer relays his experience with Kyrgyz management:

> Life's gotten worse here [since the collapse] because national factors
> exist. There's discrimination on the basis of language and at work in state
> institutions. I think life's gotten worse. . . . Because in organizations, in
> institutions, the first person—this is the policy, it may be secret—but basi-
> cally this person is of the native nationality. . . . So there is oppression in
> commerce. . . . For example, I worked in one organization and when
> we needed to work we worked, we restored everything, and then when
> everything was turned around, when they began to make a profit, they
> said to us: guys, that's it, thanks, you are no longer needed. They fired us
> and in three months a person of the native nationality filled my position.[90]

Linguistic discrimination is another reason the labor market has
shrunk for Russians. Though formal policy does not endorse linguistic

discrimination in Kyrgyzstan, it is not uncommon for managers to use lack of proficiency in the state language as a pretense to deny qualified Russians powerful positions, particularly at the level of management.[91] Although knowledge of Kyrgyz is required to fulfill some management duties, the overwhelming majority of those responsibilities are carried out in Russian, which remains the principal language of professional communication. Despite the fact that most business transactions are conducted in Russian, knowledge of Kyrgyz is a standard hiring requirement. So while professional exclusion is based on ethnicity rather than language, managers use a lack of Kyrgyz language skills as an excuse to avoid hiring Russians. The following quotation is from an interview with a fifty-year-old unemployed Russian who worked in the shuttle trade, which makes up a large part of the country's informal economy:

> There is discomfort related to the Russian language. . . . They declared that the state language would only be Kyrgyz, despite the fact that the overwhelming majority of the population spoke in Russian—and moreover, more than half of the population considers this the language in which they think. At times due to lack of knowledge of the state language—in budgetary spheres and state structures—they began to fire Russians, so discrimination began. Discrimination based on language—surely this is serious discrimination.[92]

It is difficult to find a Bishkek Russian who considers formal language policy discriminatory, but this does not mean that Bishkek Russians do not experience linguistic discrimination. A forty-three-year-old Russian lawyer who at one point worked for the Slavic Foundation and at the time of the interview worked for the Association of Ethnic Russians gives his opinion on discrimination in the following statement:

> At the state level, the official level, we do not have oppression like they have in Latvia where laws are issued which discriminate against the Russian population . . . in the constitution where the status of Kyrgyz as the state language is secured discrimination on the basis of language skills is not permitted, and in labor laws discrimination on the basis of language skills is not permitted . . . at the local level there have been cases when local managers or local bosses tolerated violations of this. If we're talking about my friends or acquaintances—they cannot occupy certain positions because they are not representatives, as we say, of the titular nation, and yes, there have been such cases, but this happens unofficially with reference to a lack of competence, ability, or knowledge. There are a few examples where we cannot become chairman of a village council, so at the local government level, can't occupy certain positions but I repeat—this is all done unofficially, everything's posed as relative connections, kinship ties—but at the official level this is not done.[93]

The issue is different in Latvia, where formal language policy *does* dictate who can and cannot work in various professions. Theoretically this should clarify one's chances of reaching certain professional goals, but there is a perception among Riga Russians that even if they are proficient in Latvian they will still confront obstacles in the labor market because they are "non-native." Consider the following quotation from an interview with a forty-nine-year-old Russian employee of a small firm who speaks enough Latvian to garner an official language certificate designating his level of proficiency intermediate:

> When perestroika arrived, Russians became no one here and it meant study Latvian or you are no one. The status of Russians has diminished. Even if you speak Latvian, it's unlikely you'll aspire [to anything grand], the more so because now they've passed a law that divides the highest category of language proficiency. There are not simply three [categories], this is what existed since 1990; now there are more criteria so that only a Latvian could meet them because it is possible to know Latvian this well only if you are Latvian. So there's a language problem. It's a different matter that they can discriminate because you are Russian—not always, I emphasize, not always, but there are reasons for me to say this. When a Russian, even one who knows Latvian, when they simply push him aside, they don't fire him, but they very tactfully say good-bye, you are free. . . . If a Russian knows Latvian well, there's a fifty-fifty chance he will not reach the higher levels of management even if he knows Latvian better than many Latvians. My wife knows Latvian, she's a citizen, was born here, her roots are here, but I don't think she could reach the higher levels— though of course she has advantages over Russians who do not know Latvian.[94]

Representatives of Russians in both countries emphasize the prevalence and significance of informal discrimination. Kyrgyzstan's Slavic Foundation fears that the Kyrgyz have become a *staatvolk*, a group "culturally and politically preeminent in a state, even though other groups are present in significant numbers."[95] According to a representative of the foundation, since the acquisition of independence there has been a gradual but consistent informal process in which the Kyrgyz are promoted to positions of power. During the Akayev era, Kyrgyz personnel dominated the "White House": the highest level of government was about 90 percent Kyrgyz; directors and managers of most firms were Kyrgyz; and only one university rector was not Kyrgyz.[96] The same representative of the Slavic Foundation claims that personnel discrimination is the main mechanism through which the Kyrgyz are building a state of and for the Kyrgyz: "Russians face personnel discrimination at the state and local levels, but the main thing is that there are no Russians in government at the state level. Tax inspectors, judges, prosecutors— they're all Kyrgyz. Look at the government: Russians comprise about 12 percent of the population, but there are only two Russians in parliament."[97]

Representatives of Kyrgyzstan's Union of Russian Compatriots also deem informal nationalization practices highly problematic because they deprive Russians of the opportunity to influence affairs of the state. One former vice president considers the exclusion of Russians from powerful positions detrimental to Russian interests: "Slowly they forced us from our positions. . . . Russians were pushed out of the state structure and other organizations such as the police, justice department, legal field. . . . The oppression is hidden and gradual."[98] The union's chairman agrees with these sentiments: "Over the last fourteen years they have forced Russians out of state positions . . . it's not a secret that they fill positions with their own. If the manager is of the titular nationality, he attracts his own and looks not at professional qualities but at nationality."[99] Similarly, a representative of Kyrgyzstan's Public Association of Russians asserts that informal personnel practices make finding a job extraordinarily difficult for Russians: "It's easier for Kyrgyz to find work because disdain for Russians exists. I wouldn't say Russians face blatant oppression, but the Kyrgyz have gradually forced Russian specialists out of the state structure and large enterprises."[100]

Representatives of Latvia's Russian minority population also underscore the injurious consequences of informal aspects of nationalization. One representative of the Party of National Harmony claims that "There are both official norms and unofficial administrative practices that put Russians in a far more vulnerable position than Latvians."[101] Similarly, the president of the Association of Latvian-Russian Cooperation acknowledges that Russians have trouble working for the state even if they are citizens and have mastered Latvian.[102] The president of Russian Society echoes these sentiments in an assertion that while language policy is the primary means of discrimination, informal personnel practices serve the same purpose. When asked if Russians in Latvia face oppression, she answered, "Yes, but language knowledge is only the first moment. Even if you study Latvian and demonstrate that you have mastered the language, it's all the same—you'll have trouble finding work."[103]

Interviews reveal a widespread sense of perceived ethnic discrimination among Bishkek and Riga Russians that stems from informal personnel practices privileging the core nation. They also suggest a pervasive awareness among Bishkek and Riga Russians that such practices guarantee core nation domination of management, which curtails economic opportunity. However, the interaction of formal nationalization policies and informal nationalization practices influences Russian minority politics in Kyrgyzstan and Latvia differently. In Kyrgyzstan, elites implement formal policies that promote Kyrgyz interests but simultaneously accommodate Russian interests. Yet the interaction of formal policies and informal practices thwarts the realization of such accommodation because personnel decisions privilege Kyrgyz at the expense of Russians. These competing informal institutions contradict the intended aim of formal institutions. The high level of Russian exit illustrates that detrimental effects of informal practices trump potential merits of formal policies. In Latvia, elites implement formal policies that promote Latvian interests and dismiss Russian interests. The interaction of formal policies and informal practices contributes to the advancement of Latvians because personnel decisions privilege Latvians at the expense of Russians. These complementary informal institutions reinforce the intended aim of formal institutions. Surprisingly, unfavorable consequences of formal policies and informal practices have not generated a high level of Russian exit from Latvia. In order to understand why Russians remain in a state that implements antagonistic policies and condones discriminatory practices we must explore the role of informal networks.

Informal Networks in Kyrgyzstan and Latvia

The Latvian case suggests that inherited dense informal networks can alleviate minority discontent in the context of a developed post-Soviet economy. Whether a minority inherits such networks depends on its socioeconomic status during the Soviet era. The fundamental difference between Russians in the Latvian SSR and the Kyrgyz SSR is that by the late 1980s Russians dominated state and party organs in the former but had been ousted from such organs in the latter. As discussed previously, in the late 1960s Central Asian elites began to implement affirmative action policies that privileged "their own." Moscow allowed this behavior because it did not consider such personnel changes a threat to the regime. The region was incorporated into the Soviet Union fairly early, had always been undeveloped, and had never known independent statehood. The chances of a regional challenge to the center were slim. Because Moscow was not particularly concerned about compliance, it did not deem it necessary to extend excessive power to Russians. The center's willingness to tolerate such affirmative action policies gave regional elites the green light to oust Russians from key positions within the party, Komsomol, and KGB. Lacking alternatives to the system from which they had been ejected, Russians began to migrate from Central Asia to Russia in the 1970s.

In sharp contrast, Moscow brutally suppressed attempts by Baltic elites to implement affirmative action policies that privileged "their own." The Baltic republics were incorporated into the Soviet Union fairly late, had always had relatively strong economies, and were home to nationalistic populations that had tasted the sweetness of independent statehood. As a result, Moscow took special measures to maintain strict control over them. The center ensured compliance by granting Russians it sent to the region after World War II excessive power, and Russians retained the institutional dominance they acquired in the immediate aftermath of the war throughout the Soviet era. Institutional dominance, a high standard of living, and economic opportunity meant that migration to Russia was nonsensical for most Baltic Russians. They remained in a region where they enjoyed power, prestige, and economic opportunity.

When the influence of Soviet institutions began to crumble in the early 1990s, informal networks based on previous state and party affiliations began to emerge. These networks are made up of colleagues from Soviet political institutions who rely on each other's expertise and resources to resist efforts made by post-Soviet elites to exclude Russians from power. The networks are informal because the party and state organs within which members congregated previously disintegrated shortly after the union's collapse and because they operate on the basis of a single, unwritten, foundational rule, which is that a minority must take care of its own in an environment of discrimination. This mentality is a logical reaction to the realization that independent statehood forced Russians in non-Russian successor states into a seemingly fixed disadvantageous position.

The Latvian case illustrates how institutional dominance allowed Russians to transform capital associated with Soviet state and party organs into foundations for new political and economic activity in the early post-Soviet era. Informal networks enabled Russians in post-Soviet Latvia to organize on a political basis and to enter the country's vibrant private sector. Moreover, the utilization of such networks has proved longstanding and effective in terms of preserving a strong Russian presence in the country's business sector. Many Russians prefer to hire "their own" whenever possible, and this contributes to the growth of mono-ethnic private companies. The main reason for ethnic segregation in Latvia's business sector is a tendency among Russian companies to rely on informal contacts when hiring.

In contrast, Russians in post-Soviet Kyrgyzstan reside in an environment where jobs are scarce. Private sector jobs are in short supply because the economy is undeveloped. Without dense informal networks, Russians cannot mitigate the effects of being frozen out of both public and available private sector jobs by informal nationalization practices. Sparse informal networks impede their ability to organize collectively, and as a result their prospects of improved opportunity are minimal. Whether Russians in post-Soviet states have inherited dense informal networks influences the degree to which they can evade nationalization policies and practices, and thus reconfigure the boundaries of their respective opportunity structure.

The Critical Importance of Dense Informal Networks

> [F]or the most part, it was money from the Komsomol and party, and access to Soviet property.

Dense informal networks have provided Russians with the means to reconfigure the opportunity structure Latvian elites created with the implementation of their post-Soviet nationalization project. Russians in independent Latvia are part of dense informal networks because they dominated local state and party organs during the Soviet era. The ethnic division of power that characterized the Latvian SSR, where non-Latvians were overrepresented in the party and key areas of administration, ensured Russian control over key decision-making organs. In 1986 only four of the thirteen Central Committee members were Latvian.[104] In 1989 Russians occupied 46 percent of the republic's state and party positions, Latvians occupied 34 percent, and Belarusians, Ukrainians, and Poles occupied 16 percent.[105] The occasional Latvian who did hold a critical position was "shadowed" by a Russian to guarantee compliance with center demands.

However, by the early 1990s Russians were forced to rely on their own devices because nationalization policies and practices had pushed them out of the state sector. Russians established a niche in independent Latvia by transforming political capital associated with Soviet state and party organs into economic capital that was then used as a basis for new commercial activity in the emerging private sector.[106] This process was not inherently ethnic in nature—Latvians participated in the process as well. But in the immediate aftermath of the Soviet Union's demise Russians were in an advantageous position because they had dominated local institutions for the previous fifty years. Though Russians converted political capital into economic capital in three different ways, these methods were not necessarily utilized independently of one another. Most Russians relied on a combination of methods to establish new businesses including (1) pillaging raw materials in Russia and Latvia, (2) participating in *nomenklatura* privatization in Latvia, and (3) taking advantage of connections in Russia.

The pillaging of raw materials occurred in the early 1990s when prices were still artificially low in Russia and Latvia. The process of raiding Russia's raw materials was rather straightforward. Former party, Komsomol, and KGB personnel in Riga worked closely with colleagues in Moscow who had access to Russia's natural resources to purchase raw materials, particularly metals, at excessively low prices. These budding entrepreneurs then sold the raw materials to the West at market prices and earned a generous profit.[107] The process of pillaging Latvia's raw materials was similar. Individuals with access to natural resources, such as Red Army soldiers living on military bases, acquired and sold raw materials to small "businesses" that appeared in urban areas during the early 1990s. These outfits purchased scrap metals and timber at low prices and then sold these items to the West at global prices.[108] People with access to natural resources, many of whom were Russian, success-fully transformed previous positions within the Soviet apparatus into bases of capital for new commercial activity: "The heyday seemed to be the 'colored metals' craze that saw the stripping of factories, and even railroads, for their metal content which was then sold on the world mar-ket. No doubt, many managers and former communists translated their previous position to comfort in the new order, but this is inevitable in any period of radical transition."[109] The raiding of Latvia's raw materials ceased by 1995 because the Red Army had departed, local authorities had cracked down on metal and timber purchasers, and market reform processes had begun to take hold in Russia.

Russians in Latvia also converted political capital into economic capi-tal through *nomenklatura* privatization. This term refers to a general process in which members of the former *nomenklatura* or privileged class use personal knowledge, access, expertise, and connections to benefit from the economic and political uncertainty that characterizes the ini-tial stage of post-communist reform. Particularly prevalent in the indus-trial sector prior to the implementation of effective privatization legislation, *nomenklatura* privatization was endemic in Latvia as it was in most post-Soviet states in the early 1990s.[110] According to a journalist who writes for *Chas*:

> There were a few sources of initial capital. First there was Komsomol, party, and KGB money that launched some businesses. But many small and mid-size businesses, and even some large ones, were established by people who bought part of a former Soviet enterprise and then entered the market. For example, take the construction firm Tilts Civil Engineer-ing. There were people who worked in construction during the Soviet era who obeyed Moscow, and when privatization began they simply gathered resources—like a fragment of a large enterprise—and established their own firm. Then there was the cooperative movement during perestroika. Some cooperatives turned into firms and joint stock companies. But for the most part, it was money from the Komsomol and party, and access to Soviet property.[111]

This quotation alludes to a typical type of *nomenklatura* privatization facilitated by perestroika. Economic restructuring policies created conditions for the establishment of private enterprises, or cooperatives. In the late 1980s it was not uncommon for a director of a state enterprise to establish a co-op in his name and then purchase raw materials and/ or finished products from the state enterprise at artificially low prices. The private enterprise then sold the raw materials and/or finished products to the West at market prices, and profits accrued to the private enterprise while losses condemned the state enterprise. When the state enterprise in question became available for purchase, its director used capital accumulated through the private co-op as well as knowledge, expertise, and connections to manipulate the parameters of the sale to his advantage, and then purchased the state enterprise for a fraction of its worth.[112] One independent journalist experienced in tracking the country's rich and famous confirms the prevalence of this method of privatization in newly independent Latvia: "For example, there might be a large state-owned factory around which private cooperatives were built. These cooperatives manufactured on the basis of the factory's equipment, and then sold the products. As a rule, directors of state factories built these cooperatives and gradually acquired personal capital. In the end, they bought the state factory and it was privatized."[113]

Finally, Russians in Latvia transformed political capital into economic capital by tapping into connections they had in Russia. Russian managers in Latvia's industry and transport sectors had close ties with their counterparts in Russia during the Soviet era, and this put them in a favorable position when the union collapsed.[114] Research supports Aadne Aasland's argument that because Baltic Russians worked in large state enterprises that received administrative direction from Moscow, they had connections with business communities in former republics, such as Russia, that should have created opportunities at home in the post-Soviet era.[115] Indeed, Russian entrepreneurs in Latvia continued to use these Soviet-era connections in private business activity. According to a representative of Latvia's Association for the Support of Russian-Language Schools: "Former *Komsomol* activists in Latvia had very good contacts with the Moscow *Komsomol nomenklatura*. To this day they have good contacts with those former Moscow *Komsomol* members who now work in Moscow commercial banks and are influential in this sector."[116] This individual acknowledges that many Russians, particularly those affiliated with the party and Komsomol, relied on connections they had in Russia to establish private businesses in Latvia after the federation's demise.[117] For example, one prominent, wealthy Russian-speaking entrepreneur in the oil industry who worked for the Latvian Academy of Sciences during the Soviet era tapped into academy connections with factories in Urlask and Saint Petersburg to generate start-up capital for his new company in the early post-Soviet era.[118]

Participation in Latvia's private sector enables Russians to make a living despite constraints imposed by nationalization policies and practices designed to preserve an all-Latvian public sector. A revealing study conducted in 2004 states the following:

> One of the interviewees was a Russian woman who had tried several times to find a job in government institutions, and her experience shows that it is incomparably easier for non-Latvians to find a job in the private sector: *At first I looked for jobs at state institutions, I wanted to be a civil servant. I studied at the University of Latvia, my language skills improved, I started to speak Latvian, and I thought that would be enough to find a job at a high-ranking state institution. I think I went through four or five job competitions, and always I was rejected. Then I came to understand that I simply wanted a different job, because those state employees were poorly paid. I found a job in a month's time afterward. Later on acquaintances told me that when it comes to those job competitions in state institutions, someone wrote down after my interview that I don't speak Latvian well enough, but at the time I spoke the language better than I do now.*[119]

Scholars and local experts on the Russian minority question agree that Russians play an active role in Latvia's business sector, where they do not confront restrictions based on ethnicity.[120] According to Anatol Lieven, "For the moment [Russian businessmen] are doing very well in Latvia, and more and more intelligent and determined young local Russians are rising to join their ranks. So far, they have faced no serious obstacles in the economic sphere."[121] Excluded from the state structure, Russians have established a strong presence in the private sector. As Helen Morris states, "Indications are that Russian-speaking non-citizens have been able to circumvent some of the citizenship and language restrictions through engagement in private enterprise and political relationships with Russian Federation companies."[122] And according to Pal Kolsto, "In political and cultural terms, then, we may note a marginalization of the non-Latvian population. In socioeconomic terms, however, no such marginalization seems evident. . . . Whereas the Russians have few opportunities for improving their societal status qua group, they do have considerable possibilities for making careers within private enterprise."[123] Writing about Russians in Estonia and Latvia, Graham Smith states the following: "Rather than struggle to retain their occupational niches within public sector management, many have moved over to the private sector, making up what constitutes one of the fastest growing social groups within the Baltic states, a new Russian business elite."[124] In 2004 a small group of entrepreneurs established a nongovernmental organization called OKROL (the United Congress of Russian Communities of Latvia) to represent this growing social group in Latvia. According to one of its cochairmen, "Ninety-five percent of Russian-speakers living in Latvia either have their own business or work as employees in the non-government sector. We therefore create a large part of our state's budget. Because of this, one of OKROL's main goals is to unite small and medium-sized Russian businesses."[125]

One member of Latvia's parliament who represents the Party of National Harmony characterizes Russian activity in the private sector in terms of the Jewish model of behavior, which posits that Jews in Europe engaged in commercial activity for years in response to both the denial of political rights and exclusion from the state sector. Russians in post-Soviet Latvia confront similar circumstances and, according to this deputy, have adopted the same coping mechanism: "Russians see that they have no chance in Latvia's state structure. This I call the Jewish syndrome. . . . Today young talented Russians who are inclined toward working for the state or at the management level are forced to enter the private sphere or to migrate from Latvia. The private sphere allows them to break through, to build a good career."[126] The rigidity of Latvia's antagonistic nationalization strategy raises the question of why elites would allow Russians to engage in private sector activity, which is often more lucrative than public sector employment. Aina Antane and Boris Tsilevich argue that the Jewish model of behavior is compatible with aggressive nationalization because it gives Russians incentive to worry about politics only if and when politics affect business. In the absence of this condition, the model suggests that Russians will leave politics to Latvians.[127] However, the massive demonstrations against the controversial education policy that was implemented in 2004 contradict this prediction since the policy had nothing to do with commercial activity and everything to do with identity politics and cultural preservation. The demonstrations, which I discuss in Chapter 6, suggest that Russians *do* worry about politics that are unrelated to business. I argue in Chapter 7 that what allows elites to permit Russian activity in the private sector is the fact that they have reached a satisfactory threshold of political hegemony; in other words, they have secured control of the public sector.

It is difficult to measure the economic power of Russians in Latvia. In the early 1990s Rasma Karklins suggested that non-Latvians owned approximately 80 percent of the country's privately owned businesses.[128] This outdated estimate is probably too high to characterize present conditions. Although Russians did dominate the private sector at that time, as the decade progressed increasing numbers of Latvians opened new firms, and today neither group dominates the private sector.[129] But survey data do suggest that Russians are active in the business community: 64 percent of employed Russian respondents who participated in the 2000 Baltic Barometer Survey were employed in the private sector, which means they were self-employed or worked for privatized firms, new private enterprises, or self-owned businesses.[130] And while the survey's categories changed slightly, 53 percent of employed Russian respondents who participated in the 2004 Baltic Barometer Survey were employed in the private sector, which means they worked for a privatized enterprise or a private enterprise that was established after 1990.[131] It appears that Igor Zevelev was right when he argued that Russians "have adopted behavior typical of a diaspora by starting business enterprises, primarily in trade and financial operations, and are therefore thriving economically."[132] The following quotation from an interview with a twenty-eight-year-old Russian who worked for a private firm in Riga at the time supports this conclusion:

> I understand that I can't work for the state if I don't have the status of citizen. In the private sphere there is no difference [for Russians versus Latvians], in business there is no problem. But there, in government, they fired them [Russians]. And who do they fire first? Russians, noncitizens. If there are cuts, then who is the first to lose his job? A Russian. Second, a noncitizen. If you are both, you are the first candidate to be fired. So it is almost impossible for Russians to get state jobs. Then if a Latvian starts up a business it is harder for a Russian there—but not impossible. I work in a purely Latvian firm, with ten Latvians and one Russian. For the most part, Russians engage in small business.[133]

Informal networks contribute to the preservation of a strong Russian presence in the country's private sector because Russians tend to hire "their own." This propensity has generated a number of Russian companies. One study finds that minorities are active in the private sector and that there are ethnically mixed firms as well as mono-ethnic firms: "First, there is a significant proportion of minorities in the private sector and there are many companies with mixed staff, including ethnically mixed management in large companies. Second, there are also many companies that are mono-ethnic. There are many cases in which the job seekers and possibly also employers focus on ethnic origin, which is often closely linked to a person's native language."[134] Another study finds that although there are increasing numbers of ethnically mixed companies, segregation continues to typify a portion of the business community.[135] Various representatives of Latvia's Russian minority population confirm the existence of mono-ethnic companies. According to a representative of the Socialist Party, "In the early 1990s nationalism was very developed here, and it still exists. If you are Russian, a Latvian firm will not hire you or will do so only with difficulty; and if you are Latvian, a Russian firm will hire you only with difficulty. We have a stratification of society, a division into two societies . . . Russians work for Russian businessmen, Latvians work for Latvian businessmen."[136] A representative of the Association of Latvian-Russian Cooperation concurs: "A two-community system exists. One structure consists of Latvian organizations which are comprised primarily of Latvians, while the other consists of Russian-speaking organizations which engage in business and commercial activity—and they hire Russians."[137] Similarly, a representative of Latvia's Association for the Support of Russian-Language Schools argues the following:

> Firms are organized according to nationality. Managers hire people with whom they work comfortably. And naturally they choose them from their own circle of acquaintances, specialists with whom they're acquainted. Very often they do this on the basis of historical, mature ties. And in our country ties are built according to ethnicity. Latvians with Latvians, Russians with Russians. Therefore there are firms where primarily Latvians work, and firms where only Russians work.[138]

Finally, a representative of the Party of National Harmony claims that Russian firms emerged with the collapse of the Soviet Union and continue to exist because both Russian and Latvian entrepreneurs "aspire to hire their own."[139]

Ethnic segregation stems from the fact that Russian companies tend to rely on informal contacts when hiring. Latvian companies engage in the same practice, but to less of an extent. One of the studies mentioned above finds that "Russian businesses are more oriented towards searching for employees through acquaintances, which is explained by the experts by their desire to maintain 'their own environment' thus endorsing segregation."[140] And it is ethnic and/or linguistic criteria that determine who belongs in one's "own environment:"

> Taking into account that friendship and personal relations in Latvia's society are largely based on language, which is a source of identification, one can say that minorities and ethnic Latvians, when they need to find work, often see an opportunity to get a job through informal connections. Taking into account that friendship and close relations often exist within the confines of a group that speaks the same language, in most cases the search for work also takes place within the confines of one ethnic and/or linguistic group.[141]

The following quotation, which is from an interview with a Moscow-educated, forty-five-year-old Russian entrepreneur who ran a flower business and an automobile business in Riga while he served as a leading spokesman for OKROL, sums up the tendency Russians have to take care of each other: "I try to support Russians when hiring because they face very difficult circumstances. At the end of the 1980s, the proportion in the state sector was approximately equal, but now it's 95 percent to 5 percent. They have forced Russians out, deprived them of work. . . . My accountant and one of my managers used to work for the state statistic department. . . . Naturally we take care of each other."[142] The Russian-speaking entrepreneur mentioned previously who worked for the Latvian Academy of Sciences during the Soviet era has a mainly Russian-speaking staff—about 25 percent of the staff is Latvian. The staff's ethnic composition stems from connections he made while working at the academy, which was a predominantly Russian institution.[143]

Informal networks have also facilitated the emergence of political parties and nongovernmental organizations that defend the interests of Russians in post-Soviet Latvia. In the late 1980s, individuals affiliated with the Communist Party formed various parties, such as the Equal Rights Party and the Socialist Party, as well as nongovernmental organizations that managed to survive the chaos of transition. At the end of the Soviet era, Russians in the Latvian Communist Party worked with colleagues in Moscow to form a pro-Russian alternative to the Latvian Popular Front. This movement, which I mentioned in Chapter 3, was called Interfront. It opposed independence and in the likely event of the Soviet Union's collapse aimed to represent the interests of Russians. Though Interfront was short-lived, its presence and the toleration of its existence encouraged the growth of independent organizations that work on behalf of local Russians. In 1990 Interfront leaders and like-minded deputies of Latvia's Supreme Soviet such as Tat'iana Zhdanoka formed the Equal Rights Movement, which became a political party that supports noncitizens. Supreme Soviet elections that year ushered in a People's Front majority faction dominated by Latvians who supported independence, and an Equal Rights minority faction dominated by non-Latvians who supported the preservation of the Soviet Union.[144] In 1993 the Equal Rights Movement registered as the Equal Rights Party. This party continues to defend minority rights and participates in protests against discrimination. For example, Zhdanoka flew to Riga from Strasburg, where she is a deputy of the European Parliament, to attend a demonstration on 1 September 2004 against the implementation of the controversial education policy mentioned previously.[145]

The roots of Latvia's Socialist Party also lie in Soviet-era political connections. Although incarcerated at the time, the current chairman was an essential ingredient for the party's emergence. In 1959 Al'fred Petrovich Rubiks became secretary of the Komsomol Committee at the factory in which he worked; he continued to climb the political ladder and eventually became, in 1990, first secretary of the Latvian Communist Party Central Committee.[146] His connections with dedicated socialists in Latvia and Russia, including Gorbachev, facilitated the formation (1993) and registration (1994) of Latvia's Socialist Party. Rubiks has been the party's chairman since 1999. The party supports socialist equality and the notion of Latvia as a common home. According to its program:

The Party consistently supports the formula adopted by the people of Latvia but rejected by the authorities: Latvia—our common home. With rude legislation and arbitrariness, the division of inhabitants of Latvia into citizens and non-citizens has been established. . . . All permanent residents of Latvia since May 4, 1990 must receive the right to citizenship of the Latvia Republic . . . it is essential that the state support national minorities, and assist in the preservation of their national identity.[147]

Given the Socialist Party's dedication to equality, it is not surprising that it considers Latvian nationalization detrimental to minorities. As one representative of the party put it, "The main problem Russians have is pure nationalism. We oppose the banning of teaching in Russian, we fight for the availability of education in Russian, and we support the zero-option citizenship policy."[148]

In spite of antagonistic policies and discriminatory practices, Russians in Latvia are in a strong socioeconomic position because they were well connected to Soviet state and party organs. In the post-Soviet era, informal networks stemming from those connections facilitated Russian entry into Latvia's business sector, as well as the founding of political parties and nongovernmental organizations that defend the interests of Russians. This has provided Russians with the means to reconfigure the opportunity structure they confront on a daily basis.

The Price of Sparse Informal Networks

> It is to the detriment of industry and private businesses to hire a Kyrgyz only because he's Kyrgyz. But this is what happens in Kyrgyzstan.

Unlike their counterparts in Latvia, Russians in Kyrgyzstan lack the means to reconfigure the opportunity structure they became acquainted with shortly after the collapse of the Soviet Union. The roots of contemporary Russian isolation from informal networks in Kyrgyzstan lie in the Soviet era. Most Russians who migrated to the Kyrgyz SSR did so prior to World War II. Although Russians were privileged for a few decades after the war, as stated previously their dominance of state and party organs in the republic diminished during the 1970s and 1980s as a result of two factors: (1) competition from the Kyrgyz, an increasingly urbanized and educated population that was growing rapidly as a result of naturally high birthrates, and (2) affirmative action policies that promoted Kyrgyz to high-level positions. In reaction to decades of Russification, elites began to implement a local *korenizatsiya* that fostered the Kyrgyzification of university student bodies, key positions in the economy such as industrial enterprise directorships, and republic and local-level political posts. This process, which Moscow did not obstruct, greatly restricted Russian mobility.

Russians in the Kyrgyz SSR occupied far fewer positions in the 1980s than they had in the 1950s and 1960s. By 1989 Kyrgyz were overrepresented in universities, enterprise directorship positions, and the republican Supreme Soviet.[149] The Kyrgyz proportion of total students enrolled in local universities remained at 47 percent in 1960 and 1970 but had increased to 65 percent by 1989.[150] While the Kyrgyz comprised 52 percent of the republic's population in 1989, they comprised 65 percent of the republic's university student body and 55 percent of the republic's economic enterprises directors.[151] Moreover, while the Kyrgyz comprised 64 percent of the republican Supreme Soviet and 69 percent of the local soviets, Russians comprised 19 percent of the Supreme Soviet and 15 percent of the local soviets.[152] On the eve of the federation's collapse, Russians dominated only low- and mid-level positions in industry.

By the early 1990s, nationalization practices had forced Russians from local state and party organs and thus deprived them of a basis for new commercial activity. Russians in independent Kyrgyzstan have been unable to establish a societal niche because they lack political capital associated with the party, Komsomol, and KGB. Even if they had such capital, it is important to note that privatization processes occurring in the context of Latvia's growing economy were not occurring in Kyrgyzstan at this time. Moreover, as the decade advanced clan politics became increasingly important as a means to ensure Kyrgyz control over the state *and* the emerging private sector.[153] Clans provide a substitute for official bureaucracies and market institutions in post-Soviet Central Asia.[154] As a potent actor with distribution power, the clan creates a social safety net that helps members survive a transition and prosper in its aftermath. In promoting its own the clan excludes nonmembers, including Russians who "are by definition clanless," from political and economic activity it controls.[155]

This is not to say that the Kyrgyz did not suffer from the economic crisis that gripped the newly independent country or that the Kyrgyz do not endure vicious clan conflict. In the aftermath of the Soviet Union's demise, the state sector shrank dramatically: from 1990 to 2001, the proportion of the population employed by the state decreased from 74 to 21 percent.[156] As a result, many Kyrgyz lost jobs. According to one statistic, between 1989 and 1999 the percent of Kyrgyz working for state enterprises and institutions shrank from 65 to 19 percent.[157] Nevertheless, Kyrgyz still dominated the public sector. And in comparison to Russians, Kyrgyz were situated to benefit from privatization and the emergence of new firms owing to their control of the public sector and their possession of close-knit clan ties. By the same token, clan conflict has become a dominant feature of post-Soviet Central Asian society. According to Edward Schatz, "Unlike the Soviet period, however, when clan politics remained subordinated to other high-stakes struggles, in post-Soviet Central Asia clan conflict flourished. The state-building and nation-building efforts of newly independent Kazakhstan now included intense competition for control of the state, and, consequently, for resources that were increasingly valuable on international markets."[158] As rival clans jockey for power, resources, and influence, Russians in independent Kyrgyzstan remain marginalized because they are clanless and because they lack the dense informal networks that Russians in post-Soviet Latvia rely on in order to prosper.

The absence of a clan, or an informal network that functions like a clan, makes participation in the country's private sphere difficult. One sixty-year-old Bishkek Russian engineer who at the time of the interview worked for a geology agency put it this way: "Kyrgyzstan must give equal rights to people in terms of hiring. It is to the detriment of industry and private businesses to hire a Kyrgyz only because he's Kyrgyz. But this is what happens in Kyrgyzstan because there's a highly developed clan system in which relative connections matter despite the fact that a Russian may be a highly qualified specialist. And this is to the detriment of everyone, in any field."[159] Although Russians are not entirely excluded from the country's business sector, they have a tough time breaking into that sector. According to a representative of the Slavic Foundation, most Russians are shuttle traders who work on a sporadic basis and earn a living by selling cheap products they purchase in China at local markets.[160] One reason Russians work in the shuttle trade is that it is difficult for them to obtain credit to establish business firms. A thirty-nine-year-old Russian woman who at the time of the interview worked for the Association of Ethnic Russians on a volunteer basis explains: "Capitalism is supposed to work like this: if you have a head on your shoulders, you can earn a living. But in Kyrgyzstan they give credit to national [Kyrgyz] personnel, and they give them a low percent in order to get compensation later . . . and everything depends on credit, so what kind of business can we open? It's very difficult for Russians to get credit."[161] We do not know the precise extent to which Russians work in the emerging private sector, but research suggests that Kyrgyz dominate that sector. According to a representative of the Slavic Foundation, only a fraction of the Russian population works in the private sector.[162] A representative of the Union of Russian Compatriots of Kyrgyzstan agrees: "I can't say for certain, but it seems that the indigenous nationality owns most of Kyrgyzstan's private firms. If 60 percent of the population is Kyrgyz, then about 85 percent of the country's businesses are in their hands. There are very few Russians in small and medium-sized businesses, and none in large businesses."[163] A chairman of the Public Association of Russians does not dispute this point: "There are very few Russians in small business, and the managers and owners of most small businesses are Kyrgyz. And of course, they hire their own whenever possible."[164] One thirty-seven-year-old Russian woman who worked as a finance specialist at the time of the interview expressed her view as follows:

> It's much more difficult for Russians to find work because state enterprises and organizations hire Kyrgyz. In addition, although Russians are in private business there are very few of them, and most businesses hire Kyrgyz . . . Are the rights of Russians oppressed? I don't think our rights are oppressed openly, but there is a secret policy to not hire [Russians], and to give preference to the Kyrgyz. Although this is not registered anywhere, it's simply how it is. Oppression is unofficial, there are no laws that oppress our rights; it's simply that a Kyrgyz manager gives preference to a colleague of his nationality, it's easier for them to communicate, to find a common language.[165]

Sparse informal networks render both entry into the private sector and the establishment of organizations that defend the interests of local Russians arduous. Although the constitution permits the creation of "political parties, professional unions, and public associations on the basis of free expression of will and common interests," and establishes that the state "protects the observance of the rights and legal interests of these public associations," there are only four nongovernmental organizations that represent local Russians, and there are no political parties with the same objective.[166] In contrast to representatives of Latvia's Russian population who tend to hail from the political sector and are thus well connected, representatives of Kyrgyzstan's Russian population tend to hail from the industrial sector. For example, the president of the Slavic Foundation was a geologist who led expeditions to investigate potential environmental problems in the mountains.[167] An electronic engineer who lost his job at a factory shortly after the collapse of the Soviet Union runs the Union of Russian Compatriots of Kyrgyzstan.[168] And the chairman of the Public Association of Russians was a technician in the semiconductor industry.[169]

When the republic became an independent state in 1991 Russians were in a weak socioeconomic position because they were excluded from state and party organs and thus far removed from the nexus of power. Russians remain isolated from informal networks that facilitate coordinated activity because they remain outside the circle of power and are not part of the Kyrgyz clan system. This prevents them from reconfiguring their opportunity structure and establishing a niche in Kyrgyz society.

Informal Networks and the Potential for Improved Opportunities

The Kyrgyz and Latvian cases suggest that whether or not a minority is connected to dense informal networks affects its ability to restructure the boundaries of its opportunity structure. Russians in Latvia have a far greater potential for improved opportunities than do their counterparts in Kyrgyzstan because the collapse of the Soviet Union provided them with informal networks that facilitate collective action that aims to resist policies and practices that exclude them from power. In the Latvian case, complementary informal institutions reinforce the intended effect of formal institutions, which is to privilege Latvians. However, the fact that Russians are connected to dense informal networks that encourage participation in the economic sphere of society and thus contradict the intended effect of these institutions diminishes adverse effects of nationalization policies and practices, and encourages Russians to invest in a future in Latvia.

In the Kyrgyz case, competing informal institutions diminish the merits of formal institutions for Russians. Informal practices favor the Kyrgyz and thus work against Russians, and sparse informal networks hinder economic and political organization. For many Russians, adverse effects of informal institutions—the presence of discriminatory personnel practices and the lack of connections that promote collective action—generate negative perceptions of socioeconomic opportunity and a subsequent decision to migrate. The next chapter addresses Russian perceptions of Kyrgyz and Latvian nationalization.

Part II

Chapter 5
Native Versus Non-Native: Russian Perceptions of Post-Soviet Nationalization

To the Kazakh who divides us into "native" and "non-native"

This stupid favorite troubles your soul?
But his age is short—he knows this.
Chokan and Abai don't agree with you.
They would recognize me as native.
　　　　　　—Svetlana Nazarova, *Ne ostavliaite na potom . . . .*

This stanza from Nazarova's poem is an attempt to connect with the Kazakh soul through references to cultural icons like Chokan Valikhanov, a nineteenth-century Russian army officer whose scholarly interests included the history of Central Asia, and Abai Kunabev, a nineteenth-century Kazakh poet who launched Kazakh as a literary language. In Nazarova's opinion, Chokan and Abai would recognize Russians as native and their view should influence contemporary Kazakhs to do the same. But Chapter 7 shows that according to Almaty Russians, this is not happening because thinking in terms of native and non-native provides Kazakhs with moral justification for the disproportionate reservation of economic opportunity in the public sector for "their own." Similar processes are occurring in Kyrgyzstan and Latvia.

In its analysis of Russian perceptions of various aspects of post-Soviet nationalization in Kyrgyzstan and Latvia, this chapter illustrates that informal institutions have a stronger impact on Russian views of socioeconomic opportunity and corresponding decisions regarding exit and voice than do formal institutions. Data from interviews with Russian likely permanent residents suggest that Bishkek and Riga Russians consider themselves victims of nationalization who suffer from a crippling inability to work in certain sectors of the economy and to occupy management positions in the private sphere. For example, Kyrgyzstan's Ministry of Foreign Affairs informed one twenty-three-year-old Russian that his "foreign" status restricted him to mundane work at a low salary: "Of course I've faced oppression. I wanted to work at the Ministry of Foreign Affairs, and when I applied they said, 'Of course you can work here but you'll have no future, you won't become a manager because we give preference to our own.' They said, 'You can work as a translator or fulfill some other kind of job, but we'll pay very little because you are a foreigner to us.' They said this openly."[1] Russians confront similar obstacles in Latvia. In the following quotation, a forty-four-year-old Russian engineer explains that even if she naturalizes, she expects to confront hurdles in the labor market because of her nationality: "We Russians cannot work where we want because of citizenship issues, and this is outrageous. I do not feel free here because of this. Although I may naturalize, I don't think I'll be free and equal even if I become a citizen because priority is given to the titular nation. They want to hire their own, so they give preference to their own."[2]

Perceptions of Informal Nationalization Practices

> We can't work for any government organization. Nor can we work as managers. . . . We can't do anything!

Figure 5.1 reveals that while informal practices aggravate both Bishkek and Riga Russians, formal policies antagonize only the latter. When asked how the Soviet Union's collapse has affected Russians, the overwhelming majority of Bishkek responses (80.5 percent) emphasized negative effects of informal personnel practices favoring the Kyrgyz. Despite the fact that the Akayev government implemented accommodating policies and promoted the slogan *Kyrgyzstan: Our Common Home*, informal nationalization practices convey the notion of Kyrgyz state ownership. These practices have generated a consensus among Russians that their status vis-à-vis the Kyrgyz has diminished significantly. According to a forty-eight-year-old Bishkek Russian woman who at the time of the interview taught Russian to foreigners at a local university:

> Officially, of course, our policies are about equality for everyone, but everyday nationalism is clearly expressed and therefore I consider Rus-

sians to be second-class. It's harder for Russians; life has gotten worse. Take any organization—the director will be Kyrgyz but the deputy will be Russian. Why is the Russian the deputy? Because he does everything while the Kyrgyz director receives a salary. Or the Russian isn't the deputy but he's an ordinary worker who still does everything. Russians work in enterprises and organizations, but Kyrgyz manage.[3]

While a lack of state-language skills does not legally define who can work in certain professions or hold particular positions, it is often used as an excuse to prevent competent Russians from obtaining respectable jobs. This contributes to the creation of a state of and for ethnic Kyrgyz, as well as a perception among Russians that they are, at best, guests in Kyrgyzstan.

Riga Russians are also adversely affected by informal nationalization practices. When asked how the Soviet Union's collapse has affected Russians, 33 percent of the responses accentuated detrimental effects of informal personnel practices favoring Latvians (see Figure 5.1). A representative of the Socialist Party considers these practices one component of a broad effort to squeeze Russians from important positions "like toothpaste from a tube."[4] Personnel decisions that privilege Latvians are motivated by a shared understanding that Latvians must hire "their own" and fire "outsiders" in order to correct historical wrongs related

Figure 5.1. Responses to the question, How have conditions changed for Russians since the collapse of the Soviet Union?

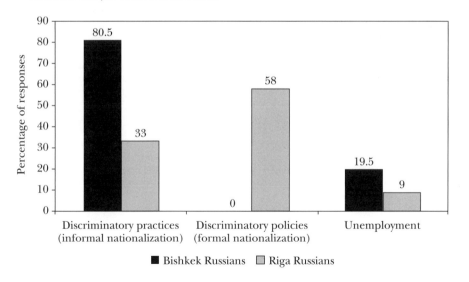

Note: Number of respondents = 90 (50 Bishkek respondents, 40 Riga respondents).

to the Soviet occupation and its consequences. When asked if it is difficult for Russians to find work in Latvia, a forty-seven-year-old Russian
woman who taught Russian at a private institute at the time answered,
"Without a doubt, yes. First, because it's necessary to know Latvian per-
fectly. Second, I think there is discrimination based on nationality—in
any case, in all state agencies and even in schools there is no doubt that
preferences are given to Latvians. No, this is not an open situation, but
it does exist. Today they will not hire a Russian in a state agency, even if
he speaks Latvian, simply because he is Russian."[5]

Perceptions of Formal Nationalization Policies

> And the rest turned out to be guests.

In addition to informal nationalization practices, formal nationalization
policies privileging the core nation have an adverse impact on Riga Russians. When asked how the Soviet Union's collapse has affected Russians, more than half of the Riga responses (58 percent) mentioned the
introduction of discriminatory legislation (see Figure 5.1). The effects of
informal practices and formal policies are highly intertwined in Latvia.
Because language and citizenship policies guide personnel decisions to
a considerable extent, they can disguise hiring and firing actions that
may in fact be based solely on nationality. The following quotation,
which is from an interview with a fifty-year-old Russian man who at the
time taught chemistry in Latvian, illustrates how various bases of discrimination are conflated:

> Life's changed for everyone, little depends on nationality—but there's a
> higher percent of unemployed among Russians. And if before this there
> was proportional representation of the Latvian and Russian nationalities
> in the government, then after independence there are practically no Rus-
> sians among the bureaucrats. Without a doubt it is harder for Russians to
> find good work. Somewhere around 1987 when all these changes began
> the main slogan was *Latvia, Our Common Home.* After independence, in
> June 1991, the slogan changed to *Latvia for Latvians.* And the rest turned
> out to be guests. All the managing positions in the state apparatus and in
> the business structures closely linked to the state apparatus are filled by
> Latvians. The selection, unfortunately, of an employee depends to a great
> extent upon nationality.[6]

Regardless of the motivations behind personnel decisions favoring Latvians, language policy undoubtedly hurts Russian-speakers. Thirty-three
percent of the responses that referred to the introduction of discriminatory legislation as a post-Soviet phenomenon that adversely impacts Russians discussed Latvia's linguistic regime. Consider the following

quotation from an interview with a forty-one-year-old Russian man who operated a boiler at a factory all day:

> I think it is harder for Russians to find good work. Only when there is a private firm with a Russian manager—then Russians will be hired. But if it's a purely state enterprise, then no. And in the government, the leadership, there are no Russians—you have to know Latvian. I sit at a boiler and I must have a language category, although only the lowest [category]—but I am one person sitting at a boiler. I don't get out, I sit at an apparatus, I'm alone—yet they demand, demand, demand knowledge of Latvian, though only the lowest category. They just never take into consideration a person's professional skills. Nationality plays a role.[7]

Latvia's exclusive citizenship policy and increasingly restrictive education policy has rendered issues related to citizenship and education salient for Russians. Twenty percent of the responses that referred to the introduction of discriminatory legislation as a post-Soviet phenomenon that adversely impacts Russians discussed Latvia's citizenship regime, while 5 percent discussed the country's education system. Although naturalization requirements softened as a result of the 1998 referendum mentioned in Chapter 4, most Russians remain outside the Latvian demos. As of July 2005, Latvians composed 74 percent of the country's citizens and Russians composed 19 percent; while Latvians composed less than 1 percent of the country's noncitizens, Russians composed 67 percent.[8] The main reason Russians do not join the Latvian demos is that they find the notion of naturalization humiliating and offensive.[9] As one fifty-one-year-old Russian woman who naturalized in order to land a job at a bookstore put it:

> Naturalization is fine for people who came to Latvia, say, two or three years ago, but what about those who were born here and have lived here ever since? I don't understand why there is such an attitude toward this group of people. I naturalized. I cannot live in Russia because I've lived here my whole life, and I'm close to the local culture, to the local people. I don't understand why I must go and prove my loyalty—I haven't violated any laws, I was born here, I speak Latvian; to whom and what must I prove? I was born here, and I was not born yesterday, it was fifty years ago![10]

Russians also consider the history exam naturalization applicants are required to pass offensive because it acknowledges the Soviet occupation. The following excerpt from an interview with a thirty-five-year-old Russian who was born in Latvia but does not have Latvian citizenship provides a typical interpretation of the situation:

> Why don't I want to naturalize? First, I have to pay around 30 Lat to naturalize. Second, the language exam doesn't bother me because I could pass it, but the main thing is that I don't want to take the history exam. I

absolutely don't agree with the history of Latvia as it is conveyed in the exam . . . for example, [the exam] claims that Russians are invaders, it represents us in a negative light. . . . For all practical purposes I'm forced to say things I absolutely don't believe.[11]

Not surprisingly, this male likely permanent resident of Riga who was working as an engineer at the time of the interview did not intend to naturalize. Finally, logistics discourage Russians from joining the Latvian demos. Many Russians lack the resources, time, and energy required to complete a process that necessitates visiting a number of agencies, taking two exams, swearing an oath of loyalty, and paying a considerable fee. In 1995 the average net monthly wage in Latvia was 77 Lat in the public sector and 69 Lat in the private sector; the naturalization fee was 30 Lat.[12] The government reduced the standard naturalization fee to 20 Lat in 2001, but it is worth noting that the average net monthly wage in Latvia that year was 129 Lat in the public sector and 106 Lat in the private sector.[13] Thus, a naturalization applicant will spend between 16 and 19 percent of his net monthly income on this fee depending on whether he works in the public or private sector. In addition to financial resources, time is a factor naturalization applicants take into account. One Russian remarks with sarcasm on the length of the naturalization process: "From the submission of documents to the moment you receive that eagerly sought-after passport, about one year passes! How proudly one of the workers at the Bureau of Naturalization remarked that they do not award citizenship in one European country as quickly as in Latvia."[14] While it is not unusual for countries to have naturalization requirements for immigrants, Latvia's requirements usually pertain to individuals who were born and raised in Latvia. Naturalization is offensive to such Russians who, as this book suggests, regard themselves as native.

Latvia's evolving education policy also contributes to Russian dissatisfaction because it asserts the state's intention to eliminate an individual's right to choose the language in which he and/or his children are educated. In the following quotation, a forty-three-year-old Russian parent who worked in advertising at the time of the interview expresses her dismay regarding that intention:

Are the rights of Russians oppressed? Yes, I think so, and even if my rights personally are not infringed upon, look at my child—he's in school, in the first class, and I see how they do not provide education in Russian for my child. So there is a problem with getting an education in our native language. And the right to work is oppressed—work and education are the main problems. . . . We are taxpayers, we have the right to teach our children in our native language—if they are born into a Russian family, they must learn in their native Russian language. In general, Russian schools exist on money, you must pay additional money to send your child to them—the state does not finance Russian schools, it only finances its own schools. And now everything is aimed to close Russian schools entirely.[15]

Russians consider the state's aim to eliminate their right to choose the language in which their children are educated a violation of human rights, as well as a step toward assimilation. As a result, nongovernmental organizations representing Russians like the Association for the Support of Russian-Language Schools oppose the state's position. In the following quotation, a representative of this organization sums up Russian perceptions concerning policies that compel Russians to learn Latvian: "It is understandable that this system of measures to protect Latvian is perceived by Russians as evil. We realize that it's necessary to know Latvian; we are against the fact that they force us to study it. This is undemocratic. Our association does not consider this a state for Latvians, but a state *for* all of us and *fed* by all of us. We all pay taxes at the same rate, citizen or noncitizen. Current education policy is unjust."[16] Frustration with the state's determination to eliminate Russian education finally found public expression in May 2003 when demonstrations made up of activists, schoolchildren, parents, teachers, and politicians broke out in urban areas across the country. Despite their tenacity, the protestors failed to influence policymakers, who do not buy the taxpayer argument made by organizations that represent local Russians.

Perceptions of Unemployment

> One factory, which is now closed, employed five thousand people who were one day suddenly unemployed.

Figure 5.1 shows that unemployment, which is directly related to post-Soviet industrial collapse, also contributes to Russian grievances in Kyrgyzstan and Latvia. When asked how the Soviet Union's demise has affected Russians, almost 20 percent of Bishkek responses and 9 percent of Riga responses referred to unemployment. Although Riga Russians are less affected by job scarcity than are Bishkek Russians because they have opportunities in the private sector, thousands of Russians in the post-Soviet region lost jobs they had held for years as newly independent states experienced major decreases in industrial production. The disintegration of economic linkages between republics, which was a logical consequence of the Soviet Union's demise, forced countless enterprises to shut down. In the following quotation, a thirty-five-year-old Riga Russian who worked in a factory prior to its closure and then found a construction job discusses a problem that plagues the entire post-Soviet region: "Many factories have closed, and for the most part Russians came to Latvia as specialists who were trained in other republics. They were sent here to work in factories. One factory, which is now closed, employed five thousand people who were one day suddenly unemployed. And for the most part the Russian-speaking population was concentrated in factories."[17] The massive closure of factories had a particularly calamitous effect on Russians because of the ethnic division of labor that characterized most of the union republics. The economic impact of the federation's collapse on Russians outside of Russia was devastating: "Russians outside of Russia tended to be highly concentrated in heavy industries of all-Union significance that frequently depended on external raw materials and external markets for their finished goods. These factories have tended to suffer most from the economic dislocation associated with the disintegration of interrepublican economic ties, and so unemployment among Russian blue-collar workers tends to be relatively high."[18] Unemployment related to industrial collapse plagues Russians disproportionately in most of the post-Soviet states, and it clearly contributes to Russian grievances in Kyrgyzstan and Latvia.

Perceptions of Oppression

> [T]hey gave citizenship only to those who were citizens in 1939 and their descendants—the rest became second-class citizens, or as we say—Negroes.

Another factor contributing to dissatisfaction among Russians is the belief that their rights are infringed upon. Sixty-six percent of Bishkek Russian respondents and 95 percent of Riga Russian respondents answered affirmatively when asked if they felt that their rights were oppressed. The right to choose a profession was the most frequently cited infringement among both sets of respondents. Figure 5.2 indicates that 67 percent of Bishkek responses and 34 percent of Riga responses emphasized the right to choose a profession when asked which rights, if any, are infringed upon. Riga Russians stressed this infringement less than Bishkek Russians because although they are unwelcome in the public sector, they are able to pursue careers in the private sector. Nevertheless, respondents from both samples claimed that Russians are judged in the labor market first on the basis of nationality, and then on degree of proficiency in the state language. Restrictions imposed by informal nationalization practices and/or formal nationalization policies prevent Russians in both countries from choosing a profession without restraint.

Figure 5.2. Responses to the question, Which of your rights, if any, are infringed upon?

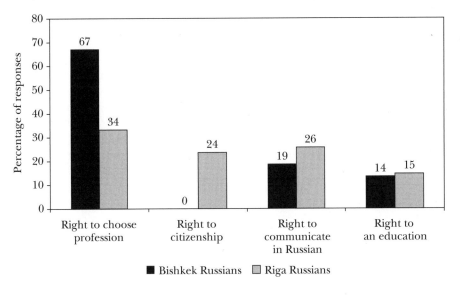

Note: Number of respondents = 90 (50 Bishkek respondents, 40 Riga respondents).

The following quotation from an interview with a thirty-seven-year-old Russian woman who worked as a finance specialist at the time illustrates how informal personnel practices hinder Russian mobility in Kyrgyzstan: "Our rights are not oppressed openly, but there is a secret practice to not hire Russians and instead to give preference to Kyrgyz. Although this is not registered anywhere, it's simply how it is. Oppression is unofficial, there are no laws that oppress our rights; it's simply that a Kyrgyz manager gives preference to a colleague of his nationality—it's easier for them to communicate, to find a common language."[19] The situation is more complex in Latvia, where formal policies *and* informal practices violate the right to choose a profession. In addition to citizenship and language requirements, informal personnel practices dictate access to a variety of careers. Consider the following quotation from an interview with a fifty-one-year-old Russian who worked in hotel administration for fourteen years until she was forced to give up her state-sector job:

> Latvians have prospects; they can work in state institutions. But Russians cannot work in state institutions and the factories are closed, so where can they work? In addition, Russians for the most part are not citizens, their status is noncitizen—what is a noncitizen? No one. Plus, Russians do not

have complete knowledge of Latvian and they are Russian—when they [Latvians] look at a person, they see a Latvian as the high nationality and you as a Russian. For example, I was at the state employment agency and I asked if I could apply for a particular position, and they said to me: we hire only Latvians. Nationality matters.[20]

In general, citizenship is not a salient issue for Russians in Kyrgyzstan because they acquired citizenship automatically in 1991.[21] But it is an issue for Russians in Latvia: When asked which rights, if any, are infringed upon, 24 percent of Riga responses emphasized the right to citizenship.[22] The following quotation is from an interview with a fifty-three-year-old Russian woman who taught computer skills for a local firm and had not naturalized because she found the process degrading:

> They must give equal rights, they must give citizenship to people so we can live normally. . . . We need the zero-option policy—this was one of the main points of the People's Way, that Latvia is our common home. Many Russians voted for independence, and due to this Latvia became independent. But after this they gave citizenship only to those who were citizens in 1939 and their descendants—the rest became second-class citizens, or as we say—Negroes, noncitizens, or local Negroes.[23]

Some Russians in Latvia, including representatives of the Equal Rights Party, refer to noncitizens as Negroes. The clever reference obviously compares the status of Russians in Latvia to the status of African Americans in the United States, but it also derives from the Russian word for noncitizen, which is *ne* grazhdanin (masculine) and *ne* grazhdanka (feminine). The Russian word for Negro is *negr.*

Bishkek and Riga Russians agree that the authorities violate their right to speak in their native language and their right to receive an education. Figure 5.2 shows that 19 percent of Bishkek responses and 26 percent of Riga responses acknowledge that the state has already restricted, or intends to restrict, the right to communicate in Russian. Bishkek Russians are less preoccupied with the issue because they do not face legislation that curbs the use of their native language, but they are worried that the government will eventually demand the publication of all official documentation in Kyrgyz. This anxiety is rooted in the Akayev government's currently unfulfilled promise to implement a ruling that reflects such a mandate by 2005: "The Russian-speaking population reacts with alarm to the ruling concerning the introduction of all official documentation in Kyrgyz from 2005 because it has not mastered Kyrgyz, and therefore those who have jobs might lose those jobs."[24] A former director of the Federal Migration Services of Russia in Kyrgyzstan claims that discussion surrounding the government's intention "rouses the migration mood" because it implies that all permanent residents must know the state language.[25] The following quotation, from an interview with a thirty-six-year-old Russian woman who worked for the International Slavic Institute—where Russian rather than Kyrgyz is spoken—supports this observation:

> Life's changed for everyone, but Russians began to leave, and why? The first wave of emigration was 1992–93, when my parents left. I think only because there was uncertainty about tomorrow. First, there were economic reasons—a lack of work. Then the question about introducing Kyrgyz in schools arose—how will this occur? Will children study in Russian? Then the introduction of Kyrgyz not only in the system of education but as a state language [arose], meaning that office work will be in Kyrgyz. *This* is not easy for people to adjust to; this encouraged Russians to leave.[26]

While it remains unclear as to whether Akayev's successor, President Kurmanbek Bakiyev, will curtail the use of Russian, it is clear that the Latvian government does not intend to alter the essence of its language policy, which is to prohibit the use of Russian in the public sphere.[27] Existing legislation and impending implementation of a policy requiring schools for national minorities to teach 60 percent of all classroom hours in Latvian generated widespread fear of assimilation among Russians in the late 1990s and early 2000s. Figure 5.3 indicates that when asked what they fear most in terms of the future of Latvia's Russian pop-

Figure 5.3. Responses of Riga Russians to the question, What do you fear most in terms of the future of Latvia's Russian population?

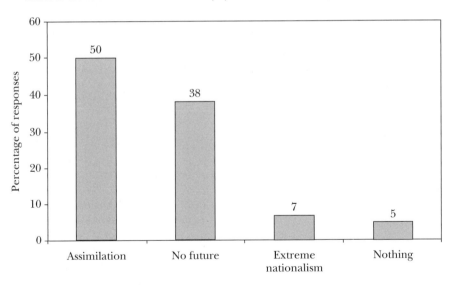

Note: Number of respondents = 40.

ulation, the most frequently cited answer—mentioned by half of the Riga responses—was assimilation. The next most often cited responses were a lack of a future (cited by 38 percent) and extreme Latvian nationalism that could generate ethnic conflict (cited by 7 percent).

One fifty-two-year-old retired Riga Russian expresses frustration with the state's determination to assimilate Russians:

> Yes, I've heard of the state's integration program and I think it's closer to assimilation. Often we here in Latvia say one thing but do another. Why is it necessary to have everything in Latvian by 2004? There's no need to pressure us—in reality, people understand that without Latvian we cannot live here. This is a wonderful stimulus to study Latvian! Based on the signs, everything's leading toward assimilation, not integration. The majority of Russians were born here, grew up here, and have lived here ever since—excuse me, but what kind of assimilation is needed? My children were born here and they speak Latvian well. What kind of integration is needed if you were born here?[28]

Nongovernmental organizations and political parties that represent local Russians also consider language and education policies assimilative. For example, Russian Society works to preserve Russian-language schools in Latvia because it considers the state's intention to liquidate these schools a step toward assimilation. As one Russian Society representative explained, "The liquidation of Russian-language schools is assimilation. If Russian-language schools are preserved and if children study the history of Russia in their native language, this does not threaten the state or Latvian culture. They assure us that this threatens the Latvian people, but we disagree. If the opportunity to use the Russian language is preserved, this does not threaten the state."[29] The Party of National Harmony agrees. According a key representative, the policy to liquidate education in the Russian language encourages assimilation:

> Although we support the idea of bilingual education, we think the form it takes must be entirely different from the form we have now. We categorically reject the liquidation of high school education in languages of minorities. High school education in languages of minorities, and in the first place Russian, must be preserved. We fight for this and hope for success . . . but the policies are directed not so that children study Latvian but so that they assimilate—and this is wrong.[30]

Figure 5.2 indicates that Russians in both states feel that the right to receive an education is infringed upon: 14 percent of Bishkek responses and 16 percent of Riga responses acknowledged that the authorities oppress this right. However, Russians in Latvia confront different issues than do Russians in Kyrgyzstan. Riga Russians claim that their right to receive an education in their native language is infringed upon. Four years prior to the implementation of the controversial education policy mentioned above, a forty-five-year-old teacher claimed that she could not educate her child in his native language. What follows is this Riga Russian's response to the question, Are the rights of Russians oppressed?

> Naturally—how can they not be oppressed if I do not have the same chance of being hired as a Latvian? Second, if I am not a citizen of this country I do not know who I am. Third, my child already cannot receive an education in Russian. This is a big problem. I want him to know Latvian so that he can feel free here, so he can communicate easily in Russian or Latvian. But I want him to receive an education in his native language. His father is Russian, I am Russian, his ancestors were Russian. Therefore, I want him to receive an education in Russian. I don't want him to be cut off from Russian culture.[31]

In Kyrgyzstan the concern is that higher-education enrollment decisions are based on nationality rather than merit.[32] In 1993—the peak of Russian exit—75 percent of students admitted to institutes of higher education in the country were Kyrgyz.[33] While statistics on age group by nationality are scant, approximately 55 percent of the country's total population was Kyrgyz in 1993.[34] This indicates that the Kyrgyzification of university student bodies that began in the 1960s did not cease with the Soviet Union's collapse. A twenty-three-year-old Russian man provides a personal example: "When I applied to the Slavic University in Bishkek, the International Relations Department told me that the department generally accepts Kyrgyz students because it wants to produce Kyrgyz diplomats and therefore doesn't need Russian students."[35] Depending on the specific institution, professor, and group of students in question, Russian students who are admitted to university face various challenges. The following excerpt is from an interview with a twenty-three-year-old Russian woman with a university degree in economics who worked for the International Slavic Institute: "My friends have faced oppression when they've enrolled in the Kyrgyz State University. They are in lecture and if the group consists of a majority of Kyrgyz, then the teacher begins to lecture in Kyrgyz although the Kyrgyz speak Russian. So the Russians say—excuse me, we don't understand. But half the lecture has already been led in Kyrgyz—this kind of oppression happens often, and they feel oppressed."[36]

An Ideal Post-Soviet Society

> If earlier a Kyrgyz without an education worked in a factory making sausages, now this same Kyrgyz is a director.

In order to elicit clues as to what an ideal post-Soviet society might look like, I asked respondents what would need to change in order for the welfare of Russians to improve. Figure 5.4, which reflects responses to this question, shows that Bishkek Russians are most dissatisfied with informal practices and the economy, while Riga Russians are most dissatisfied with formal policies and informal practices. Forty-five percent of Bishkek responses suggested that Russians are frustrated with certain aspects of the economy such as a low standard of living, industrial collapse, low and/or unpaid salaries and pensions, job scarcity, and instability. In addition, 43 percent of Bishkek responses suggested that Russians are highly dissatisfied with pervasive informal nationalization practices that restrict access to jobs that do exist and would be far less frustrated if personnel and education enrollment decisions were based on merit rather than nationality. The following quotation from an interview with a fifty-year-old Bishkek Russian who managed a laboratory responsible for developing systems of automation before his factory shut down illustrates how industrial collapse—combined with the emergence of informal nationalization practices—destroyed Russians' prospects in Kyrgyzstan:

> Life's gotten a lot worse and there are two reasons for this: economic and political. In terms of the economy, the Russian population comprised 90 percent of the republic's industrial sector but the main industry was high-tech manufacturing, which operated in the war production complex. After the collapse [of the Soviet Union] practically all orders were canceled and the result was that a mass of people ended up unemployed, without any means to survive—and for the most part these were Russians. The second reason, politics—immediately after the collapse and acquisition of independence there was a rotation of personnel, which replaced the managing stratum—not only in the political sphere but also in the industrial sphere since practically all enterprises were state owned. From the moment of independence there were appointments of representatives of the titular nation to posts of directors and so forth, which prior to independence they could not aspire to. Therefore, when this rotation occurred it went according to nationality not to professionalism.[37]

One thirty-four-year-old Russian engineer put it this way: "If earlier a Kyrgyz without an education worked in a factory making sausages, now this same Kyrgyz is a director."[38]

In contrast, Riga Russians are satisfied with their country's economy: only 5 percent of Riga responses mentioned a stronger economy as a factor that would improve the welfare of local Russians. Given the country's economic prosperity, accession to the European Union, and, most important, the government's toleration of Russian participation in the private sector, this is not surprising.[39] But Riga Russians are highly dissatisfied with formal nationalization policies and informal nationalization practices that privilege Latvians. When asked what needs to change in order for the welfare of local Russians to improve, 54 percent of Riga

Figure 5.4. Responses to the question, What would need to change in order for the welfare of Russians to improve?

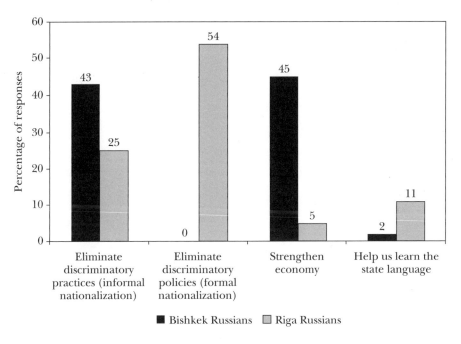

Note: Number of respondents = 90 (50 Bishkek respondents, 40 Riga respondents).

responses mentioned the need to eliminate formal policies and 25 percent referred to the need to abolish informal practices. In particular, Russians would like automatic citizenship, the designation of Russian as an official language, the opportunity to be educated in Russian, access to subsidized Latvian-language courses, and personnel decisions based on merit rather than nationality.

The data presented thus far suggest a number of conclusions. First, despite the fact that Russians confront accommodating policies in Kyrgyzstan and antagonistic policies in Latvia, there is a widespread sense of perceived ethnic discrimination among Russians in both states. In Kyrgyzstan this perception stems from informal personnel practices that privilege the titular nation. At the end of the day, Bishkek Russians feel that their ethnic identity compromises their ability to earn a living in what is already a challenging economic situation. In Latvia the perception of ethnic discrimination is rooted in formal policies and informal practices that hinder Russian mobility. Second, Russians in both countries are adversely affected by informal nationalization practices.

Even in Latvia, where formal policies restrict mobility, Russians underscore the deleterious result of informal personnel practices on their prospects in the labor market. Finally, a sentiment that the respective core nation has forced Russians out of the public sector contributes to a strong sense of relative deprivation among Bishkek and Riga Russians. The next chapter analyzes Russian responses to perceptions of socioeconomic prospects.

Chapter 6
Russian Responses to Perceptions of Socioeconomic Prospects

To the Kazakh who divides us into "native" and "non-native"

An evil will has made it so more than once already:
Broken fates scattered,
Shaking, dangling, buried around the world
In a foreign land, on a foreign shore. . . .
LEAVE? I DON'T WANT TO, I CAN'T!
—Svetlana Nazarova, *Ne ostavliaite na potom* . . . .

The last line of this stanza from Nazarova's poem suggests that migration is a suboptimal solution for Russians in Kazakhstan to problems posed by post-Soviet nationalization. This sentiment depicts reality for Russians in Kyrgyzstan and Latvia as well. Many Russians who migrate from non-Russian successor states to Russia do so with reluctance. In reference to Russians moving to Russia from various successor states, Hilary Pilkington states that "the majority, while not 'fleeing' from homes under threats to their lives, feel forced to move and were willing to accept any opportunity which allowed them to 'get out.' . . . [this] places Russian returnees closer to refugees on the refugee-economic migrant continuum than to voluntary labour migrants."[1] This chapter, which is based on interviews designed to discern motivations for exit and to determine causes for variation in degree and type of voice, analyzes Russian responses to diminished socioeconomic opportunity in Kyrgyzstan and Latvia.

We know there is significant variation in terms of the degree to which Russians in post-Soviet states exercise exit, but the Kyrgyz and Latvian cases reveal a counterintuitive finding, which is that out-migration is more prevalent in the context of accommodating nationalization than antagonistic nationalization. Table 6.1 shows the number of Russians who migrated annually from Kyrgyzstan and Latvia since the collapse of the Soviet Union. Given the almost identical number of Russians in Kyrgyzstan (916,600) and Latvia (905,500) at the time of the last Soviet census (1989), the total number of Russians who had left by 2003 indicates that Russians in Kyrgyzstan were three times more likely to exercise the exit option than were Russians in Latvia.

As suggested in Chapter 1, a potential explanation for this finding concerns regime type. Holding all other factors constant, we expect people to flee from an authoritarian state and remain in a democratic state. While the international community considers Kyrgyzstan the most liberal state in Central Asia, Latvia is far more democratic than Kyrgyzstan ever was under Akayev or is under Bakiyev. Yet the data presented in this chapter indicate that regime type does not influence the propensity of Russians to migrate from either country. When Russians migrate from Kyrgyzstan to Russia, which is the most popular exit destination, they are not necessarily moving to a more liberal state. In 1994, right around the peak of Russian exit from Kyrgyzstan, Freedom House deemed Kyrgyzstan and Russia "partly free," and gave the two countries almost identical scores: the former earned a 4 for political rights and a 3 for civic liberties, while the latter earned a 3 for political rights and a 4 for civic liberties.[2] Rather than regime type, the causes of Russian out-migration from Kyrgyzstan concern informal personnel practices, poor economic conditions, and isolation from local networks. These three factors generate negative perceptions of socioeconomic opportunity, which in turn stimulate exit.

Out-migration has had a detrimental effect on Kyrgyzstan. There are many problems associated with Russian exit, including the rupture of familial ties and the deterioration of the country's international image, but the most injurious consequence is the outflow of skilled labor.[3] There was a clearly demarcated ethnic division of labor in the Kyrgyz SSR where Kyrgyz dominated agriculture and Russians dominated the intelligentsia and industry. Post-Soviet Kyrgyzstan has lost educated and skilled Russians "who were born in Kyrgyzstan, or who had lived [in Kyrgyzstan] five to ten years, had secured a home and a job, and had a defined socioeconomic status."[4] Workers, technical specialists, academics, engineers, doctors, musicians, and teachers have moved to Russia in search of equal opportunity, work, and a higher standard of living. According to a former director of the Federal Migration Services of Russia in Kyrgyzstan, "The Kyrgyz are losing a skilled labor force, they are losing technical workers. We see who is leaving, and it's the skilled labor force. I have in mind drivers, builders, doctors, and teachers."[5] One source claims that in 2000 the country lost 1,460 doctors, 1,803 economists, and 5,340 engineers as a result of Russian exit.[6]

Table 6.1. Russian Migration from Kyrgyzstan and Latvia

	1992	1993	1994	1995	1996	1997	1998	1999	2000	2001	2002	2003	Total
Russian Exit from Kyrgyzstan	59,294	89,984	41,463	18,718	14,020	9,891	7,869	9,281	17,485	20,217	20,351	11,994	320,567
Russian Exit from Latvia	30,740	19,694	14,223	8,395	6,264	5,606	3,442	1,904	3,787	3,645	1,333	984	100,017

Sources: Natsional'ny statisticheskii komitet Kyrgyzskoi Respubliki; *Demographic Statistics in the Baltic Countries* (Tallin, Riga, Vilnius: Statistical Office of Estonia, Central Statistical Bureau of Latvia, Lithuanian Department of Statistics, 1996), 57 (1992–94 data); *Demographic Yearbook of Latvia* (Riga: Central Statistical Bureau of Latvia, 2000), 159 (1995–99 data); and *Statistical Yearbook of Latvia 2004* (Riga: Central Statistical Bureau of Latvia, 2004), 44 (2000–2003 data).

The out-migration of skilled personnel in the early 1990s produced a brain drain that has had devastating economic consequences: "The main loss is human capital, highly skilled workers. . . . The migration of the population from the Kyrgyz Republic means a loss of labor resources, of highly-skilled personnel. This 'brain-drain' reduces the chances of a quick reconstruction of state enterprises, and also of an intensive growth of the private sector."[7] Scarce funding and the loss of potential mentors pose challenges to the creation of a vocational training program to replace Russian specialists who have left. According to one local scholar, Russian out-migration has generated "losses among the intelligentsia and first and foremost among the industrial intelligentsia. As a result, a niche has appeared that most likely cannot be filled in the near future."[8] Despite Akayev's campaign to reduce the rate of Russian out-migration, which manifested itself in a decree stipulating (1) the legal use of the Russian language in certain economic sectors, (2) just representation of the Russian-speaking population in government organs and enterprises, (3) a reconsideration of the deadline for transferring documentation into Kyrgyz, (4) an agreement between the Kyrgyz and Russian ministries of foreign affairs on simplifying procedures to acquire Russian citizenship, and (5) a renewed fight against manifestations of Kyrgyz nationalism, the exit phenomenon continues.[9]

The Latvian case differs from the Kyrgyz case in this context on two counts. First, the low level of Russian out-migration has not adversely affected the economy: Latvia has not experienced a brain drain. Second, both formal nationalization policies *and* informal nationalization practices stimulate the exit that has occurred. The most interesting aspect of this case is the fact that most Russians stay in Latvia because dense informal networks counteract the intended effect of nationalization policies and practices. A flourishing economy and access to such networks open doors to the private sector, and opportunities in that sector outweigh unpleasant consequences of antagonistic nationalization. The ability to prosper in spite of policies and practices designed to hinder mobility discourages Russian out-migration from Latvia.

Russian Exit from Kyrgyzstan: Why Russia?

Since acquiring independence, Kyrgyzstan has lost a significant portion of its Russian population, which diminished by 34 percent between 1989 and 1999.[10] Based on a fairly constant life expectancy rate, this decrease can be attributed primarily to migration.[11] Table 6.1 shows the number of Russians who migrated from Kyrgyzstan annually from 1992 to 2003, which totals 320,567. The majority of Russians who migrate from Kyrgyzstan choose Russia as a destination. According to the country's Department of Demographic Statistics, about 80 percent of the Russians and

Tatars who leave Kyrgyzstan move to Russia.[12] Interview data suggest that potential migrants identify Russia as a suitable destination because (1) they consider it their historic homeland, and (2) they believe that a move to Russia will improve their economic situation and help reunite their families.

When I asked Bishkek potential migrants why they had chosen Russia as a migration destination, respondents identified three reasons: 42 percent of the responses highlighted an affinity toward Russia, 41 percent emphasized economic opportunity, and 17 percent stressed a desire to live closer to relatives who reside in Russia. This sense of affinity toward Russia is often expressed in terms of historic homeland. While Bishkek Russians born in Russia tend to consider Russia their homeland, those born in Kyrgyzstan view Russia as their *historic* homeland. As one twenty-seven-year-old male potential migrant who was born in Kyrgyzstan explained, "Russia is my historic homeland, where people will treat me like people should treat people."[13] Although this individual has a vocational education and was working in sales at the time of the interview, he was leaving Kyrgyzstan in order to ensure a better future for his children. Sometimes this sense of affinity is connected to an abstract sense of belonging related to a shared nationality and language. When I asked why she had chosen Russia as a migration destination, a fifty-year-old female potential migrant born in Kyrgyzstan expressed this sense of belonging as follows: "Where else? I'm not young, I speak the language, and Russia is closer to my soul."[14] This woman has a vocational education, was a salesclerk at the time of the interview, and had children in Russia.

Bishkek Russians associate a move to Russia with economic opportunity for various reasons, the most obvious being the fact that Russia is far more developed than Kyrgyzstan on the basis of almost every standard indicator. The 2005 Human Development Report reflects this in ranking Russia 62 and Kyrgyzstan 109.[15] Table 6.2 shows that shortly after the Soviet Union collapsed, the Russian economy was almost six times as large as the Kyrgyz economy on the basis of GDP per capita.

By 2004 Russia's GDP per capita was more than eight times the size of Kyrgyzstan's GDP per capita. Moreover, as Table 6.3 shows, while Kyrgyzstan's annual growth rate was higher than Russia's for most of the 1990s, by 1999 Russia's economic growth had surpassed Kyrgyzstan's. An assessment of public goods not directly subjected to ethnic discrimination testifies to the fact that Russia is more developed than Kyrgyzstan. Average life expectancy, infant mortality rate, and public health expenditure statistics are either more optimistic or not considerably worse in Russia than in Kyrgyzstan. For example, Russia's life expectancy (65.4) is only slightly lower than Kyrgyzstan's life expectancy (66.8).[16] And although Kyrgyzstan's infant mortality rate has decreased since 1970, it

Table 6.2. GDP/GNI Per Capita (US$)

	1992	1993	1994	1995	1996	1997	1998	1999	2000	2001	2002	2003	2004
Kyrgyzstan	514	435	348	325	343	372	374	382	280	417	—	340	400
Russia	2967	2713	2375	2280	2208	2235	2131	2255	1720	2609	—	2610	3410

Sources: *World Development Indicators, 2003* (Washington, D.C.: International Bank for Reconstruction and Development/World Bank, 2003); World Bank Group, http://www.worldbank.org/.

Table 6.3. GDP Annual Percentage Growth

	1992	1993	1994	1995	1996	1997	1998	1999	2000	2001	2002	2003	2004
Kyrgyzstan	−14	−15	−20	−5	7	10	2	4	5	5	—	7	7
Russia	−15	−9	−13	−4	−3	1	−5	5	10	5	—	7	7

Sources: *World Development Indicators, 2003* (Washington, D.C.: International Bank for Reconstruction and Development/World Bank, 2003); World Bank Group, http://www.worldbank.org/.

remains significantly higher than Russia's infant mortality rate: in 2003 Kyrgyzstan's infant mortality rate was fifty-nine per one thousand live births, while Russia's was sixteen per one thousand live births.[17] Finally, public health expenditure is greater in Russia than in Kyrgyzstan: in 2002 Russia devoted 3.5 percent of its GDP to public health, while Kyrgyzstan devoted 2.2 percent.[18]

The second reason Bishkek Russians associate a move to Russia with economic opportunity is that they believe they will face less discrimination in their destination country than in Kyrgyzstan, and that this will allow them to prosper in Russia's labor market. I interviewed one thirty-five-year-old female potential migrant who, although she is a university graduate, was unemployed at the time of the interview because the kindergarten where she worked decided to replace her with a Kyrgyz. She explained that she was moving to Russia because Russia is her historic homeland and because "In Russia everyone is Russian so there's the possibility to find work and earn money; here in Kyrgyzstan we can't do this."[19] But the expectation that Russians will not discriminate against Russians is unrealistic. In fact, Russian immigrants are often perceived as outsiders and thus poised to confront the same kind of discrimination they faced in the countries from which they migrated. In her analysis of Russian migration to post-Soviet Russia, Pilkington finds that local Russians tend to view immigrant Russians as newcomers, strangers, migrants, or refugees. Alternatively, they perceive immigrant Russians in terms of the republic from which they migrated, so a Russian migrant from Kyrgyzstan is considered Kyrgyz rather than Russian. According to Pilkington, "It was this which migrants found most hurtful, since it denied their Russianness and thus any sense of having returned 'home.' "[20]

Finally, Bishkek Russians are optimistic about Russia's future because of the country's abundant supply of natural resources. When asked why he had chosen Russia as a migration destination, one fifty-two-year-old male potential migrant who is a university graduate but was unemployed at the time of the interview answered as follows: "Already a democracy, more or less, is beginning in Russia; there are many parties there and they argue with each other which is good for the people. In addition, Russia is one of the richest countries in the world because it has woods, gas, oil, and gold."[21] The fact that Russia's economic growth is largely due to the 1998 devaluation of the ruble and rising world oil prices suggests that the economy may suffer when positive effects of devaluation wear off and oil prices drop, but vast oil and natural gas reserves will remain highly valued commodities even in the event of these circumstances. Furthermore, should President Medvedev conquer the corruption that continues to plague Russia, rates of foreign and domestic investment may increase.[22]

In contrast, economic growth is a serious challenge for Kyrgyzstan: foreign aid disappears into corrupt environs, the country is not rich in natural resources and thus has trouble attracting foreign direct investment, and the economy is based primarily on agriculture:

> The republic's domestic product has derived from four main sources: irrigated cotton and grain agriculture, livestock raising, mining, and some machine-building for the textile and energy industries. However, Kyrgyzstan has not traditionally created a large share of output even within Central Asia for most of these categories, let alone any significant portion of USSR production, with the exception of a few selected areas in which Kyrgyzstan has concentrated: wool production, horse-raising, refined sugar (from sugar beets), machinery for the meat industry, and electric motors. Overall, agriculture is still the mainstay of the Kyrgyz economy.[23]

The structure of the Kyrgyz economy has not changed a great deal since 1995 when Kathleen Braden's essay containing this assertion was published. In 2001 the country's main economic activity remained agriculture and livestock: agriculture employed 53 percent of the labor force. This sector was followed by retail/wholesale trade and then gold mining and processing.[24]

Russian Exit from Kyrgyzstan: Three Phases

Figure 6.1 depicts Russian exit from Kyrgyzstan between 1991 and 2003. This phenomenon had three phases, the first of which occurred prior to the Soviet Union's demise. Approximately 65,000 Russians left the Kyrgyz SSR between 1990 and 1991.[25] The impending collapse of the federation as well as violence between Uzbeks and Kyrgyz in Osh generated this wave of exit. In 1989 Russians comprised 22 percent of the Kyrgyz SSR's population, while Kyrgyz comprised 52 percent.[26] An increasingly nationalistic environment in which various politicians, political parties, and nongovernmental organizations voiced anti-Russian sentiment contributed to Russians' anxiety about their future as a minority in a newly independent state. The ethnic conflict that emerged in southern Kyrgyzstan, which was "one of the largest and most violent on the territory of the former USSR," also made Russians apprehensive.[27] In response to decisions made by local authorities in Osh to transfer land inhabited by Uzbeks to homeless Kyrgyz in 1990, outspoken Uzbeks demanded the designation of Uzbek as the region's official language and the annexation of parts of southern Kyrgyzstan to Uzbekistan. Rejection of these demands sparked widespread violence that resulted in over 5,000 crimes and between 171 and 230 casualties.[28] Both heightened concern regarding how independent Kyrgyzstan would treat Russians as well as fear of further conflict in the Ferghana Valley, a trou-

Figure 6.1. Number of Russians who migrated from Kyrgyzstan annually.

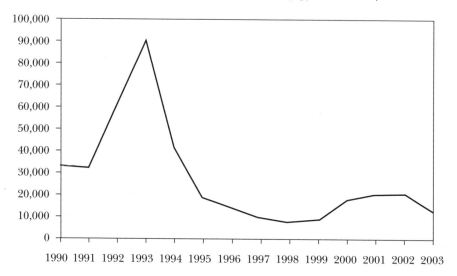

Source: Natsional'ny statisticheskii komitet Kyrgyzskoi Respubliki.

blesome region that had already witnessed violence between Uzbeks and Meskhetian Turks in 1989, drove Russians from Kyrgyzstan during this phase of exit.

The second phase of exit, which lasted from 1992 to 1994, saw the outflow of almost 200,000 Russians. In 1993, the peak year of out-migration, 89,984 Russians abandoned their homeland.[29] By this time unemployment had become an acute problem and the authorities had begun to "Kyrgyzify" local and state levels of government via informal linguistic discrimination: "From the moment of the proclamation of independence in 1992, they [the Kyrgyz] began to build a national state in which all key posts in political and economic structures were filled by representatives of the titular nationality."[30] Rather than fight a losing battle to acquire a presence in the public sector, which was the only sector where one could earn a steady income, many Russians left. This phase of exit was a reaction to unemployment, the introduction of informal personnel practices favoring the Kyrgyz, the dismissal of Russians from management positions, and the constriction of the Russian language's sphere of influence.[31]

Although the intensity of Russian out-migration diminished after 1994, Figure 6.1 shows that Russians continued to leave Kyrgyzstan throughout the 1990s: almost 8,000 Russians left in 1998, which was the decade's lowest point of exit. The third phase began in 1999. The director of the Federal Migration Services of Russia in Kyrgyzstan at the time, V. I. Ostapchuk, attributes the quickened pace of out-migration to "a whole series of unresolved problems in the Republic" including unemployment, low and/or unpaid salaries and pensions, and a lack of basic services such as the provision of natural gas.[32] Despite the fact that he served as an invited guest of the Kyrgyz Republic, Ostapchuk acknowledges political aspects of the "unresolved problems," such as the law on civil service requiring public servants to know the state language and the government's plan to publish official documentation in Kyrgyz by 2005. Ostapchuk also asserts that informal nationalization practices contribute to Russian out-migration: "Furthermore, the expulsion of the Russian population from power structures at the federal and local levels, law enforcement agencies, and the judicial branch causes a negative reaction and hinders the ability of our compatriots to obtain legal protection."[33]

During 1999 more than 10,000 individuals visited the Federal Migration Service of Russia, and over 9,000 Russians actually migrated from Kyrgyzstan.[34] In the following quotation, a local journalist compares the number of people who visited the institution in 1999 to the number who visited in 1998: "If last year five to seven people visited representatives of the Federal Migration Services of Russia in Kyrgyzstan every day to receive permission for a move, then this year sixty to seventy people do so. While some fill out applications and receive consultations inside, others patiently stand outside in the small courtyard."[35] Interview data suggest that the increase in Russian exit during 1999 was due primarily to a heightened sense of distress regarding widespread nationalization practices, poor economic conditions, and the perceived effect of these factors on the next generation.

Russian Exit from Kyrgyzstan: Three Main Motivations

> Nothing is changing because of their mentality: Kyrgyz help Kyrgyz.

The data suggest that a constant motivation for Russian exit from Kyrgyzstan is a widespread perception of ethnic discrimination stemming from informal nationalization practices. I asked potential migrants in Bishkek the following questions in order to identify their motivations for migration: (1) Which factors influenced your decision to migrate from Kyrgyzstan, and (2) What must change in order for you to remain in Kyrgyzstan? Figure 6.2 reflects responses to the first question.

Informal nationalization practices, poor economic conditions, and the perceived impact of these factors on the next generation arose in 77

Figure 6.2. Responses of Bishkek Russians to the question, Which factors influenced your decision to migrate from Kyrgyzstan?

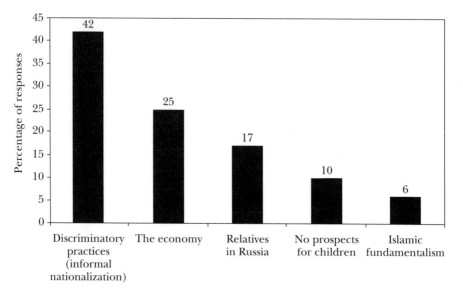

Note: Number of respondents = 115.

percent of the potential migrant responses. The first factor, which arose in 42 percent of the responses, was the most frequently cited motivation for migration. Interviews indicate that Russians believe that their ethnicity hinders their ability to find a job and that informal personnel practices promoting the Kyrgyz generate grievances that motivate exit. In the following quotation, a Russian potential migrant who at the age of twenty-seven felt he could not earn a living in his country explains his situation: "Nothing is changing because of their mentality: Kyrgyz help Kyrgyz. The Kyrgyz are a community of fellow countrymen. The fact that I am now a member of a national minority is a problem. I can't find work because of this status. Recently, I went to an office to apply for a position. The manager was Kyrgyz. It was immediately clear that I am second-class. Now I'm moving to Russia with pleasure."[36]

Russians are also troubled by the economy, a motivation for exit that arose in 25 percent of the responses. But Kyrgyz also worry about job scarcity, inflation, unpaid and/or low salaries and pensions, a lack of basic services, instability, and financial stresses of daily life. And Kyrgyz migrate from Kyrgyzstan as well. According to Zafaar Khakimov, director of the Department of Migration Services under the Ministry of Foreign Affairs, more than 600,000 Kyrgyz live abroad: 370,000 reside in Uzbekistan, 160,000 in China, 56,000 in Tajikistan, 42,000 in Russia, 11,000 in Kazakhstan, 2,000 in Turkmenistan, and 2,500 in Turkey.[37] What renders Russians distinct from Kyrgyz in this context is the fact that they are victims of industrial collapse *as well as* informal nationalization practices. The extent to which Russians were psychologically and economically devastated by the collapse of industry cannot be overstated. Even Kyrgyz acknowledge the problem. In the following quotation a Kyrgyz author laments the country's inability to create jobs for Russians: "Slavic out-migration is a huge loss for our country, it's a question of losing the able-bodied population, and I'm very sorry that it's turned out that for the most part the reason is that we are still not able to provide jobs for our Russians. During the Soviet era, the Kyrgyz worked in the fields and herded sheep, while Russians worked in plants and factories, which unfortunately now stand idle."[38] During the Soviet era Russians domi-nated heavy industry, technology, and science, while the traditionally pastoral Kyrgyz worked in agriculture and light industry. In 1989 there were 1.6 employed Russians for every employed Kyrgyz. Russian workers outnumbered their Kyrgyz counterparts in industry by a ratio of 2.1:1. In heavy industry, the ratio was 2.7:1 in favor of the Russians, and in mechanical engineering and metalworking the ratio was even higher at 3.2:1.[39]

The disintegration of economic linkages between the union republics had a detrimental impact on every republic's industrial sector, but the Kyrgyz SSR was particularly dependent on other republics for natural resources. In 1991 the source of roughly 12 percent of the republic's GDP was transfers from the union budget, about 98 percent of the republic's trade was with other Soviet republics, and over 40 percent of the republic's imports came from Russia.[40] The Soviet Union's demise severed trade links that had kept the Kyrgyz economy afloat for decades, and as a result of this phenomenon many industrial enterprises had to shut down. One example is a glass factory in Tokmak that relied on deliveries from other republics for survival. Its liquidation forced approximately 1,300 people of predominantly Slavic origin to either compete in a tight labor market that offers few opportunities and favors Kyrgyz or to eke out an existence via the informal economy.[41] The fol-lowing quotation, which is from an interview with a fifty-year-old unem-ployed Russian potential migrant with a vocational education who worked in a factory that now stands idle, illustrates the two-pronged effect of industrial collapse and informal nationalization practices: "The reason I'm leaving is job related. When I call up someone regarding a job in Bishkek, they say, 'We don't need Russians.' I can't find work because of nationalism. At least everyone looks like me in Russia."[42]

Concerns regarding informal personnel practices, a poor economy, and the next generation's future are interdependent. When potential migrants cited distress related to their children's future, a motivation for exit that arose in 10 percent of the responses, they expressed anguish regarding how informal practices and poor economic conditions will shape that future. Parents worry that there will be a dearth of jobs in general *and* that informal practices will prevent their children from landing jobs that are available. One thirty-two-year-old female potential migrant who has a vocational education but was unemployed at the time of the interview described the interdependent nature of concerns regarding informal practices, a poor economy, and the next generation's future as follows: "Life has changed for everyone, for all people—in general it's difficult to find work, especially for Russians . . . I'm moving to Russia for the future of my children, so they can get a better education. . . . It's possible to study Kyrgyz, but why? Even if you speak Kyrgyz you still will not get a good job because you don't have the same eyes."[43]

The desire to live near relatives who reside in Russia, a factor that arose in 17 percent of the responses, also contributes to Russian exit. Many Russians in Kyrgyzstan have relatives in Russia because of previous waves of migration; 90 percent of the potential migrants I interviewed had relatives in Russia. As part of a strategy to prevent continued exit, Kyrgyzstan's former president did occasionally ask Russians who had left to return to their homeland: "To Russians who still remain in Russia, I say: 'Return to your native land. You must miss your native mountains, Ala-Too, and the summits of the Tian'-Shan, and your native lake Issyk-Kul'."[44] But the data presented here suggest that in order to be persuasive such appeals must be accompanied by the elimination of informal nationalization practices and improved economic conditions.

Finally, fear of Islamic fundamentalism arose in 6 percent of the responses to the first question I asked potential migrants. Events in Batken, a region of southern Kyrgyzstan, generated this concern. In August 1999 a militant guerrilla group affiliated with religious fundamentalists who oppose the Karimov regime in Uzbekistan entered Kyrgyzstan from Tajikistan and captured about 320 local villagers, the commander of the Kyrgyz Interior Ministry Forces, and four Japanese geologists. The hostages were released by October. The fact that the kidnappings had less of an impact on residents of northern Kyrgyzstan than on residents of southern Kyrgyzstan[45] accounts for the low frequency of this response in Bishkek. As the president of the Dzalal-Abad Association of Ethnic Russians explains, Russians in the north "do not see threats to their existence, but we in the south realistically feel them. . . . We have in the south powerful Islamization. . . . Earlier we had one mosque in the city, but now they've built around 40 in three years. And surely this is not only a spiritual center, but also an ideological center."[46]

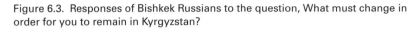

Figure 6.3. Responses of Bishkek Russians to the question, What must change in order for you to remain in Kyrgyzstan?

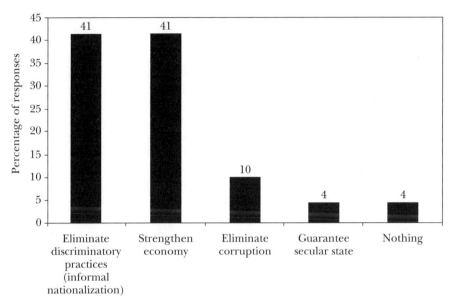

Note: Number of respondents = 115.

Figure 6.3 reflects responses to the second question I asked potential migrants: What must change in order for you to remain in Kyrgyzstan? The results reveal that President Bakiyev must eliminate discriminatory practices *and* improve the economy if he wants to preserve a Russian presence in Kyrgyzstan. When asked what must change, respondents emphasized the need to crack down on informal nationalization practices and strengthen the economy: each factor arose in 41 percent of the responses. Russians clearly view themselves as victims of discrimination in the labor market. Related to this concern is apprehension that the eventual publication of official documentation in Kyrgyz will further diminish their status in the labor market. Many adult Russians, like the thirty-nine-year-old male potential migrant quoted below who has a vocational education and worked as a radio technician at the time of the interview, worry that they will not be able to master the Turkic language: "Russian must be a second state language because my generation cannot learn a new language well enough that we'll be able to work as managers. Soon all documentation will be in Kyrgyz and we [Russians] won't be able to understand anything or work anywhere, which means we'll have no prospects in Kyrgyzstan."[47]

Moreover, many Russians consider the intention to publish official documentation solely in Kyrgyz a reflection of anti-Russian sentiment. The events that propelled President Akayev out of office in March 2005 suggest that anti-Russian sentiment, though less ubiquitous than in the early 1990s, still exists. The "Tulip Revolution," which was partially rooted in a political power struggle between northern and southern clan divisions, did not include Russians. Excluded from the political arena by informal nationalization practices, Russians observed the revolutionary events from the sidelines. Most telling in terms of the salience of the Russian minority question in contemporary Kyrgyz society was the appearance during the chaos surrounding the political turmoil of leaflets in Bishkek, where Russians are most heavily concentrated, that were "of the most disgusting content—urging ethnic strife."[48] The following paragraph is from such a leaflet: "Kyrgyzstan is for the Kyrgyz, this is our land on which we must build our lives. Why do the majority of our residents lack access to civilization—hot water, communication? Because these things are used, first and foremost, by 'arrivals' . . . Kyrgyz people, do not purchase apartments or homes from Russians! They will run from here very soon, and you will get their apartments for next to nothing."[49] Though Russians promptly discarded these leaflets, the International Crisis Group acknowledges that they "were said to be distributed in some areas of Bishkek calling on Kyrgyz not to buy property from Russians, 'because they would be leaving anyway.'"[50] And references to such leaflets did appear in local newspaper articles. For example, a *Vechernii Bishkek* piece on the increased number of people visiting the Russian Embassy to inquire about migration procedures after the revolution asserted that recent events including the revolution, subsequent illegal land seizures in Bishkek, and "conversations going on in provocative leaflets" severely frightened many people.[51] The March 2005 events did stimulate a rise in out-migration that was predominantly, though not exclusively, Russian. During the first five months of 2004, 4,722 individuals migrated from Kyrgyzstan to Russia; during the same period in 2005, 7,035 individuals migrated from Kyrgyzstan to Russia. In 2005, 57 percent of the migrants were Russian; 19 percent were Kyrgyz.[52]

In addition to anti-Russian sentiment, economic development is critical to potential migrants who underscored the need for job creation, paid and higher salaries and pensions, the provision of basic services, industrial development, and stability. Potential migrants linked corruption, which was mentioned in 10 percent of the responses, to a lack of economic development. Respondents insisted that officials terminate corrupt practices that rob the public of its meager assets. One twenty-six-year-old female potential migrant who has a high school education and was working in construction at the time of the interview put it this way: "The government must change. It's corrupt—the people pay taxes, yet the government has nothing but debt. Officials ride around in nice cars, while we sit around without gas."[53]

Finally, Figure 6.3 shows that the preservation of a secular state is of some importance to Bishkek Russians. The need for Kyrgyz authorities to guarantee a secular state, which arose in 4 percent of the responses, echoes the fear of Islamic fundamentalism that motivates Russian exit. It is important to note, however, that Kyrgyz fear Islamic fundamentalism as well. One study on general migration processes in the republic finds that "the invasion of criminal thugs and religious extremists into Kyrgyz territory" as well as deteriorating economic conditions sparked the wave of out-migration that began in 1999.[54]

Thus, the third wave of Russian exit is due to a set of interrelated motivations that includes informal practices that favor the Kyrgyz, poor economic conditions, and the perceived effect of these factors on the next generation. In contrast to their counterparts in Latvia, Russians in Kyrgyzstan lack dense local networks that facilitate coordinated activity; in other words, they lack the means to reconfigure their respective opportunity structure. The Latvian case illustrates how such networks discourage Russian exit.

Russian Exit from Latvia: One Short Phase

Despite the fact that Russians are highly dissatisfied with antagonistic nationalization policies and practices, on the whole they have not chosen to migrate from Latvia. A small number have left since the collapse of the Soviet Union. Between 1989 and 1999, Latvia's Russian population diminished by only 22 percent.[55] A fairly consistent life expectancy rate suggests that this change is due primarily to migration.[56] Moreover, Table 6.1 shows that with the exception of one year—2000—there has been a steady decrease in the level of Russian exit from Latvia since 1992. Figure 6.4 shows the number of Russians who left Latvia annually from 1992 to 2003, which totals 100,017.

The peak occurred in 1992, when approximately 3 percent of the Russian population migrated from Latvia.[57] Economic decline and the introduction of nationalization policies and practices motivated the exodus of 64,657 Russians who left during the country's only wave of out-migration, which spanned 1992 to 1994. Two factors contributed to industrial collapse—the disintegration of the all-union economy and the implementation of market reforms. As one journalist put it: "Deep social and economic reforms of the last years led to the quiet death of Latvian industry (and there's still no hope for its revival). People left. Thousands and thousands of specialists, whose knowledge and skills are

Figure 6.4. Number of Russians who migrated from Latvia annually.

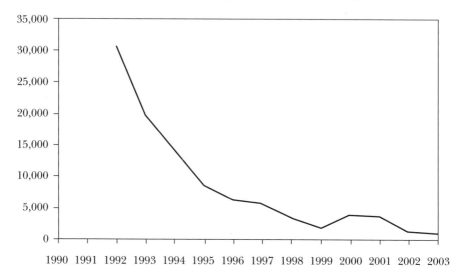

Sources: *Demographic Statistics in the Baltic Countries* (Tallin, Riga, Vilnius: Statistical Office of Estonia, Central Statistical Bureau of Latvia, Lithuanian Department of Statistics, 1996), 57 (1992–94 data); *Demographic Yearbook of Latvia* (Riga: Central Statistical Bureau of Latvia, 2000), 159 (1995–99 data); and *Statistical Yearbook of Latvia 2004* (Riga: Central Statistical Bureau of Latvia, 2004), 44 (2000–2003 data).

now in other countries and on other continents. What remains are the ruins of Latvia's former industrial potential—and those residents who either view Latvia as their homeland, or have no one waiting for them."[58] Industrial stagnation hurt the economy in general but devastated the Russian population in particular. As noted in Chapter 3, many of the Russians Moscow sent to the Latvian SSR to resolve the labor shortage problem after World War II worked in industry. Consequently, Russians were the primary victims of unemployment generated by post-Soviet industrial collapse.

Antagonistic nationalization policies also motivated Russian exit in the early 1990s. The 1991 ruling on citizenship status excluded most Russians from the Latvian demos, and subsequent citizenship and language laws further demoralized local Russians. According to a former director of the Federal Migration Services of Russia in Latvia, out-migration was in large part a reaction to the implementation of aggressive policies:

There was a tendency beginning in 1991 after the Soviet Union's collapse—policies were implemented in successor states that did not always meet the hopes of every Russian population. In Latvia, restrictions were introduced regarding the use of the Russian language and the possibility to naturalize. . . . Russians interpreted this as an oppression of their rights. . . . When there was this period of strong discomfort, when there were difficult problems with language and with policies that oppressed their rights, Russians who were not able to find themselves were forced to leave.[59]

However, the rate of Russian exit from Latvia has slowed dramatically since the early 1990s. Not only did local economic conditions improve as the Soviet Union's demise faded into history and market reforms took effect, but, more important, connectedness to informal networks that facilitate coordinated activity enabled Russians to participate in the country's private sector.

Russian Exit from Latvia: Three Main Motivations

> They saw segregation, a form of apartheid, a hidden or Western form of apartheid.

The data suggest that formal policies *and* informal practices motivate those Russians who do see out-migration as a logical response to antagonistic nationalization to leave Latvia. I asked potential migrants in Riga the same questions I asked their counterparts in Bishkek: (1) Which factors influenced your decision to migrate from Latvia, and (2) What must change in order for you to remain in Latvia? Figure 6.5 shows that Russians who planned to leave Latvia at the time of the interview were equally dissatisfied with formal and informal aspects of post-Soviet nationalization.

The most frequently cited motivations for Russian exit from Latvia are nationalization policies and practices. Formal policies related to language, education, and citizenship arose in 32 percent of the responses: language policy and education policy each accounted for 12 percent, and citizenship policy accounted for 8 percent. Informal personnel practices privileging Latvians arose in 31 percent of the responses.

Potential migrants cited offensive aspects of language policy, such as the government's determination to eliminate the use of Russian in as many spheres of communication as possible, as a key reason for exit. One highly educated potential migrant between the ages of forty-six and fifty-five at the time of the interview was moving to Russia in search of a job. She claimed she had been unemployed for seven years because she does not speak Latvian.[60] This respondent's situation illustrates the inimical impact language policy can have on Russian-speakers in the workplace. The following anecdote from my research journal suggests that

Figure 6.5. Responses of Riga Russians to the question, Which factors influenced your decision to migrate from Latvia?

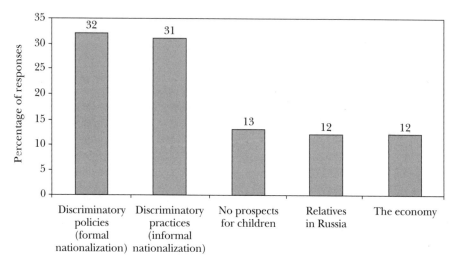

Note: Number of respondents = 65.

language policy can also complicate simple, routine activities like reading public notices: "One day an elderly man asked me, in Russian, to translate a notice hanging on our apartment building. He explained that he could not read the notice, which may have pertained to him as a building resident, because it was written in Latvian. When I explained that I could not read Latvian either, the man nodded and walked away." These and other related problems encourage Russian exit. Some issues such as the desire to preserve ethnic identity, which also contributes to Russian out-migration, are more abstract. According to a representative of the Center for the Preservation of the Russian Language, "Further deterioration of the linguistic situation will cause more Russian out-migration. Beginning in the 1990s, people abandoned their apartments and left the country in order to preserve their Russian identity. They saw segregation, a form of apartheid, a hidden or Western form of apartheid."[61] This individual's personal story is revealing. Born and raised in Latvia, he considers Latvia his homeland. But post-Soviet nationalization caused problems for his brother, who was unable to find a job, as well as his children, who were unable to study in their native language. By 2005 his family had moved to Russia in order to preserve its ethnic identity.

Another concern for potential migrants, which arose in 12 percent of the responses, is whether parents can and/or will be able to educate their children in Russian. Parents who observe trends in education policy promoting Latvian-language schools at the expense of Russian-language schools are troubled by the thought of their children studying in a foreign language. One highly educated potential migrant between the ages of thirty-six and forty-five at the time of the interview spoke Latvian well and had a steady job selling women's clothing but was moving to Russia so her child could study in his native language.

OKROL, the organization that represents Russian businesses, is also concerned about developments in education policy restricting the use of Russian in public institutions. According to one of its cochairmen, the organization seeks to protect Russian rights related to education, language, and citizenship: "OKROL's goal is to create comfortable conditions for Russians in Latvia, so we have three tasks. First, preserve education in Russian at all levels. Unfortunately, we're losing this battle. Second, resolve the issue of noncitizens. Third, ensure that the Russian language is on equal footing with Latvian in terms of preservation and use."[62] As part of its battle to preserve Russian education, OKROL played a leading role in the demonstrations discussed below.

Despite the fact that they can naturalize, Russians do cite problems related to citizenship as a motivation for exit. One young, well-educated potential migrant who worked as an engineer for a power plant at the time of the interview was moving to Russia because she was offended by restrictions placed on noncitizens. As stated previously, the Latvian Human Rights Committee has compiled a list of fifty-seven legal differences between citizens and noncitizens. For example, members of the National Guard, customs officers, civil servants, judges, public prosecutors, jurors, court bailiffs, policemen, firemen, security officers, pharmacists, private detectives, and aircraft and ship captains must be citizens. In addition, only citizens are guaranteed legal assistance and have the right to possess firearms. Citizens may travel to thirty foreign countries without a visa, but noncitizens can only travel to four. Finally, citizens have the right to establish political parties and participate in local and state elections, but noncitizens are deprived of these rights.

The committee's publication does not address the impact of informal nationalization practices on non-Latvians because it is impossible to prove the existence of such practices. But informal practices privileging Latvians in the labor market, which arose in 31 percent of the responses, are the second most frequently cited motivation for Russian exit. When asked if it is more difficult for Russians to find work than Latvians, 83 percent of potential migrants said yes, 8 percent said no, and 9 percent were unsure. One potential migrant who sold bread at Riga's central market at the time of the interview identified obstacles in the workforce as one of the most serious problems Russians confront. When asked what must change in order for her to stay in Latvia she simply replied, "The attitude toward the Russian population."

Like their counterparts in Kyrgyzstan, potential migrants in Latvia linked perceptions of discrimination to anxiety regarding the next generation's future. When asked about reasons for exit, the "children have no future" factor arose in 13 percent of the responses. This motivation stems directly from nationalization policies and practices. Russians worry about educating their children in their native language as well as the degree to which their children will suffer in the labor market from formal and informal aspects of post-Soviet nationalization.

Though a desire to live near relatives who reside in Russia motivates migration from Latvia less than formal policies, informal practices, and the effect of these factors on the next generation, it did arise in 12 percent of the responses. This is not surprising given the fact that 99 percent of the potential migrants I interviewed had relatives and/or friends in Russia. Personal connections in Russia can be a powerful pull factor because the Soviet Union's collapse severed links between Russia and Latvia, and thus rendered travel between the two countries prohibitively expensive. Moreover, relatives and/or friends provide a support network for migrants upon arrival. Pilkington finds that migrants are attracted to Russia "by the presence or advice of friends, family or acquaintances . . . knowing that their presence would provide a support network in the immediate period which would assist them in acquiring residence rights, finding housing and employment, supporting themselves financially and caring for pre-school children."[63]

Finally, the data reveal that local economic conditions hardly encourage Russian exit: the economy arose in only 12 percent of the responses. Furthermore, Figure 6.6 shows that nationalization policies and practices are *far* more important to potential migrants than is the economy. When I asked potential migrants what needed to change in order for them to remain in Latvia, nationalization policies and practices arose in 59 percent of the responses, while the economy arose in a mere 18 percent of the responses.

Riga Russians do not consider economic conditions in Latvia a push factor for various reasons. First, Latvia has a higher standard of living than Russia, which remains the most realistic and popular migration destination for residents of Latvia. According to data for 1995, 2000, 2001, 2002, and 2003, on average 48 percent of migrants choose Russia as a destination.[64] Table 6.4 shows that while Latvia's economy has grown since 1995, Russia's economy has experienced inconsistent growth. Moreover, Latvia's economy has experienced very high levels of growth since 2000. Negative repercussions of the 1998 Russian financial crisis caused lower growth rates in Latvia in 1998 and 1999, but the economy

Figure 6.6. Responses of Riga Russians to the question, What must change in order for you to remain in Latvia?

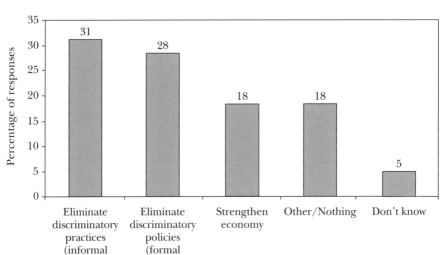

Note: Number of respondents = 65.

grew substantially thereafter because Latvia diminished its trade dependency on Russia.

Table 6.5 shows that while Latvia's GDP per capita was slightly lower than Russia's GDP per capita in the immediate aftermath of the Soviet Union's collapse, by 1997 the former had surpassed the latter. By 2004 Latvia's GDP per capita was 62 percent greater than Russia's GDP per capita.

In addition, important human development indicators including average life expectancy, infant mortality rate, and public health expenditure are either more optimistic or not much worse in Latvia than in Russia. Average life expectancy is six years longer in Latvia (71.4) than in Russia (65.4), and the infant mortality rate is lower in Latvia (10 per 1,000 live births) than in Russia (16 per 1,000 live births).[65] Both countries allocate about the same percent of GDP to public health. In 1990 Latvia devoted 3.3 percent of GDP to public health, while Russia devoted 3.5 percent; in 2002 Latvia allocated 3.3 percent of GDP to public health, while Russia allocated 3.5 percent.[66]

Second, Latvia's economic prospects are good. The 2005 Human Development Report ranks Latvia 48 and Russia 62 out of 177 possible rankings.[67] While Latvia is not as endowed with natural resources as

Table 6.4. GDP Annual Percentage Growth

	1992	1993	1994	1995	1996	1997	1998	1999	2000	2001	2002	2003	2004
Latvia	−35	−15	1	−1	3	9	4	1	7	8	—	8	9
Russia	−15	−9	−13	−4	−3	1	−5	5	9	5	—	7	7

Sources: *World Development Indicators, 2003* (Washington, D.C.: International Bank for Reconstruction and Development/World Bank, 2003); World Bank Group, http://www.worldbank.org/.

Table 6.5. GDP/GNI Per Capita (US$)

	1992	1993	1994	1995	1996	1997	1998	1999	2000	2001	2002	2003	2004
Latvia	2193	1900	1941	1950	2035	2247	2373	2418	2603	2816	—	4420	5460
Russia	2967	2713	2375	2280	2208	2235	2131	2255	1720	2609	—	2610	3410

Sources: *World Development Indicators, 2003* (Washington, D.C.: International Bank for Reconstruction and Development/World Bank, 2003); World Bank Group, http://www.worldbank.org/.

Russia, 45 percent of its territory is forest.[68] Harvested wood feeds the paper, plywood, and furniture industries, and is increasingly used for combustion as oil prices climb. Year-round ports are also a key source of growth: Riga services Japan via Siberia, and Ventspils is the end of the Volga-Urals oil pipeline.[69] Finally, integration with Western institutions has opened the door to further development, while political stability, democratic processes, and minimal corruption render the country more attractive to foreign investors than almost any other non-Baltic post-Soviet state. In 2003 foreign direct investment was 2.7 percent of Latvia's GDP and 1.8 percent of Russia's GDP.[70]

Finally and most important, Russians are active in Latvia's flourishing private sector: in short, they have adapted to industrial collapse and exclusion from the public sector by turning to commerce. A journalist who founded a large publishing company in 1994 that produces various Russian publications including the newspaper *Chas* explains this phenomenon: "The system has been constructed in such a way that it is simpler for Russians to achieve success in business rather than in the public sector, which entails a set of restrictions including a series of professions that are closed to noncitizens."[71] In the following quotation, a representative of the Party of National Harmony emphasizes the Russian presence in the country's private sector: "The absolute majority of Russians work in private business, and this trend started in the early 1990s. Large factories and scientific research institutions closed, and as a result a Russian workforce emerged. The state didn't hire them, so they adapted and went into private business. Many organized their own firms. And since then, the participation of Russians in private business has been quite considerable."[72]

Thus, the principal motivations for Russian out-migration from Latvia are antagonistic nationalization policies and practices, and the perceived effect of these factors on the next generation's future. While industrial collapse motivated Russian exit in the early 1990s, steady economic growth has diminished the degree to which local economic conditions stimulate exit. And what is critical to this analysis is the fact that connectedness to dense informal networks has enabled Russians to create a vibrant economic niche in post-Soviet Latvia. Access to the private sector encourages Russians to invest in a future in Latvia, and political mobilization represents one manifestation of that investment.

Different Explanations for Variation in Level and Type of Russian Voice

Russians respond to post-Soviet nationalization with varying degrees and types of voice. In Latvia, grievances generated by nationalization policies and practices as well as the presence of dense informal networks produce a high level of contentious voice. There are four political parties and numerous nongovernmental organizations that represent local Russians through a confrontational form of voice. In Kyrgyzstan, grievances generated by informal nationalization practices and a lack of dense informal networks produce a low level of amicable voice. There are only a handful of organizations that represent local Russians, and they adopt a nonconfrontational form of voice. Once again, we might expect regime type to make a difference: all else being equal, people should be more willing to mobilize in a democratic context than in an authoritarian context. In part, people are more willing to mobilize in Latvia than in Kyrgyzstan because Latvia's system provides legitimate political space for organization. While the Kyrgyz government is far less authoritarian than the Uzbek government, it is not nearly as democratic as the Latvian government. However, two historical factors suggest that regime politics are not the main variable driving variation in level and type of voice in these cases. First, although Latvia has been a parliamentary democracy since the early 1990s, Russians who have had grievances since then did not protest collectively until 2004. Second, the "Tulip Revolution" indicates that the Kyrgyz public is not as docile or apolitical as we might have thought given the less than democratic regime it coexists with on a daily basis.

We might also expect external actors to influence level and type of voice. Perhaps Russian voice is amicable in Kyrgyzstan because European Union membership is not even a remote possibility; in other words, Russians avoid clashes with the authorities because they have no confidence in the EU's willingness to come to their aid. And perhaps Russian voice is confrontational in Latvia because Russians hope EU membership might force parliament, or the Saeima, to take accusations of human rights abuses seriously; in other words, Russians risk clashes with the authorities because they have confidence in the EU's willingness to come to their aid. Some scholars, including Klara Hallik and Pal Kolsto, make this kind of argument. Hallik claims that Russians in Estonia hoped EU accession would generate a liberalized version of the country's citizenship policy, which closely resembles Latvia's citizenship policy.[73] For his part, Kolsto acknowledges that Latvia's yearning to join international organizations like the EU represents "an important safety valve for frustrations in the Russophone community."[74] There are two problems with this type of argument. First, there is little—if any—empirical evidence supporting the claim that Russians in either Estonia or Latvia actually count on EU support. Second, there is empirical evidence supporting the claim that authorities in the Baltic states do not fully yield to pressure from international institutions, including the EU, to lessen the intensity of their respective nationalization policies.

Though the Organization for Security and Cooperation in Europe (OSCE) convinced elites in Latvia to amend the 1998 citizenship law, it failed to persuade them "despite immense pressure from the OSCE mission and the EU" to make further concessions.[75] And because it desperately wanted NATO to include the Baltic states, the United States exerted a kind of pressure that generated "an equivocal pursuit by the EU of moderation in Estonia and Latvia."[76] According to James Hughes, this policy of moderation dampened the EU's original dedication to minority protection.[77] It seems likely that Russians in Latvia were at least somewhat cognizant of the fact that international pressure failed to prevent the implementation of antagonistic nationalization policies, and thus were not under the illusion that parliament might respond to human rights demands because it worried about jeopardizing EU accession. Lastly, it is unlikely that Russians in Latvia thought that Russia, also an important external actor, would support antiregime protests. While Russia has voiced concern over the treatment of Russians in the Baltics, it has done nothing substantive to improve the welfare of its compatriots abroad.

Amicable versus Contentious Russian Voice

The explanation for variation in type of Russian voice has a great deal to do with sources of blame. The social movement literature speaks to three questions concerning post-Soviet Russian voice: (1) Why is Russian voice amicable in Kyrgyzstan but contentious in Latvia, (2) what accounts for the wave of Russian political mobilization that swept Latvia in the early 2000s, and (3) what explains the abrupt cessation of this episode of Russian voice? I argue that representatives of Latvia's Russian minority population are able to adopt contentious rhetoric and tactics because they have a concrete source of blame for grievances, while their counterparts in Kyrgyzstan adopt amicable rhetoric and tactics because they lack a concrete source of blame for grievances.

Sidney Tarrow's classic definition of contentious politics states that "Contentious politics occurs when ordinary people, often in league with more influential citizens, join forces in confrontation with elites, authorities, and opponents."[78] Based on this definition, Russian voice in post-Soviet Kyrgyzstan is not at all confrontational. Nongovernmental organizations representing Russians do not aim to politicize their constituency, do not frame issues in a confrontational manner, and seek to work within the established political system. The amicable nature of Russian voice is surprising given Russian dissatisfaction with various aspects of Kyrgyz nationalization.

The absence of a concrete source of blame accounts for the cordial quality of Russian voice in Kyrgyzstan. According to the social movement literature, highly charged injustice collective action frames contribute to contentious politics. A collective action frame is "an interpretive schemata that simplifies and condenses the 'world out there' by selectively punctuating and encoding objects, situations, events, experiences, and sequences of actions within one's present or past environment."[79] Thus, collective action frames

> punctuate or single out some existing social condition or aspect of life and define it as unjust, intolerable, and deserving of corrective action. . . . But the framing of a condition, happening, or sequence of events as unjust, inexcusable, or immoral is not sufficient to predict the direction and nature of collective action. *Some sense of blame or causality must be specified as well as a corresponding sense of responsibility for corrective action.*[80]

The injustice component of a collective action frame expresses moral indignation that is burdened by emotion and requires human actors such as government agencies to take responsibility for causing harm and distress.[81] An effective injustice collective action frame must therefore be aimed at a specific, concrete target: "The heat of a moral judgment is intimately related to beliefs about what acts or conditions have caused people to suffer undeserved hardship or loss. The critical dimension is the abstractness of the target. Vague, abstract sources of unfairness diffuse indignation and make it seem foolish. . . . When we see impersonal, abstract forces as responsible for our suffering, we are taught to accept what cannot be changed and make the best of it."[82] The essence of these arguments is that an injustice collective action frame that is not aimed at a specific target will fail to generate the level of emotion—whether anger, fear, or desperation—required for mass mobilization.

Russians in post-Soviet Kyrgyzstan believe they suffer from a severe loss of status vis-à-vis the Kyrgyz that manifests itself as undeserved hardship in the labor market. As one thirty-seven-year-old Russian woman who worked as a financial specialist and had no intention of migrating at the time of the interview explained, "I don't think the rights of Russians are oppressed openly, but there is a secret policy to not hire [Russians], and instead to give preference to the Kyrgyz. Although this is not registered anywhere, it's simply how it is. Oppression is unofficial. There are no laws that oppress our rights, it's simply that a Kyrgyz manager gives preference to a colleague of his nationality."[83]

But Russians in Kyrgyzstan lack a concrete source of blame for the informal practices that fuel their grievances. While a single Russian can undoubtedly blame a particular manager at a particular firm for the realization of discriminatory personnel decisions, at the aggregate level Russians cannot identify a specific individual or agency responsible for tolerating such practices. The post-Soviet government cannot be portrayed as a legitimate source of blame because it has refrained from implementing antagonistic policies and has made concessions to Russians. Representatives of Kyrgyzstan's Russian population cannot create an effective injustice collective action frame without a specific target. Knowing that they cannot generate the level of emotion required for mass mobilization, they do not aim to politicize Russians; instead they work with the government to create a society based on equal rights and responsibilities. Given this context, amicable voice is the most effective method to redress grievances.

In contrast, Russian voice in Latvia is contentious—ordinary people join influential individuals to confront the authorities. Political parties and nongovernmental organizations representing the country's Russian population aim to politicize their constituency, frame issues in a confrontational manner, and work within the established political system only when compromise seems realistic. In Latvia the authorities are the specific, clearly identifiable target: "At the other extreme, if one attributes undeserved suffering to malicious or selfish acts by clearly identifiable persons or groups, the emotional component of an injustice frame will almost certainly be there. Concreteness in the target, even when it is misplaced or directed away from the real causes of hardship, is a necessary condition for an injustice frame."[84] The existence of a concrete source of blame explains the contentious nature of Russian voice in Latvia.

Russians hold the Latvian government responsible for the implementation of antagonistic policies. Although formal nationalization policies and informal nationalization practices generate grievances, it is much easier and far more effective for activist Russians to focus on the unjust nature of concrete policies rather than the unjust nature of intangible practices. At the aggregate level, Russians *can* identify a specific agency responsible for the implementation of hostile policies. The following statement, which refers to citizenship and language restrictions that prevent most Russians from working for the government, is from an interview with a forty-three-year-old Russian woman who managed an advertising firm at the time. It clearly identifies the government as a source of blame for grievances: "The policies of the government must change. The government does not want to notice that half the population is Russian-speaking! It's important that the government realizes that we are all the same, that we need equal rights because we are all the same."[85] Not only does the government implement such policies, but it also refuses to alter the nature of its nationalization program. Representatives of local Russians aim to politicize their constituency because they know they can stir up the level of emotion required for mass mobilization. In the early 2000s, they were successful in this endeavor.

"The collective mobilization of heightened emotion" accounts for this historic episode of contentious Russian voice.[86] The catalyst was the impending realization of the controversial policy discussed previously to curtail the number of classroom hours taught in Russian *within schools for national minorities*. As the date of implementation approached, Russians became increasingly emotional about the future of their identity in Latvia. Anger was widespread. But anger alone will not generate organized collective action; it must be accompanied by hope for the possibility of change.[87] As Milton J. Esman put it more than thirty years ago, "grievances alone are insufficient to mobilize protest at a level that threatens existing arrangements. To be effective, grievances must be associated with rising expectations, with credible hopes for personal and group improvement."[88] Various phenomena including cultural shifts, political opportunities, transforming events, small victories, threats to the quotidian, and assaults on group meaning and membership can create a sense of hope.

A transforming event (the first large protest) and a threat to the quotidian (fear that they would lose their already dwindling right to study in their native language) stimulated hope for change among Russians in Latvia. Local newspapers covered the first massive protest, which occurred in May 2003, extensively. That attention, and the fact that the authorities did not subdue the demonstrators, generated hope for change and sparked a wave of protests that did not subside until shortly after the policy went into effect sixteen months later. The government's divisive policy evoked pervasive fear among Russians that they would have to assimilate. Ron Aminzade and Doug McAdam's assertion that "the dominant emotion animating the threat/action link is fear" is borne out by evidence presented later in this chapter.[89]

This episode of Russian voice ended shortly after the policy went into effect. Various emotions contribute to the cessation of confrontational politics, including pride and satisfaction in the achievement of objectives. But more often than not "feelings of despair may lead people to abandon their early idealism, become cynical or apathetic about prospects for an alternative future, and focus their energies on individual pursuits and the demands of daily life."[90] At the end of the day, pride and satisfaction were absent from Russians' emotional repertoire: the protests failed to stop the authorities from curtailing the use of Russian in schools for national minorities. The policy's implementation created feelings of despair among Russians, who quickly lost hope and returned to the demands of daily life. Anger and hope for change contributed to the emergence of mass Russian protests, while despair contributed to the cessation of those protests. The Latvian case supports the social movement literature's assertion that we need to bring emotion into the study of voice.[91]

Russian Voice in Latvia: Concrete Issues to Protest, Specific People to Blame

Because Russians in the Latvian SSR maintained a strong presence in state and party organs throughout the Soviet era they were an integral part of the power nexus in the immediate aftermath of the union's demise. Entrepreneurial Russians took advantage of this window of opportunity to form political parties that represent local Russians. Since the reinstatement of independence, representatives of Latvia's Russian population have adopted a contentious stance toward the government. Although nongovernmental organizations and political parties representing Russians aim to improve their constituency's welfare by working within the political system, they simultaneously frame issues in a confrontational manner and promote politicization.

Representatives of local Russians assume a defensive strategy based on the notion that contentious organization is the only recourse available in an environment hostile to negotiation. The few minor concessions the government has made have not convinced activists that compromise regarding the intensity of antagonistic nationalization is on the agenda. For example, results of the 1998 referendum on citizenship relaxed but did not eliminate naturalization requirements. And while parliament invited suggestions regarding the government's societal integration program mentioned previously, it failed to incorporate alternative ideas into the official program. This track record has led representatives of local Russians to conclude that there is little opportunity for negotiation with an unyielding regime that insists on antagonistic nationalization. Instead of focusing on informal practices, which are abstract and disconnected from a concrete source of blame, they focus on tangible policies implemented by the government. The very existence of such policies allows them to create effective injustice collective action frames.

Nongovernmental organizations representing Russians in Latvia, such as Russian Community and Russian Society, aim to unite Russians on the basis of a shared language, culture, and history.[92] Both of these associations initially sought to protect Russian interests through dialogue with the authorities and to build harmonious relationships with other nationalities in Latvia.[93] But experience revealed that dialogue did not produce change, and the organizations subsequently began to challenge decisions made by the authorities. According to a representative of Russian Community, "We are not against compromise, but we do have goals. Russian must be an official language, Russians must have the opportunity to receive information and education in their native language, and the state must finance Russian education. We will not deviate from these principles."[94] Russian Community adopts contentious rhetoric in response to the discussion and/or implementation of antagonistic policy. For example, the organization deems the state's rejection of the Russian language unacceptable: "If they introduce a second state language, Russians would be able to speak, write, and study in their native language—and still study Latvian. But the rejection of Russian, which almost half the population speaks, is offensive and unacceptable."[95] The organization also attempts to politicize Russians. Not only did it advocate a civil disobedience campaign in response to the 1999 language law, but it continues to acknowledge the potential for Russian retaliation against the state: "Russians are becoming increasingly radical . . . they wait for the right moment to at least not support the state, if not turn against the state. . . . Russians are strangers in Latvia because the state alienates them; it reminds them that they are invaders who must obey. . . . There is a Russian proverb: nothing nice or kind comes from force."[96]

In response to antagonistic policies like the 1999 language law, Russian Society also adopts a confrontational posture, which manifests itself in demonstrations and letters of protest. Although this organization opposes Latvia's language policy, it encourages Russians to master the state language. The following quotation from an interview with a Russian Society spokesperson sheds light on this position: "I work in a school, and at one point I observed language testing. Lessons were going on, and suddenly a group of people appeared to verify state language skills. . . . They tested one teacher—they asked questions, the teacher shook, it was horrible. Tears flowed from fear that she would forget everything she knew. It was a horrible scene. So we try to help by providing free Latvian language lessons."[97] Although this organization hopes to increase the number of Russians who speak the state language, it opposes the government's societal integration program because it identifies the Latvian language as the glue that will hold an integrated society together: "We didn't like the initial program so we criticized it severely. It was assimilation, and humiliating because it insisted that we prove our loyalty. Why must we prove our loyalty? Latvians don't prove their loyalty; why must Russians? They've written a new program, which is not better, just written differently. We don't consider the state's program integration; it is a justification for assimilation."[98]

Issue-based nongovernmental organizations representing Russians such as the Association for the Support of Russian-Language Schools in Latvia, the Center for the Preservation of the Russian Language, and the Association of Latvian-Russian Cooperation also aim contentious rhetoric and tactics at the authorities. The Association for the Support of Russian-Language Schools seeks "to contribute to the support and development in Latvia of education in the Russian language."[99] Its president argues that it is the democratic right of all residents, *regardless of nationality*, to choose the language in which their children are educated: "We demand that parents have a choice. If a parent wants his child to remain Russian and study in his native language, this opportunity must be protected."[100] The association encourages Russians to master Latvian and supports the integration of minorities into society but considers language and integration policies ethnocentric and assimilative: "Integration is very important for Latvia—there is no alternative. But it is an historical process. Minorities must integrate, but the state's program reflects a very ethnocentric political course and is, in essence, a program of assimilation. We submitted many changes, but they didn't incorporate anything we proposed. We continue to criticize the program because we cannot support the notion of mandatory education in Latvian."[101] The association also acts independently to forge change. For example, it has developed an alternative to the state's bilingual education program, which it deems "very simplified and vulgar," and it sponsors conferences for parents who are eager to influence policymakers.[102] In its attempt to persuade the authorities to abandon the 2004 education policy, the association argued that the state is guilty of depriving parents of choice: "The position of our organization is that parents—meaning taxpayers—must choose the language in which their children will study, and that the state cannot dictate to them the language in which their children will study. . . . The state has provided the proportion: 60 percent in Latvian, 40 percent in Russian."[103]

The Center for the Preservation of the Russian Language aims to secure a legal status for Russian in Latvia, even if it is only language of interethnic communication. As one representative put it, "We aim to preserve Russian at the subjective level—we want people to proudly wear the banner of the Russian language. This is a very important instrument in preserving Russian identity. . . . If we are deprived of our native language, we are lost."[104] The center also wants the authorities to preserve Russian-language schools and alter the societal integration program, which it deems discriminatory, assimilative, and conducive to apartheid. Suggestions the center submitted to parliament did not appear in the final version of the program. Not surprisingly the center rejects the program's content, which it considers ultraradical and anti-Russian. In the following quotation, a center representative accuses the state of implementing a societal integration program that embraces assimilation, segregation, and apartheid:

> They offered representatives of Russians the opportunity to submit changes to the integration program, so we did. Our suggestions didn't oppress the rights of Latvians, but we did defend our rights in accordance with international standards. These modifications did not appear in the program. Instead, they adopted the most radical, anti-Russian integration program. We are categorically against the program because it encourages assimilation, segregation, and apartheid.[105]

Although the center opposes the state's approach to integration, it acknowledges that Russians must master Latvian and that the state must protect Latvian: "Russians living in Latvia must know Latvian well so that we have one common community instead of a two-language state that discriminates."[106] So while the center opposes the 1999 language policy discussed in Chapter 4, it supports the preservation of Latvian *if* the means to safeguard it do not hinder the functioning of other languages: "We consider the law on language unacceptable; it is discriminatory toward Russian-speakers so we oppose the new law in its entirety. It is pure discrimination. It is necessary to preserve Latvian because it is deteriorating, but not to the detriment of another language."[107]

While most organizations represent Latvia's Russian population as a whole, the Association of Latvian-Russian Cooperation represents permanent residents of the Latvian SSR who became citizens of the Russian Federation after the Soviet Union's demise.[108] The association's goal is to normalize relations between Latvia and Russia, assist Russian citizens in Latvia, and appeal to Russia on behalf of its compatriots abroad. A leading representative of the association emphasizes Russia's obligation to its compatriots:

> Since the collapse of the Soviet Union, a lack of proficiency in Latvian has created problems in the workforce. Unemployment among Russians in Latvia is high. . . . Russians who took Russian citizenship disagree with the processes occurring here, like the suppression of linguistic rights. In accordance with its law on compatriots, Russia is obliged to assist its compatriots legally and economically. We would like Russians in Latvia to benefit from this policy.[109]

The association opposes language and education policies in general, as well as "draconian measures" associated with linguistic legislation that force Russians to study Latvian: "We oppose the language law . . . there is no need to forbid us to study in our native language. Our children must study Russian culture and be educated in their native language. Our language cannot be ignored."[110] Speaking with remarkable foresight in 2000, this Association of Latvian-Russian Cooperation representative anticipated future confrontation between local Russians and a state unwilling to weaken the intensity of its nationalization program: "A fight for our rights lies ahead. The harsher the policies, the harsher a fight for our language, culture, and rights."[111]

In addition to these nongovernmental organizations, four political parties represent Latvia's Russian minority population: the Russian Party, Socialist Party, Party of National Harmony, and Equal Rights Party.[112] These parties used to comprise an opposition faction in parliament called For Human Rights in a United Latvia, but with the exception of the Equal Rights Party each entity eventually abandoned the faction.[113] Today the faction consists of the Equal Rights Party and For Free Choice of the Peoples in Europe.

According to a leading representative, the basis of the Russian Party's conviction regarding whom it represents is the difference between Russians, who can integrate into Latvian society, and Russian-speakers, who are in the process of assimilating into Latvian society:

> We represent Russians who consider themselves Russian, rather than the many former Soviet peoples who call themselves Russian-speakers. There is a difference and it is significant . . . Russians will be able to *integrate* into Latvian society if they remain Russian, while Russian-speakers are an intermediate group. This group went from Russian to Russian-speaker, and now finds it is much easier to assimilate. Russian-speakers are already half assimilated because they are not Russian.[114]

The Russian Party aims to ensure the integration of Russians into Latvian society without a loss of national identity; to prevent the dismissal of teachers and directors of Russian-language schools on the basis of language or nationality; to guarantee the teaching of basic subjects in Russian-language schools in Russian; and to persuade the authorities to designate Russian an official language.[115] Its broad objective is to maintain a respected sense of Russian identity in Latvia: "Our main goal is to have Russians remain Russian—not Soviet, but Russian—and to have this identity respected rather than persecuted."[116]

The party opposes the state's designation of Russian as a foreign language and considers the 1999 language law discriminatory: "How is it possible that here, in Riga, where more than half the population is Slavic, they can say that there is only one language? This is blatant discrimination."[117] The Russian Party works to influence policymaking in order to eliminate such blatant discrimination. In particular, it seeks to prevent the liquidation of Russian-language schools, which it considers a step toward assimilation: "We are 100 percent against the language policy, how it stipulates the end of education in Russian. Let children study in Russian, in Russian schools. . . . We oppose the transfer of education into Latvian. It is not right, and it is a huge mistake."[118] The party's position on the societal integration program is similar to its position on language policy: it supports the notion but opposes the formal program because it facilitates the liquidation of Russian-language schools.

While the Socialist Party, Equal Rights Party, and Party of National Harmony do not represent Russians exclusively, they do represent noncitizens who are, as stated previously, overwhelmingly Russian. These parties adopt a similarly contentious approach and identify the same source of blame. The Socialist Party does not hesitate to name the government as the agent responsible for the design and implementation of nationalization politics. One of its representatives put it this way: "The authorities invent these politics. Nationalists devised a slogan: 'Latvians, don't surrender!' This means Latvians don't surrender, Russians are leaving! But this was at the top [of society—at the official level], not at the bottom [of society]."[119] As this individual explained, the Socialist Party seeks to improve the socioeconomic welfare of the country's entire population including its noncitizens: "The citizenship problem has not been resolved, and the situation is absurd. My wife is Russian, and although we were married in 1941 and she has lived and worked here ever since, she is not a citizen. Our children have citizenship through me, but my wife is a noncitizen. This is groundless and undeserved. So the struggle continues."[120] One aspect of that struggle is a determination to convince the authorities to designate Russian an official language. While the Socialist Party does not oppose the identification of Latvian as the sole state language, it insists that the authorities give Russian official status and rejects certain aspects of the 1999 language law it considers discriminatory: "We oppose the new language law because it bans education in Russian . . . Russians need to know Latvian. . . . If you live in Latvia you must know Latvian, but there is no need to impose the use of Latvian."[121] The party also objects to the societal integration program: "The program is against Russians and the Russian language—everything is against, against. This and that is forbidden."[122] The Socialist Party advocates resistance because it faces an uncompromising regime that implements antagonistic policies on a regular basis. Not surprisingly, its slogan is: "Our fate—in our hands! There are no victories without struggles!"[123] According to the party's chairman, "We are not afraid. Without a sensation, without such a serious attitude toward the issues from the population, nothing will change."[124]

The Equal Rights Party adopts at least as confrontational an approach as the Socialist Party. Its platform is candid about the possibility of violent confrontation, as well as the source of problems faced by its constituency. According to its program, "The protest of the Russian community boils down to parliamentary activities and peaceful acts of protests—meetings, pickets, signature collecting. *However, the marginalization of the Russian community and the growth of linguistic pressure from the state do not eliminate a transition to conflict in a violent phase.*"[125] This party promotes social justice, human rights, and the interests of minorities. Every year it protests the 1991 ruling that created a second-class society of noncitizens, and periodically it submits petitions opposing citizenship policy to parliament.

According to one of its leading representatives, the Equal Rights Party also opposes Latvia's language policy because it violates the rights of the Russian minority population: "Our Party opposes the new [1999] law because it declares all languages except Latvian foreign. . . . The law and its regulations violate the rights of and discriminate against the Russian minority. . . . We are against the fact that all other languages have been ostracized to the kitchen, so that they can be used only at home."[126] Although it rarely forges policy change by appealing to international actors, the party does issue complaints to the United Nations Commission for Human Rights and the European Court regarding the government's position on citizenship and language. Russian voice acquired greater potential to garner international attention when the party's chairman, Tat'iana Zhdanoka, was elected to the European Parliament in 2004.

The party is against the liquidation of Russian-language schools, the curtailment of subjects and classroom hours taught in Russian, and the government's societal integration program. In the party's view, "The integration program is a thesis of assimilation; there is no equality or mutual respect. According to the program, integration is based on the Latvian language and one view of history. For all practical purposes, it orders non-Latvians to integrate."[127] The following statement made by a leading representative most accurately sums up the party's position on the Russian minority question: "Russians in Latvia are second-class; Negroes. There is discrimination based on ancestry. If you don't have ancestors who were born here in 1940, then you are a Negro. This is pure discrimination on the basis of ethnic affiliation."[128]

Although it tends to avoid such extreme rhetoric, the Party of National Harmony also fights for the rights of noncitizens in a contentious manner. This party aims to secure "the freedom, prosperity, and security of the people and of every individual on the basis of the revival of the people's economy in a free and independent state—Latvia."[129] As one spokesperson explained, the task is to build a society based on equal rights: "We seek a situation in which non-Latvians are recognized as equal citizens, where the attitude toward every individual does not depend on language or ethnicity. . . . Today the dominant notion is that Latvia is a state founded by Latvians for Latvians. Historically this is understandable, but the situation is harmful and dangerous."[130] Like the parties discussed thus far, the Party of National Harmony opposes formal policies that restrict the rights of Russians and argues that the state actively encourages assimilation: "The party opposes the state's education policy and rejects the liquidation of high school education in languages of minorities. We continuously fight for the preservation of education in Russian and continuously hope for success . . . but the policies facilitate assimilation and this is wrong."[131]

The party characterizes the societal integration program in terms of assimilation as well. According to the same representative, "There are certain sections, particularly the part on education, that are undoubtedly assimilative. . . . Although we support the idea of integration, we cannot support the program. Forced assimilation is forbidden."[132] Although the party views the 1999 language law as more liberal than it might have been, it opposes many aspects of it including the fact that it is illegal to submit documentation to the authorities in Russian. The individual I interviewed elaborates on this point:

> This policy contains a series of concrete norms that, from our point of view, oppress Russians. The problem with this law is that it forbids the submission of documentation by a private person to a state institution in another language, which means that people will not be able to defend their rights—they are giving every bureaucrat the possibility to violate the rights of people who cannot write well in Latvian and cannot pay for a translator. This is a violation of our constitutional rights.[133]

The following quotation from my interview with this representative sums up the party's view of post-Soviet nationalization: "I don't want to oversimplify things, but I am convinced that policies and practices pursue the goal of favoritism. Through policies and practices, they extend privileges to Latvians in a whole series of spheres. . . . Unfortunately, we cannot say that in Latvia rights and opportunities do not depend on ethnic origin and/or native language."[134] After the 2003–4 protests came to an end, this party spokesperson argued that the main problem Russians have is their government because it is unwilling to discuss the issues or treat Latvians and Russians equally:

> I would say that the main problem is the relationship of the Russian-speaking minority with its own government, which doesn't want to have a dialogue, which doesn't want to recognize Russian-speaking residents and citizens of Latvia as equal to Latvians, and which doesn't want to resolve their problems conscientiously. . . . And that relationship not only with this government but toward the state itself has gotten worse every year.[135]

The wave of large-scale demonstrations that swept Latvia in the early 2000s suggests that many Russians share this view. In the midst of these protests, an article appeared in *Chas* entitled, "What Do Russians of Latvia Want?" The author's straightforward answer focused on the authorities: "Russians want the government to hear them and to finally begin a dialogue with almost half the population."[136] According to the article, Russians want the authorities to (1) amend the law on education, (2) stop playing the de-occupation card, and (3) start relying on discussion rather than coercion. A few months later, the Latvian Association for the Support of Russian Schools and the Union of Teachers from Russian Schools announced to the Riga legislature that "Pressure and repression from the majority of parliament and the government" have weakened positive motivation among Russians to master the state language.[137] According to data provided by the State Inspection Board for Education, compared to the 2003–4 academic year, the number of students in the tenth class during the 2004–5 academic year that wanted to learn Latvian decreased by 12 percent.[138] As early as 1998, an outspoken deputy of parliament named Iakov Pliner issued a warning in his book about the state's intention to restrict, if not eliminate, the use of Russian in the education system: "Higher education in the Russian language has already been curtailed; now secondary schools are turning in this direction."[139] Six years later, the authorities implemented legislation mandating that 60 percent of classroom hours in schools for national minorities be taught in Latvian.

This policy generated widespread emotion among Latvia's Russian minority population that initially manifested itself as anger. But as I said, anger is a necessary but insufficient ingredient for organized collective action—there must be hope for change in order for coordinated political mobilization to transpire. Two factors created a sense of hope in this case: (1) fear that Russian education and thus Russian identity were at risk, and (2) a transforming event that occurred in May 2003. In the context of education policy, Russians often express fear in terms of ethnic extinction. One woman gave a local newspaper her opinion of education policy as follows: "We cannot support the 60–40 percentage! If there's no Russian culture or Russian language, we as Russians will perish here."[140] Representatives of local Russians express this sentiment as well. For example, OKROL links education to cultural preservation: "Education is a means of reproducing culture. Without education there will be no culture. And if there's no culture, there will be no awareness that a person belongs to a certain nationality or a certain commonality."[141] The transforming event that made Russians optimistic about their future occurred on 23 May, when approximately ten thousand people—the overwhelming majority of whom were Russian—participated in a protest organized by the Association for the Support of Russian-Language Schools in Latvia. The demonstration was marked by the slogan "For Free Choice of Language of Education!"[142] The authorities did not block the protest, and local newspapers covered the event extensively.

The protest's success mobilized hope for change that triggered a series of large demonstrations. Russian activists, schoolchildren, parents, and teachers participated in the demonstrations, which did not cease until the policy's implementation. On 11 February 2004, approximately 30,000 young people from Riga, Yurmala, Liepa, Elgavi, Ventspils, and Daugovpils gathered in front of the presidential palace in Riga;[143] on 1 April approximately 15,000 schoolchildren, parents, and teachers went on strike all over the country for two days—around 10,000 schoolchildren participated in Riga alone.[144] A few days later a number of activists decided to directly address the source of blame: a long column of students marched toward the building that houses the Cabinet of Ministers, and upon arrival a leading Headquarters for the Defense of Russian Schools activist presented the minister of education with an appeal, which was signed by 6,800 students, parents, and teachers representing six different cities, asking the minister to refrain from implementing the education policy.[145]

With a concrete source of blame in hand, representatives of local Russians created a highly charged injustice collective action frame in the early 2000s that generated a surge of emotion that propelled thousands of people into the streets on an almost daily basis. Headquarters for the Defense of Russian Schools, a nongovernmental organization created in the spring of 2003, planned the demonstrations.[146] The following statement made by a leading Headquarters representative sums up the organization's message: "Our children have proven with their actions that they are not and never will be slaves. They are truly free people who want to live, and will live, in a free country which they themselves will create. . . . We congratulate parents and teachers who have decided to stand next to our children and students."[147] Activists who have battled the authorities on behalf of Russian interests since the emergence of Latvian nationalization in the early 1990s participated in the opposition movement. But it is Iakov Pliner, a cochairman of For Human Rights in a United Latvia, who made the most provocative statement during the protest era: "Even in the period of the Nazi occupation of Latvia it was possible to receive a full-fledged high school education in Latvian or Russian. The current norms fail to guarantee this."[148]

On 1 May 2004, approximately fifty thousand people—schoolchildren, parents, teachers, and activists—held a demonstration in Riga to protest education policy. At the same time, people celebrated Latvia's accession to the European Union on the other side of the Daugava River.[149] A prominent Headquarters activist proclaimed the following at the anti-education policy demonstration: "They're raising the flag of the European Union and drinking beer over there . . . and that's precisely why we're over here! So the world's television cameras can see that Russians will not surrender."[150] Three months later, Headquarters organized a small "field trip" to Strasbourg: thirty-five schoolchildren and five supervisors demonstrated in front of the European Parliament.[151] Students held large banners sporting bold slogans such as *Stop Apartheid in Latvia, Hands off Russian Schools!* and *Equal Taxes, Equal Rights!* Then, just prior to the policy's scheduled implementation, Headquarters activists went on a three-week hunger strike to honor the right of Russian students to study in their native language.[152] But the protests failed to generate change: the government implemented the controversial policy on 1 September.

The last large-scale demonstration occurred on that day when more than thirty thousand people gathered in front of Riga's Freedom Monument to protest the policy's implementation. Mikhail Tiasin, a prominent activist, gave a short speech in which he emphasized the futility of appealing to the source of blame for Russian grievances: "For the last thirteen years the government has proven that it does not care about us. They don't give a damn about us. Moreover, they want things to be more difficult for our children than their children. During the time of our hunger strike, not even one small unimportant bureaucrat paid us a visit . . . I call on every one of you—don't count on the government, but believe in yourself and cross the line of humiliation and fear."[153] The policy's implementation created a prevailing sense of despair among Russians that brought this episode of contentious politics to an end. As they lost their sense of idealism, children and teachers went back to school while parents returned to the demands of daily life.

The long-term effects of this critical juncture in the history of Latvia's political development, when a self-proclaimed democratic regime ignored the voice of thousands of people who took to the streets on a recurring basis, are still unknown. Nevertheless, certain politicians are willing to speculate on the nature of long-term consequences. According to one representative of the Party of National Harmony, "So the government can ignore the demands of thirty to fifty thousand people who took to the streets? This undermines our belief in democracy and results in a choice—either people will become further disillusioned with democracy and become apathetic, or they will lean toward radical methods."[154] Short-term effects of this critical juncture are easier to assess. As the demonstrations ceased, a group of entrepreneurs established OKROL, which is the brainchild of Headquarters for the Defense of

Russian Schools activists who saw that other measures than protest were necessary to defend the interests of Russians.[155] Members of OKROL may disagree on the means to achieve the end, but they agree that the goal is to preserve Russian culture and business in Latvia.

Whether OKROL will be able to achieve its objectives is questionable, but history suggests that it will direct confrontational rhetoric and tactics toward the government. The contentious nature of Russian voice, which manifests itself in pugnacious rhetoric and public protest, is due to the presence of a concrete source of blame for grievances. Representatives of local Russians call attention to tangible policies implemented by the government. These policies and, more important, those who implement them provide a foundation for the creation of an effective injustice collective action frame that draws on powerful emotion-generating words like Negro, apartheid, assimilation, segregation, alienation, humiliation, violation, second-class, offensive, and unacceptable. In contrast to the Russian minority population in Latvia, the Russian minority population in Kyrgyzstan lacks a tangible source of blame for its grievances and thus has trouble generating an effective injustice collective action frame.

Russian Voice in Kyrgyzstan: Nothing Concrete to Protest, No One to Blame

Although the Kyrgyz constitution grants individuals the right to establish political parties, professional unions, and public associations, Russians have not seized this opportunity. There are only four nongovernmental organizations that represent Kyrgyzstan's Russian population. This minority has not been able to organize itself effectively because local Russians were not part of dense informal networks that facilitated coordinated political activity when the Soviet Union collapsed. Nevertheless, these four nongovernmental organizations—the Slavic Foundation, Union of Russian Compatriots of Kyrgyzstan, Public Association of Russians, and Russian Cultural Center—do represent their natural constituency.

Given widespread Russian dissatisfaction with conditions in post-Soviet Kyrgyzstan, it is astonishing that these organizations adopt such amicable rhetoric and tactics. In general they strive to achieve equal rights for all ethnic groups in Kyrgyzstan, work within the established political system, and shun confrontational means to achieve their goals. The following excerpt from an editorial written by the president of the Slavic Foundation before the government designated Russian an official language illustrates the nonconfrontational manner in which organizations representing Russians communicate with the authorities:

> In principle, the submission of additions and changes to the main law of the state [the constitution] is entirely justified. Life changes . . . there are

new demands. . . . It's a different matter, how important and timely these suggested changes and additions are. Absent among the questions handed down in a referendum according to presidential decree, in our opinion, is one of the most important—about giving the Russian language official status. . . . The constitutional court of Kyrgyzstan made a positive decision about submitting changes to the Constitution. So why wasn't this question handed down in a referendum? Why aren't we asking the people's opinion on this question?[156]

The absence of a concrete source of blame renders the creation of a highly charged injustice collective action frame exceedingly difficult. Russians in Kyrgyzstan lack an unambiguous source of blame for their main grievance, which is the prevalence of informal nationalization practices that "occur in a concealed way, but nevertheless happen."[157] Representatives of local Russians cannot credibly blame the government for these practices because it has implemented accommodating policies and has made concessions to Russians ever since the republic became an independent state.

President Akayev's readiness to negotiate with representatives of local Russians during the first fifteen years of the post-Soviet era discouraged them from challenging the system. His approach encouraged these activists to frame delicate and/or controversial issues in a nonconfrontational manner, improve the welfare of Russians through dialogue, and avoid measures that promote Russians *at the expense of Kyrgyz*. While Akayev remained wholly committed to the state's nationalization project, he simultaneously made various concessions to Russians. For example, he established the Assembly of the Peoples of Kyrgyzstan, facilitated the creation of a Slavic University, and elevated the status of Russian from language of interethnic communication to official language.

According to one of its representatives, the Slavic Foundation was a reaction to Kyrgyz nationalism that arose in the immediate aftermath of the Soviet Union's demise. Founded in 1989, the organization's original purpose was to preserve Russian language and culture in Kyrgyzstan. Today it also aims to protect human rights, foster ties with Russia, form connections with local and international organizations, and resolve migration problems. In an interview, this representative underscored the fact that the foundation works on all of this "at the constitutional level."[158] The organization's inclusive philosophy is revealed in his reaction to the preamble of the constitution, which stipulates the *revival* of the Kyrgyz nation and the *protection* of the interests of other nations: "How is it possible that the Kyrgyz nation must be revived, but others will only have their interests protected? We are all people of Kyrgyzstan—Americans, Russians, Kyrgyz, Tatars, Uzbeks. If we are citizens, then we must have equal opportunities to revive our cultures. There is no need to divide us so that one nation has priority."[159]

Instead of encouraging Russians to fight for their rights, the Slavic Foundation works with the Kyrgyz government through the Assembly of the Peoples of Kyrgyzstan to foster a multiethnic society based on equal rights. Not long after the Uzbek-Kyrgyz conflict in Osh, President Akayev created the assembly to facilitate dialogue between representatives of different nationalities and government officials. The assembly functions as an institutional forum in which representatives of the country's minorities, who are excluded from the political arena by informal nationalization practices, act on behalf of their respective constituency.[160] The Slavic Foundation's representative quoted above praises President Akayev, who "plays the first violin in [the Kyrgyz] state," for creating the assembly:

> It's necessary to give credit to our president because when it comes to questions on ethnic harmony I would say that he plays the first violin in our state . . . Akayev sometimes, even two times a year, meets with us [through the assembly] and we have the opportunity to give him our comments and suggestions and as a rule he lays out a mission to figure out the problems we raise. I can say, of course, not all problems, but many problems are resolved.[161]

The establishment of a Slavic University is the foundation's most important success thus far. In the early 1990s, the foundation conducted research that led it to conclude that uncertainty regarding the future of Russian education in Kyrgyzstan contributed to Russian out-migration. To address this concern without infringing upon the state language it proposed a Slavic University, sponsored by the Kyrgyz and Russian governments, in which the language of instruction would be Russian but students would have ample opportunity to study Kyrgyz. President Akayev and President Yeltsin attended the Slavic University's opening ceremony in 1993, and a fully functioning Kyrgyz language department was established in 1999.[162]

Formerly called the Association of Ethnic Russians, the Union of Russian Compatriots of Kyrgyzstan adopts tactics similar to those utilized by the Slavic Foundation to protect the cultural interests of Russians.[163] The president of the Dzalal-Abad branch sums up the organization's motto this way: a dialogue of culture will render the survival of Russians in Kyrgyzstan possible.[164] Alluding to the informal discrimination that permeates society, a leading Union of Russian Compatriots representative suggests that clan affiliation and/or nationality determines personnel decisions: "They pushed Russians out of many spheres including the police, office of the public prosecutor, army registry, customs inspection—only a few [Russian] individuals work there although we represent 12 percent of the population and Russian-speakers are 30 percent in the republic. . . . If the manager is of the native nationality, he hires his own and frequently doesn't look for professional qualifications but for relatives or fellow countrymen."[165] Rather than attempt to mobilize Russians around nonsystemic sources of blame like one manager at one firm, the organization works with the Kyrgyz government, foreign governments, and potential investors to improve the economy.[166] The rationale is that foreign investment will strengthen the economy, and a healthier economy will gradually improve the socioeconomic welfare of Kyrgyz *and* Russians. A former Union of Russian Compatriots representative put it this way: "The only way to keep Russians here is to improve economic conditions . . . this is the only way . . . the economic task is more important than the political task because without an economic foundation it's very difficult for people to resolve basic problems."[167]

The Union of Russian Compatriots also fosters education links with Russia. The all-union system of free education disintegrated with the collapse of the Soviet Union, and independent Kyrgyzstan cannot afford to provide subsidized education. Between 1995 and 2000, public expenditure on education decreased from 6 to 4 percent of national GDP.[168] Diminished public expenditure has reduced teaching salaries considerably and this causes corruption throughout the education system, low morale in the schools, and the need for many teachers to take a second job.[169] Low salaries also stimulate migration from Kyrgyzstan: according to one source, 246 teachers migrated to Russia in search of paid work in 1999 alone.[170] Many parents either cannot afford higher education in Kyrgyzstan or simply want their children to study in Russia. The union maintains agreements with various institutes of higher education in Russia through the Russian Ministry of Education in order to partially alleviate these problems. Collaborating institutes provide students from Kyrgyzstan with a stipend and waive tuition, room, and board.

The Public Association of Russians and the Harmony Russian Cultural Center also exercise amicable voice in their efforts to protect the interests of local Russians.[171] According to a representative of the Public Association of Russians, "There are many people in this country, but the Russian-speaking population happens to consist of individuals who cannot find work. As a result, Russians leave."[172] He argues further that while there is no open, blatant oppression, "it's clear that they [the Kyrgyz] are gradually forcing us out of state organs and large enterprises."[173] The association seeks to create an informational forum for Russians, encourages Russia to assist Kyrgyzstan's industrial development, and sends students to Russia on scholarships provided by the Russian government. Similarly, the Russian Cultural Center is determined to protect the interests of Russians via amicable rhetoric and tactics. Instead of condemning the government for condoning informal personnel practices that privilege the Kyrgyz and thus contribute to Russian out-migration, the center aims to decrease the level of exit by preserving Russian culture, language, and education in Kyrgyzstan.[174]

Although the perception that informal personnel practices compromise one's ability to earn a living is widespread, it has not generated contentious voice in Kyrgyzstan. While an individual Russian might blame a certain manager at a certain firm for a personnel decision favoring a less qualified Kyrgyz, at the aggregate level Russians cannot identify a particular individual or agency responsible for the toleration of such practices. Representatives of local Russians lack the kind of specific target required to create an effective injustice collective action frame and thus do not seek to politicize their constituency. In contrast to their counterparts in Latvia, they cannot legitimately hold the government responsible for dissatisfying circumstances. Consequently, representatives of Kyrgyzstan's Russian population work with the government to create a society based on equal rights, opportunities, and responsibilities.

Toward a Theory of System Transition

Russians in Kyrgyzstan did not inherit dense informal networks from the Soviet era. A lack of such networks makes it difficult for them to organize on a political basis *and* inhibits their entry into the country's private sector. While effective nationalization has secured Kyrgyz domination of the state sector, slow economic development renders the private sector exceedingly small. The Kyrgyz continue to dominate the small private sector because they lack nonpolitical resources that can be shared with national minorities. In contrast, the dense informal networks that Russians in Latvia inherited when the Soviet Union collapsed have allowed them to organize on a political basis. Within the context of a flourishing economy, these networks also facilitated their entry into the country's private sector during the early 1990s and continue to preserve a strong Russian presence in that sector. Latvians tolerate a Russian presence in the private sector because effective nationalization has secured titular domination of the state sector and because they have nonpolitical resources that can be shared. The next chapter incorporates these themes into a theory of system transition based on three cases: (1) Latvia, which is characterized by partial control; (2) Kyrgyzstan, which is characterized by control; and (3) Kazakhstan, which is in the early phase of transition from control to partial control.

Chapter 7
Ethnic Systems in Transition

To the Kazakh who divides us into "native" and "non-native"

For centuries we shared joy and tears,
We tended our gardens and raised our children,
With roots grown into this land together with you—
What the hell kind of "non-native" am I?
            —Svetlana Nazarova, *Ne ostavliaite na potom.* . . .

This stanza from Nazarova's poem alludes to Russian resentment stemming from a concrete decision elites made in the early 1990s to create
a state of and for ethnic Kazakhs. While nationalization policies and
practices generate umbrage among Russians in Kazakhstan as they do
among Russians in Kyrgyzstan and Latvia, dissatisfaction among Russians
in Kazakhstan is beginning to fade. This chapter identifies mechanisms
that facilitate the emergence of a society in which Kazakhs and Russians
continue to tend gardens and raise children together, as they share
mutual joy and tears related to such life-affirming activities; in other
words, it specifies factors that foster stability in potentially unstable multiethnic societies.

While I explore this issue from a comparative perspective based on
the Kazakh, Kyrgyz, and Latvian cases, this chapter focuses on Kazakhstan. Comparative analysis suggests that an ethnic system can undergo a
transition in which a minority moves from a subordinate position to a
satisfactory, though not superordinate, position vis-à-vis the majority of
the state in question. A satisfactory position permits alteration of an
opportunity structure designed to restrict upward mobility such as the
one Russians in Latvia occupy. This chapter presents a theory of ethnic
system transition that captures two conditions under which a minority

can move from a subordinate to a satisfactory position in relation to a particular majority: first, elites must reach a threshold of political hegemony where they exert sufficient control in terms of the degree to which they "own the state" or dominate the public sector; second, the state in question must have a developed economy. Elites representing the ethnic majority can afford, politically, to grant minorities access to the system once they reach a threshold of political hegemony, and it is much easier for them to do so if there is a thriving private sector that creates nonpolitical resources that can be shared. Milton J. Esman hints at this proposition in the following quotation:

> When an ethnic community controls the state apparatus, it generally defines access to and control of economic assets in ways calculated to benefit its constituents. In addition to land and natural resources, such assets include factories, capital, credit, and licenses to operate commercial and financial enterprises and to practice professions and trades. If members of the dominant community possess the skills needed to compete successfully under market processes and disciplines, market rules may be allowed to prevail. Members of other ethnic communities may then participate in the competition and acquire a share of the wealth. Despite informal processes of discrimination, this policy has provided opportunities for upward mobility for members of immigrant diasporas in most Western European countries and in North America.[1]

The Problem of Classifying Multiethnic Post-Soviet States

Concepts typically evoked to classify multiethnic post-Soviet states are inappropriate for the cases examined here. For example, Pal Kolsto characterizes Kazakhstan and Latvia as bipolar societies consisting of two clearly identifiable groups that are approximately equal in size.[2] He admits, however, that this classification does not apply to any other post-Soviet state.[3] The bipolar description thus limits our ability to understand the dynamics of multiethnic states in general. Post-Soviet states can also be characterized as nationalizing states in which elites promote the language, demographic predominance, economic flourishing, and political hegemony of the core nation.[4] Yet the following analysis suggests that once elites consolidate the political hegemony of the core nation, their determination to promote the economic flourishing of that nation begins to wane. This is a critical point to consider.

Some scholars classify certain post-Soviet states, like Estonia and Latvia, in terms of ethnic democracy.[5] Ethnic democracies combine legitimate democratic institutions with institutionalized ethnic dominance.[6] Although this type of polity extends certain collective rights to minorities, its very existence depends on the core nation's maintenance of institutional dominance. Hegemony of the core nation is achieved through various means, including legislation that restricts political and linguistic rights. There are two problems with applying this concept to the cases discussed here. First, ethnic democracy fails to capture the political essence of Kyrgyzstan or Kazakhstan because neither state is based on legitimate democratic institutions. Second, Sammy Smooha highlights an important point regarding Estonia that applies to Latvia as well: Estonia may be an ethnic democracy for Russians who are citizens of the country, but it is a "non-democracy" for noncitizens.[7] So in order to classify Latvia in terms of ethnic democracy we must disaggregate the Russian minority population and, I would argue, redefine the meaning of ethnic democracy.

Other scholars entertain but usually reject consociational democracy, which is founded on the notion of power sharing, as a means to classify multiethnic post-Soviet states.[8] The four basic elements of this kind of polity are a government by a grand coalition that represents all relevant segments of society; the mutual veto, which serves to protect minority interests; the principle of proportionality, which acts to ensure proportional representation in government, civil service, appointments, and the allocation of public resources; and autonomy for each relevant segment of society to determine its internal affairs.[9] Yet the fundamental premise of consociational democracy is the missing link of politics in Kyrgyzstan, Kazakhstan, and Latvia, where elites work assiduously to *avoid* sharing power with representatives of national minorities.

In contrast to the concepts discussed thus far, Ian Lustick's notion of control furthers our understanding of ethnic dynamics in post-Soviet states. Like consociationalism, control is a means to obtain stability within potentially unstable multiethnic states, but unlike consociationalism it rests on the notion of hierarchy. A system of control is based on a relationship in which a superordinate segment of society enforces stability by restricting political opportunities for the subordinate segment(s) of society.[10] Stability is maintained via coercion or the threat of coercion, as well as political and economic institutions, legal frameworks, and cultural circumstances. Rival groups do not share power: one group dominates the political system at the expense of every other group. Whereas in a consociational context the regime acts as an umpire who translates compromises into effective legislation, in a control context the regime acts as a legal and administrative instrument of the superordinate segment of society.[11]

The relevance of Lustick's definition of control can be seen in the cases explored here, where the ethnic majority constrains Russian political opportunities through nationalization policies and/or practices. However, these cases indicate a need to distinguish control from what I have called partial control.[12] The defining characteristic of a system of partial control is that the core ethnic group controls the political sector *but shares control of the economic sector.* In such a system, collective rights in the cultural and educational sectors that allow a group to prosper as a minority are either not extended or are extremely limited. I classify the cases explored here as follows: the Kyrgyz ethnic system is characterized by control, the Latvian ethnic system by partial control, and the Kazakh ethnic system by movement from control to partial control.

The Kyrgyz Ethnic System: Control

The Kyrgyz ethnic system is made up of one group (the Kyrgyz) that is superordinate across all domains, and various groups (including Russians) that are subordinate across all domains.[13] Informal nationalization practices constrain Russians' political aspirations, while sparse informal networks and the Kyrgyz clan system restrict their economic aspirations. The following quotation, which is from an interview with a forty-eight-year-old Russian likely permanent resident of Bishkek who worked in construction during the Soviet era but was unemployed at the time of the interview, alludes to the adverse consequences of the local clan system for Russians:

> In general, all people were equal under the Soviet Union, absolutely equal. In connection with the collapse and independence there was a program that elevated the titular nationality to the first place—so the Kyrgyz—and everyone else sunk below because there was this proclamation of the state that the titular nationality had to be higher. In connection with the traditional settlement of the Kyrgyz, there are clans, families. Every relative tries to help his fellow clan community. But Russians do not have this. We thought—we live in the Soviet Union, everyone is equal—but this turned out not to be. The government of Russia has simply come unscrewed from us, and we have ended up today as the most wretched nationality, the most wretched. No one helps us, we are cut off from Russia like being cut off from a mother, and the Kyrgyz government does not need us.[14]

Equality is an outdated assumption in post-Soviet Kyrgyzstan. Nationalization practices have secured Kyrgyz domination of the public sector: in other words, they have enabled elites to reach a threshold of political hegemony. Awareness of this fact among Russians accounts for the wholly Kyrgyz nature of the Tulip Revolution discussed previously, which involved Kyrgyz from the south challenging the political dominance of Kyrgyz from the north. National minorities watched the revolution unfold from their homes; they did not participate because they have no stake in a political system of and for ethnic Kyrgyz.

Kyrgyz elites are unwilling to expand access to this system because doing so would require relinquishing *political* control. The lack of a vibrant private sector means there is a shortage of nonpolitical resources. While the private sector has grown since the collapse of the Soviet Union—it now accounts for a seemingly impressive 75 percent of GDP—a recent report prepared for the Asian Development Bank argues that strong state intervention renders it quite weak:

> The underlying problematic in private sector development is the pervasive and excessive role of the state. Although the private sector now accounts for 75 percent of official GDP in the Kyrgyz economy, the size, role and impact of the state sector in the national economy is greater than indicated by its 25 percent share of GDP. Aside from the production of goods and services in state-owned enterprises, a large but hidden or informal "stealth" state economy operates through the country's governance and public administration apparatus. . . . This stealth but sizeable state economic sub-sector, with an excessive regulatory regime used and abused for rent-seeking, official corruption and political patronage, crowds out the private sector and distorts the functioning of the market mechanism.[15]

Various scholars, including Roman Mogilevsky and Rafkat Hasanov, share this view: "A large impediment to development of private entrepreneurship and free movement of goods [in Kyrgyzstan] is the intervention of the government, which takes the form of excessive licensing and certification requirements as well as a direct intervention of officials into production processes and ownership issues."[16] Similarly, Martin Spechler argues that although the private sector accounts for 75 percent of the economy, small and medium-sized businesses suffer because they face high taxes, corrupt inspections, difficult entry regulations, and a government that still has a tendency to dictate production goals.[17] At this point, sharing economic power with national minorities would require the Kyrgyz to relinquish control of enterprises that are still at least partially owned by the state, which would necessitate a redistribution of *political* power. Kyrgyz elites are not willing to do this. The result is that Russians have negative perceptions of socioeconomic opportunity because group identity restricts their mobility.

The Latvian Ethnic System: Partial Control

If the Kyrgyz case is an example of control, the Latvian case is an example of partial control.[18] Here the position of majority and minority ethnic groups varies depending on the domain in question. Although Latvians constrain Russians' political aspirations, they do not restrict their economic aspirations. Control of the political sector is restricted to Latvians, but control of the economic sector is shared with members of the Russian minority. While nationalization policies and practices solidify Russian subordination in the public sector, they do not affect the private sector, where Russians maintain a commanding presence. By and large the political elite is essentially Latvian, while the economic elite is heavily Russian. Though group identity restricts mobility in the public sector, it does not do so in the private sector. This variable status generates positive perceptions of socioeconomic opportunity among Russians.

The Political Aspect of Partial Control

Elites established political control for Latvians in the immediate aftermath of the Soviet Union's demise through the implementation of strict citizenship requirements. The initial mechanism for securing political control was the 1991 government ruling discussed previously that restricts the demos to individuals deemed loyal to the state. While citizens of the interwar republic (as well as their descendants) are entitled to automatic citizenship, everyone else except former Soviet armed forces/security services personnel who are banned from the demos must naturalize. While most "aliens" can naturalize, elites have institutionalized various linguistic hurdles for naturalization applicants to clear. The confinement of Latvian to the kitchen for decades meant that by the time Gorbachev embraced glasnost' a critical mass of Latvians believed that their native language was in danger of extinction. Elites quickly designated the titular language the republic's sole state language and then passed legislation requiring naturalization applicants to take an oral and written language exam, a test on the constitution, and an oath of loyalty to the state.

The most important legal difference between citizens and noncitizens in terms of consolidating political control is that the latter cannot vote in national elections. Since the Russian population of newly independent Latvia was made up primarily of postwar immigrants, who as a result of the policy discussed above were denied automatic citizenship, it was mainly Latvians who voted in the first parliamentary elections. The restrictive citizenship legislation was passed in September 1991 *before* elections were held in June 1993. Citizens voted for candidates affiliated with nationalist parties like Latvia's Way, and as a result elected representatives of such parties implemented policies designed to promote the core nation.[19] One local publication explains it this way: "The Latvian invention of non-citizen status provided for the exclusion of the minority from sharing in power and stabilized majority support for radical liberal reforms carried out by right wing governments."[20] According to Anton Steen, these elections changed the ethnic composition of Latvia's parliament: "I have no figures to illustrate the ethnic composition of the [Baltic] leadership before independence. . . . But there is no doubt that a substantial ethnic change of top leaders took place, and this change was especially dramatic in Estonia and Latvia."[21] The first post-Soviet elections ushered in a parliament made up of eighty-eight Latvians, six Russians, and six individuals who were neither Latvian nor Russian.[22]

Change in the ethnic composition of parliament made the implementation of policies designed to ensure long-term political control possible. For example, parliament passed legislation that widens the sphere of communication in which the state language is required and narrows the sphere of communication in which Russian is permitted. By 1999 parliament had designated all languages other than the state language foreign. Moreover, the state utilizes language testing to determine access to a variety of professions. And while knowledge of the state language is a standard requirement for public sector employment, employees of private institutions must also use the state language when their activities affect the public interest.

These policies aim to reserve public sector positions for representatives of the core nation and thus preserve that nation's political control. By the early 1990s Latvians had solidified control of state institutions: "In the state bureaucracy and judiciary, the indigenous elite has an overwhelming majority in all three countries [Estonia, Latvia, and Lithuania], standing at between 90 and 100 per cent in 1993–94 and 1997."[23] A recent Baltic Barometer Survey suggests that less than one-third of the country's Russian population is employed in the public sector: 26 percent of employed Russian respondents work for state budgetary organizations or state-owned enterprises.[24] Political dominance within the context of a flourishing private sector enabled elites to expand access to the system.

The Economic Aspect of Partial Control

In a system of partial control a group's subordination in the political arena does not necessarily imply its subordination in the economic arena as well. Consolidation of political control allowed elites in Latvia to relinquish control of the private sector with little opposition. The country's developed economy is, in part, based on a strong private sector that offers nonpolitical resources that can be shared. The assumption that motivated elites to tolerate Russian participation in the private sector was that economic prosperity would give Russians a stake in the system and therefore foster stability.

Excluded from the public sector, well-connected Russians embraced the private sector. Scholars agree that Baltic Russians play a prominent role in local business communities because they do not confront discriminatory policies and practices in the private sector.[25] In 2000, 64 percent of employed Russian respondents who participated in a Baltic Barometer Survey worked in Latvia's private sector.[26] Four years later, 56 percent of employed Russian respondents who participated in a Baltic Barometer Survey worked in Latvia's private sector.[27]

Privatization proceeded rapidly in Latvia: by 1997 most of the country's small and medium-sized enterprises were in the private sector.[28] By 2003 Latvia's private sector accounted for 74 percent of the economy and employed 63 percent of the population.[29] As in other post-Soviet states, new businesses emerged in Latvia in response to the collapse of the all-union economy. Not only did Russians acquire many privatized firms through the means discussed in Chapter 4, but they also opened countless new firms because they were able to evade harsh citizenship and language restrictions in the private sector.[30] Many of these businesses are located in the secondary sector, where Russians were heavily concentrated during the Soviet era. According to one study, the wholesale and retail sectors house the largest number of Russian firms.[31]

As demonstrated in Chapter 4, dense informal networks contribute to the preservation of a strong Russian presence in Latvia's business community. As they try to stay afloat in a political sea characterized by antagonistic nationalization, Russians hire "their own" whenever possible. This tendency facilitates the growth of Russian companies. Ethnic segregation in Latvia's business sector stems from the fact that "there are many cases in which the job seekers and possibly also employers focus on ethnic origin, which is often closely linked to a person's native language."[32] When they hire their own, Russian entrepreneurs create opportunities for Russians who are excluded from the public sector and in so doing preserve a robust Russian presence in the local business community.

The Collective Rights Aspect of Partial Control

A critical difference between ethnic democracies and systems of partial control is that collective rights are either not extended or are extremely limited in the latter. In contrast, "the minority is accorded some collective rights and sometimes even granted autonomy with certain limitations" in the former.[33] Collective rights, such as the Arab right to a separate school system in Israel, allow a group to prosper *as a minority* in ethnic democracies. Because they encourage assimilation into the dominant culture, executors of systems of partial control do not extend collective rights.

Russians in Latvia have access to Russian media, Russian cultural organizations, and a Russian Party that represents their unique interests. But they are not granted free use of their native language, and they lack a separate school system. While they have the right to an education in their native language through private schools, regardless of nationality the average resident of Latvia cannot afford such a luxury. And while there are state schools with programs for national minorities, in 2004 elites restricted the number of classroom hours taught in Russian in these institutions. On the whole, the Latvian government does not extend to Russians collective rights that allow them to prosper as a minority.

The Kazakh Ethnic System: Transitioning from Control to Partial Control

Two things must happen in order for the movement from control to partial control that characterizes the Kazakh ethnic system to occur. First, elites must reach a threshold of political hegemony. Electoral success determined this threshold in newly independent Latvia, where citizens elected a parliament dominated by members of the core nation who quickly implemented policies designed to expand Latvian ownership of the state. Once elites had crossed this threshold, the economic flourishing of the core nation was no longer a priority because it had secured domination of the public sector and could thus afford to relinquish some control. Second, the state in question must have a developed economy. The Latvian case indicates that once elites reach a threshold of political hegemony, they create access to the system in order to foster stability *if there are nonpolitical resources that can be distributed.*

Kazakh Nationalization

> Russians have become second-class citizens. . . . Our government consists for the most part of Kazakhs, so this means when it comes to issues related to government . . . Russians are cut off.

During the 1990s, elites took concrete steps to ensure Kazakh ownership of Kazakhstan. Formal policies related to personnel, migration, and territorial administration as well as informal personnel practices favoring members of the core nation served to constrain the political and economic aspirations of Russians. Shortly after the Soviet Union's collapse, the government began to aggressively oust Russians from key city and oblast-level administrative positions.[34] This process continued throughout the decade. According to the Center for Humanitarian Research, Russians are the victims of a disproportionate representation of Kazakhs in organs of authority.[35] One scholar claims that local Russians "have every reason to expect that they may become just as politically marginalized as the Russophones in Latvia. Even today it is clear that they are being pressed out of most positions of power in Kazakhstani society."[36] Another scholar agrees: "What is most obvious (and the most worrisome for non-Kazakhs) is something that is apparently not included in the government's nationalities policy: the monopolization of all branches of power and public offices by Kazakhs."[37]

Migration policies targeting both Kazakhs who reside in southern Kazakhstan and the roughly four million Kazakhs who reside abroad are designed to dilute Russianized regions of the country.[38] The government entices Kazakhs in the south to resettle in the north and encourages the repatriation of Kazakhs who fled their homeland in the early twentieth century.[39] In the early 1990s, President Nazarbaev established annual immigration quotas to stimulate repatriation.[40] While the quotas have not entirely been met, the government has persuaded a sizable number of Kazakhs to relocate. For example, 94 percent of the quota was met in 1993; 64 percent in 1994; 73 percent in 1995; and 88 percent in 1998.[41] The Department of Migration works with various governments to facilitate repatriation and helps migrants adapt to local conditions upon arrival.[42] In addition, the state finances repatriation expenses and finds suitable areas of residence for immigrant Kazakhs.[43] The government intensified its campaign in 1997, when President Nazarbaev identified several migration priorities including "the assistance in the repatriation of Kazakhs, their settlement, and their adaptation."[44] A 1997 law on migration guarantees immigrant Kazakhs free transportation to Kazakhstan, assistance in job and school placement, vocational training, unemployment and pension benefits, help learning the state language, and the means to acquire a home.[45] The government thus funds the transportation, settlement, and adaptation of returning Kazakhs, who are known as *oralmans*, or "people who come back."[46] State assistance has paid off: approximately 170,000 Kazakhs returned to their historic homeland between 1991 and 1998.[47] This success has encouraged the government to establish higher immigration quotas as the economy has improved.[48]

Territorial administration policy is also designed to dilute Russian regions of the country. One such policy increased the percent of Kazakhs in Russian regions significantly by incorporating Russian-dominated oblasts into Kazakh-dominated oblasts and vice versa. By 1999 Akmola's population was 38 percent Kazakh (it was 22 percent Kazakh in 1989); East Kazakhstan's population was 49 percent Kazakh (it was 27 percent Kazakh in 1989); Karaganda's population was 28 percent Kazakh (it was 17 percent Kazakh in 1989); Kustanai's population was 31 percent Kazakh (it was 23 percent Kazakh in 1989); and Northern Kazakhstan's population was 30 percent Kazakh (it was 19 percent in Kazakh 1989).[49]

Another territorial administration policy transferred the capital from Almaty to Astana. The decision to move the capital from a cosmopolitan city in an ethnically diverse, relatively warm region to an undeveloped, climatically harsh city in a Russian region cost $1 billion U.S..[50] According to one former president of Kazakhstan's Association of Political Science, ethnodemographic concerns motivated the transfer: "Moving the capital to the north, to predominantly Russian-language oblasts, was in accord with the aim of stimulating the resettlement of the predominantly Kazakh political elite to the northern Russian-language region and thereby changing the ethnodemographic situation, increasing the number of Kazakhs among the population of northern Kazakhstan."[51] Several scholars agree with this interpretation.[52] For example, Taras Kuzio argues that Nazarbaev's need to strengthen Kazakh identity in the north, a heavily Russian area, was a key reason to move the capital.[53] Similarly, Henry R. Huttenbach claims that the large influx of government employees to Astana suggests "the unspoken intentions lying behind the decision to move the capital closer to the Russian population center. The emergence of a young and increasingly vibrant Kazakh capital at the doorstep of the Russian populated north speaks volumes."[54] Richard L. Wolfel concurs with this assessment and claims that motives for the capital transfer include Nazarbaev's determination to strengthen the state's ability to monitor local Russians, dilute the Russian presence in the north, and prevent secessionist movements.[55] Finally, Edward Schatz claims that part of Nazarbaev's reasoning concerned nation-building: referring to the possibility of Russian separatism, Schatz argues that "By bringing the physical apparatus of the state closer to the locus of the perceived unrest, Nazarbaev signaled his readiness to contain threats at a moment's notice."[56] Thus, despite official reasons given for the capital transfer such as geographic problems with Almaty,[57] there is a consensus among academic observers that the decision was part of a broad nationalization strategy that aims to promote members of the titular nation. In other words, contrary to official proclamations, "the primary reason . . . was the demographic predominance of ethnic Russians in the North and the possibility of separatism. A new capital represented an opportunity to create new loyal political elites and simultaneously keep tabs on the oblasts near the Russian border."[58]

Like their counterparts in Kyrgyzstan and Latvia, elites in Kazakhstan implement various policies and condone various practices that privilege the core nation. Beginning in the early 1990s Nazarbaev argued that in certain cases it is appropriate for "special provisions" to be extended to "the native nation, the Kazakhs."[59] These special provisions became pervasive and ultimately created Kazakh monopolization of "the corridors of power."[60] According to Bhavna Dave, by the time the 1997 law on languages was passed, "Kazakhstan's nationalizing state framework and various policies and directives had led to a rapid increase in the Kazakh share in the state and regional offices."[61] One scholar identifies personnel decisions in particular as the main tool used to Kazakhify the state: "The ethnocratic line of the state received its realization, first and foremost, in personnel policies—in awarding advantages for all high level positions to individuals of the titular nationality. Three quarters of all bureaucrats in the high apparatus of the country are Kazakh."[62] As a thirty-nine-year-old Russian likely permanent resident of Almaty who worked as an engineer for a security firm at the time of the interview put it:

> Russians have become second-class citizens. . . . Our government consists for the most part of Kazakhs, so this means when it comes to issues related to government—applying for vacancies in state offices, for credit from a bank, or a to study abroad—Russians are cut off. In terms of the government, Russians are always in an unfavorable position. In business it depends on the owner of the establishment—Kazakhs hire Kazakhs and Russians hire Russians. But in terms of public service, of course Russians have absolutely no chance. Of course there are exceptions, but these are special Russians who have converted to Islam—in short, atypical Russians. Now Russians are strangers in this state.[63]

When I asked Almaty Russians about their experience as a new minority, they underscored the adverse impact of these provisions, or personnel practices, on their ability to navigate the labor market. Figure 7.1 shows that 64 percent of Almaty likely permanent residents mentioned the unfavorable effect of personnel practices privileging Kazakhs; only 22 percent mentioned discriminatory policies, while a mere 14 percent spoke of unemployment. According to one forty-year-old respondent who was working in a factory at the time of the interview:

> It's much harder for us to obtain management positions because of nationalism, Kazakh nationalism, and the lack of a desire to see Russians in higher positions. The main problems Russians face are getting management positions, discrimination based on language, and getting a higher education. What is observed among Kazakh elites is a gradual ousting of Russians, smoothly. They don't make extreme movements but there's a tightening, a pressure on Russians based on language, and infringements of our rights exist.[64]

Representatives of nongovernmental organizations that defend the interests of Russians agree with this interpretation. According to a lead-

Figure 7.1. Responses of Almaty Russians to the question, How have conditions changed for Russians since the collapse of the Soviet Union?

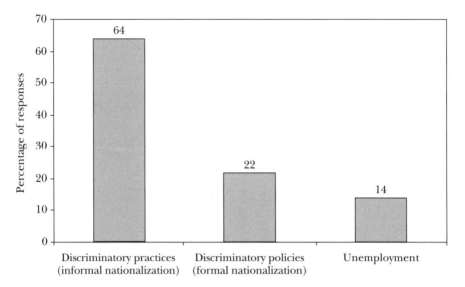

Note: Number of respondents = 50.

ing representative of one such association called Lad: "We lack representation in the state sector—in the executive, legislative and judicial branches, as well as in administration. Titular personnel dominate the state sector. . . . No one says, 'You're Russian so therefore I won't hire you,' but there are maneuvers, obstacles, barriers that make this clear."[65] Those maneuvers, obstacles, and barriers have created a situation in which a "considerable portion of Russians as they [Kazakhs] say 'left' many important spheres: state apparatus, power structure, organs of law and order, the courts, and the office of the general prosecutor."[66]

Elites have also taken advantage of unusual circumstances such as those surrounding the "Pugachev incident" to convey a strong unambiguous message regarding their determination to implement nationalization policies and condone nationalization practices.[67] In 1999 Kazakh authorities arrested twenty-two people who were accused of attempting to overthrow the local government in Ust'-Kamenogorsk in order to establish an autonomous Russian Republic. Although they did nothing illegal except smuggle a few low-grade weapons across the border, the accused were tried, convicted, and sentenced for attempting to orchestrate an unconstitutional coup. The "Pugachev incident" was a badly conceived, even farcical symbolic act intended to raise controversial issues regarding the treatment of Russians in Kazakhstan, but the government manipulated the circumstances in order to remind Russians of their status in a state of and for ethnic Kazakhs. In other words, the authorities' actions were part of a larger strategy designed to achieve political, economic, cultural, and demographic Kazakh hegemony. Robert Kaiser and Jeff Chinn summarize this phenomenon in the following quotation: "Since the collapse of the USSR and Kazakhstan's independence in December 1991, Kazakh political elites have become less accommodative, as they have become more intent on reconstructing their state to serve primarily if not exclusively the interests of the Kazakh nation."[68]

The Creation of a Partly Russian Middle Class

> Russians have begun to occupy a certain niche in Kazakhstan: small business. . . . They don't face obstacles in small business, although it's difficult for them to become managers.

Shortly after the Soviet Union's demise, Kazakhstan adopted a series of structural reforms that gradually transformed the economy from one based on central planning principles to one based on free market principles. In conjunction with the 1999–2000 increase in oil and natural gas prices, these reforms have succeeded: Kazakhstan's GDP essentially doubled between 1999 when it was almost $17 billion U.S. and 2003 when it was almost $31 billion U.S.[69] Average monthly salaries rose from $99 U.S. in 1999 to $155 U.S. in 2003.[70] In addition, the level of unemployment has steadily decreased over the years: in 2000 it was 12.8 percent, in 2001 it was 10.4 percent, in 2002 it was 9.3 percent, and in 2003 it was 8.8 percent.[71] While unemployment and low incomes continue to plague many rural areas, economic growth has created "a newly rich class . . . with their luxury automobiles and hotels they frequent."[72] Although it has not proceeded rapidly, privatization of state-owned enterprises is occurring. The share of the private sector grew from 55 percent of GDP in 1998 to 65 percent in 2003.[73] By 2006 two-thirds of the country's firms were in the private sector.[74] As these firms were privatized and new ones were established, the number of people working for small enterprises rose from 542,030 in 2000 to 748,785 in 2003.[75] Although the Kazakh economy may eventually fall ill with the Dutch Disease because of its dependence on oil exports, there is no guarantee that this will happen. There are scholars who claim that arguments concerning the Dutch Disease do not apply to Kazakhstan.[76] And most important for this analysis is the fact that the Kazakh economy did not get sick during the period under consideration.

In almost every post-Soviet society domination of the public sector ensures domination of private sector management because managers must negotiate on a regular basis with the state in order to conduct business. Kazakh nationalization was effective precisely because it secured titular domination of the management of both the public sector *and* the private sector. By 2004 Kazakhs held 79 percent of political and administrative positions within government; Russians held 14 percent.[77] Kazakh domination of private sector management made it difficult for Russians to enter the private sector during the 1990s, but by the early 2000s successful nationalization had created a strong sense of confidence among Kazakhs regarding the degree to which they own the state. This self-assurance enables elites to tolerate Russian activity in the private sector.

Like their counterparts in the Kyrgyz SSR, Russians in the Kazakh SSR were ousted from state and party organs and thus isolated from informal networks when the Soviet Union collapsed. Few Russians occupied key positions in the Kazakh republic in the 1980s as a result of Russian out-migration and locally initiated *korenizatsiya*. Resistance to Russification began in the late 1960s under the republic's first secretary, Dinmukhamed Kunaev, who gave Kazakhs incentive to apply to university, emphasized the importance of Kazakh language and culture, and, most important, strengthened political networks among Kazakhs. By the 1980s Kazakhs occupied key positions in administration, heavy industry, agriculture, and construction: "Under Kunaev, Kazakhs participated increasingly in the leadership of both party and state, whereas much of the old Russian dominance over native cadre broke down, particularly after 1971, when Kunaev became a full member of the Politburo."[78] By 1981 Kazakhs comprised 52 percent of the Kazakh Central Committee and ran 47 percent of Kazakh Central Committee departments; in addition, they occupied 60 percent of positions within the Council of Ministers and 61 percent of ministerial and state chair positions.[79] Because they tended to be workers, Russians were underrepresented in the republic's intelligentsia, legal institutions, and organs of state administration.[80] By the late 1980s there was a strong Russian presence only in low and mid-level ranks of industry.

Local *korenizatsiya* implemented by the Kazakh leadership sparked a wave of Russian exit: "Beginning in the mid-1970s, the Russians began to leave Kazakhstan at a faster rate than they were moving into the republic, a trend that further accelerated with independence."[81] Figure 7.2 shows the number of Russians who migrated from Kazakhstan annually from 1990 to 2003, which totals 2,605,148. This figure also illustrates that Russian migration picked up speed in the early 1990s following Kazakh-

Figure 7.2. Number of Russians who migrated from Kazakhstan annually.

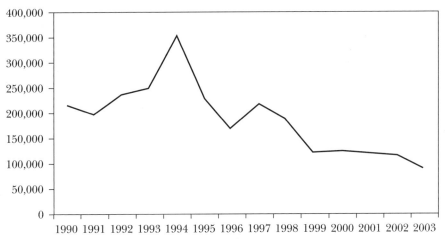

Source: Agentstvo Respubliki Kazakhstan po statistike.

stan's declaration of independence, peaked in 1994, and then declined at a fairly steady rate for the time period under consideration here. Table 7.1 tracks the number of Russians who migrated from Kazakhstan annually and shows that as of 2001 that number has decreased each year.

Regardless of their nationality, most migrants from Kazakhstan choose Russia as a destination: 70 percent of migrants moved to Russia in 2000; 67 percent moved to Russia in 2001; 66 percent moved to Russia in 2002; and 61 percent moved to Russia in 2003.[82] When asked why they had chosen Russia as a migration destination, the overwhelming majority (76 percent) of the Almaty potential migrants I interviewed identified an affinity toward Russia based on notions of homeland, language, and a sense of comfort that comes from being among "your own." Seventeen percent of the respondents cited a desire to live near relatives, while a mere 6 percent cited economic opportunity. This suggests that economic considerations were not a major reason for choosing Russia as a host country. However, Figure 7.3 indicates that in addition to discriminatory practices, the economy was a motivation for Russian exit in the late 1990s before Kazakhstan's economic situation had begun to noticeably improve and before Kazakhs had begun to welcome Russians into the private sector.

Considering that manufacturing comprised 9 percent of the Kazakh SSR's GDP in 1990, it is safe to conclude that Russians did not inherit a large slice of the republic's economic pie when the Soviet Union

Table 7.1. Russian Migration from Kazakhstan

1992	1993	1994	1995	1996	1997	1998	1999	2000	2001	2002	2003	2004	Total
232,757	247,686	352,175	225,861	170,344	215,625	186,397	120,662	124,102	118,162	114,308	88,850	88,223	2,285,152

Source: Agentstvo Respubliki Kazakhstan po statistike.

Figure 7.3. Responses of Almaty Russians to the question, Which factors influenced your decision to migrate from Kazakhstan?

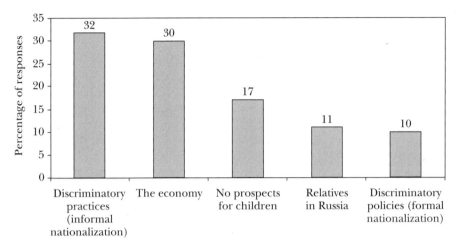

Note: Number of respondents = 115.

collapsed. A lack of dense informal networks hindered their ability to break into Kazakhstan's emergent private sector during the 1990s. Exclusion from the public and private sectors generated negative perceptions of socioeconomic prospects, which drove Russian exit. But as Kazakhs have become increasingly confident regarding the degree to which they own the state, they have expanded access to the system. This expansion created new economic opportunities for Russians that contributed to the decline in Russian exit which began in 2001.

Because they confront barriers to the public sector, Russians who stay in Kazakhstan tend to enter the private sector. Leading representatives of Lad and Russian Society, another nongovernmental organization representing local Russians, agree that Russians work in the private sector with little difficulty.[83] According to the founder of Kazakhstan's Russian Party: "Russians have begun to occupy a certain niche in Kazakhstan: small business. There are many Russians in small business—tourism, industry—they open stores, cafés, restaurants, game halls. They don't face obstacles in small business, although it's difficult for them to become managers."[84] One former president of Kazakhstan's Political Science Association asserts that although they have trouble obtaining management positions, Russians do succeed in the private sector: "Russians are discriminated against in the state sector, but many are self-employed and others do well in private enterprises, foreign firms, embassies. But the manager is always Kazakh because enterprises and firms must work with the state, and only Kazakhs can do this. Approximately 90 percent of firm managers are Kazakh—a firm comprised solely of Russians is rare. But Russians have found a niche, and they form the core of the middle class."[85]

While Kazakhs have relaxed informal personnel practices in the private sphere, a lack of dense informal networks and exclusion from a ubiquitous Kazakh clan system hinder Russians' ability to reach the level of management. A thirty-year-old female likely permanent resident of Almaty who was working as a secretary at the time of the interview sheds light on this issue: "I think people [Russians] leave because they don't see a future for their children here, especially since people of the native nationality fill management positions. If you want to manage there are certain criteria—you must be of the native nationality, and you must know Kazakh. Also there are roots of tribalism in Kazakhstan, which are rather strong, so if a Kazakh gets a job, a high position, he will hire his relatives."[86] In his discussion of the significance of kin-based access networks during the Soviet era, Edward Schatz claims that "mutual assistance among kin" differentiated Kazakhs from Russians. Moreover, according to Schatz, these networks continue to inform interactions in Kazakh society: "Political and economic structures throughout the 1990s still rewarded those with privileged access and, in this sense, belied the public façade of open politics and markets that the regime attempted to propagate. As during the Soviet period, the result was that clan networks continued to be vibrant and important, well after the demise of the Soviet state itself."[87] One thirty-nine-year-old male likely permanent resident of Almaty who was in business at the time of the interview explained the effect of the Kazakh clan system on Russians this way:

> Life's gotten worse, unambiguously. For example, many people have been deprived of work and of the lucrative part of their family budget, which enabled them to exist during the Soviet Union. Now many people lack work. But this applies to Russians for the most part because Kazakhs live by family, by clan, and if one of them advances to a management position he absolutely hires his relatives and in so doing squeezes out Russians and other nationalities. So is it harder for Russians to find good work? Without a doubt.[88]

Post-Soviet nationalization has ensured Kazakh domination of the public sector. This ensures Kazakh control of the private sector's top echelon because managers must negotiate with the state to conduct business, and Russians who lack dense informal networks and are excluded from the clan system are simply not equipped to do this.

Kazakhs are satisfied with their status vis-à-vis Russians because they dominate the public sector as well as the highest stratum of the private sector. In recognition of this fact, a fifty-two-year-old male likely permanent resident of Almaty who was working at an institute for industrial development at the time of the interview stated, "Openly Russians don't face oppression, but secretly they do. For example, in all government organs like parliament you don't see Russians. Take business enterprises—any manager is of the indigenous population, though there are more Russians in Kazakhstan than Kazakhs, but they are not represented [at the management level]."[89] Kazakh domination of both the public sector and private sector management allows elites to tolerate a heavy Russian presence in low and mid-levels of the private sector. The chance to prosper in the private sphere gives Russians a stake in the post-Soviet system.

By the early 2000s, Kazakhstan's superordinate group had reached a threshold of political hegemony where it exerted sufficient control in terms of the degree to which it owned the state. Domination of the public sector as well as the private sector's top echelon paved the way for a shift to partial control. At present, Kazakhstan is in the midst of a transition from a system characterized by control to a system characterized by partial control. Although there are few Russians in the public sector and the upper echelon of the private sector, Russians do occupy low and mid-level positions in the private sector. Their success in that arena enables them to join an emerging middle class, and the realization that they *can* become members of this group alters their perceptions of socioeconomic opportunity and contributes to a reduced level of out-migration. Despite adverse effects of nationalization, Kazakhstan's Russian population is beginning to find an economic niche. It is, in essence, following the path of Latvia's Russian population.

Implications of the Theory of Ethnic System Transition

A discontented minority's movement from a subordinate to a satisfactory position vis-à-vis an ethnic majority fosters stability in a potentially unstable multiethnic state. Systems of control are likely to be unstable because one group dominates all domains at the expense of the other, which means that the subordinate group cannot alter its opportunity structure to better suit its needs. This generates grievances. The Kyrgyz ethnic system meets the first condition required for transition. The Kyrgyz have reached a threshold of political hegemony; in short, they dominate the public sector. The system does not, however, meet the second condition because the economy is undeveloped. Though the European Bank for Reconstruction and Development's "fundamental objective in the Kyrgyz Republic remains the development of dynamic micro, small and medium-sized enterprises," the economy lacks a strong private sector.[90] There are thus few nonpolitical resources that can be shared. Moreover, it is the Kyrgyz who conduct the limited private sector transactions that do occur. Informal personnel practices that privilege the Kyrgyz, sparse informal Russian networks, and Kyrgyz clan politics render a change in this scenario unlikely. The absence of a vibrant private sector discourages the Kyrgyz from relinquishing control to one or more of the country's subordinate groups because doing so would mean relinquishing some degree of *political* control.

The status quo encourages Russian exit, which poses problems for Kyrgyzstan and Russia. Russian out-migration bleeds Kyrgyzstan of human capital: well-educated and highly skilled Russians leave because they are shut out of the public and private sectors. Russian exit does not auger well for a poor country with an economy that relies to a considerable extent on a well-educated, highly skilled Russian labor force. The current state of affairs also has negative implications for Russians who stay in Kyrgyzstan. Aggrieved Russians who do not migrate eke out a minimal existence via the informal economy and what Hilary Pilkington calls "professional de-skilling."[91] An engineer who drives a taxi for a living engages in professional de-skilling. Whether or not they are forced to de-skill, most Russians are at least compelled to supplement their income. I interviewed one Bishkek resident who augments the meager salary she earns teaching Russian at a Turkish University by tutoring foreigners. A second income allows her to pay the bills but not to purchase a luxury item like a hot plate. Quotations throughout this book reveal a degraded sense of self-worth among Russian likely permanent residents of Bishkek. This besmirched sense of dignity diminishes the level of respect Russians have for Kyrgyzstan, which weakens their desire to integrate into Kyrgyz society.

Russian exit from former Soviet republics is problematic for Russia as well. Since the Soviet Union's demise, Russia has had to confront the problem of large numbers of immigrants with considerable social welfare needs.[92] Impoverished migrants who live off the state or take jobs that local Russians feel they deserve contribute to rising nationalism, an increasingly challenging phenomenon as indicated by the existence of radical groups like the Russian Movement Against Illegal Migration. The flip side of the issue is that some members of the Medvedev administration see immigration as a critical component of a broad solution to the country's ominous demographic crisis. The trajectory of citizenship legislation adopted in Russia reflects former president Putin's ambivalent position: in 2002 he signed a law on citizenship that toughened citizenship requirements; in 2003 he submitted amendments to the law that simplified the procedure of obtaining citizenship; in 2006 he signed a bill that further simplifies this procedure in order to render the process of obtaining citizenship easier for immigrants from former Soviet republics. Russia is clearly concerned about, but undecided on, its immigration policy.[93]

In contrast to a system of control, a system of partial control can be stable because although one group dominates a particular domain such as politics other groups participate in a different arena like commerce. In the Latvian case, participation in the private sector enables Russians to alter their opportunity structure in such a way that they tend to have positive perceptions of socioeconomic opportunity. Once they had achieved political dominance, elites began to tolerate Russian activity in a private sector that emerged in the early 1990s and developed throughout the decade. A low rate of Russian exit, which stems from the ability to earn a living in the private sector, means that Latvia has avoided a severe brain drain. And Russian voice—successful or not—is healthy for the country's democracy. Not only do the 2003–4 demonstrations discussed in the previous chapter indicate a willingness and ability on the part of Latvia's Russian minority population to express itself, but the fact that the Latvian government did not stifle the activists suggests that the source of blame for Russian grievances does respect freedom of speech.

As a system in transition, Kazakhstan is increasingly stable. The fact that the level of Russian out-migration has declined since 2001 indicates a change in Russian perceptions of socioeconomic opportunity. Effective nationalization has enabled Kazakhs to reach a satisfactory threshold of political hegemony, and the country's private sector is developing quickly. As a result, Kazakhs tolerate Russian activity in the private sector and Russians benefit from that tolerance. President Nazarbaev's reelection in 2005 ensured maintenance of the status quo, which suggests that most Russians will opt to participate in the private sector rather than migrate from their homeland.

Ironically, the story of post-Soviet nationalization and its effects on Russian minority populations might have a happy ending. It is true that the impact of post-Soviet nationalization on Russians is generally negative. But under certain conditions, ethnic systems can evolve from control to partial control, and in the process a minority can move from a subordinate to a satisfactory position vis-à-vis the ethnic majority of the state in question.

Approaches to Nationalism and Contemporary Ethnic Dynamics

An important theoretical lesson learned from the Central Asian and Baltic cases explored here is that a political approach to nationalism provides more insight into ethnic dynamics in post-Soviet states than does a functional, communications, Marxist, psychological, or nationalist approach.[94] The functional and communications approaches tend to address modernization and thus do not apply to post-Soviet cases. According to the functional approach, the purpose of nationalism is to guide society through processes of modernization. Elites hijack nationalist rhetoric and manipulate nationalist sentiment in order to ease the transition toward modernity. According to the communications approach, certain aspects of modernization like a developed system of communication generate a shared sense of identity among constituents of a nation; nationalism thus emerges in conjunction with modernization. But post-Soviet states are not traditional units on the path to modernity—they are fairly developed states in the midst of political and economic transition. The problem with Marxist approaches, of course, is that they view nationalism through an economic, class-based lens that dismisses the importance of politics.

Psychological and nationalist approaches shed light on the desire of titular elites in union republics to achieve independence from the Soviet Union in the late 1980s but fail to explain actions they took thereafter. The psychological approach assumes that identification with something greater than the individual, such as the nation, is a basic human need. This school of thought argues that an important aspect of nationalism is a determination to rediscover a forgotten, abandoned, or threatened identity. The desire to revive an identity at risk helps explain why elites in some republics sought independence from the Soviet Union. The nationalist approach also illuminates this phenomenon because it argues that nations seek independence and that nationalism is an expression of this goal.

A political approach to nationalism provides insight into contemporary ethnic dynamics in post-Soviet states. The preceding analysis suggests that John Breuilly was right when he wrote the following: "To focus upon culture, ideology, identity, class or modernisation is to neglect the fundamental point that nationalism is, above and beyond all else, about politics, and that politics is about power."[95] Although Breuilly was concerned with nationalist movements that oppose the state and seek separation, reform, or unification, his focus on nationalism as a means to gain control of the state captures the essence of behavior exhibited by elites in post-Soviet states. Elites in every post-Soviet state, including Kyrgyzstan, Kazakhstan, and Latvia, have one thing in common: a steadfast resolve to enhance the degree to which the respective core nation owns its state through the implementation of nationalization policies and/or practices. Although formal nationalization policies are wrapped in nationalist flags proclaiming the right of the respective core nation to rediscover its oppressed national identity, the bottom line is that these policies and the informal practices that accompany them are designed to promote the political power of the core nation.

The Latvian and Kazakh cases suggest that once political preponderance is achieved, the superordinate group may begin to share economic power with a subordinate group. If an economy develops, a dispersion of power can discourage conflict. This finding contradicts Alexander J. Motyl's argument regarding the potential for democracy and the market to intensify ethnic animosities. In 1992 Motyl wrote the following:

> Democracy and the market are two forces that compel individuals to compete unremittingly, that produce winners and losers continually—it goes without saying that there will always be bad winners and sore losers—and that encourage groups to pursue their interests on the basis of their semiotic self-understanding, their cultural "groupness." Add to this combustible mixture the modern state, which acts as an arena within which struggles can be pursued, and another potent element contributes to conflict and competition. And if, as seems likely, the state becomes the preserve of some dominant group, we may expect ethnic animosities only to intensify.[96]

Motyl was right in the sense that post-Soviet states have become the preserve of the respective titular nation, but he was wrong in his prediction that the combination of democracy, the market, the modern state, and core nation domination of that state would intensify ethnic animosities. The cases explored here suggest that if a modern state dominated by one group implements reforms that generate economic growth and thus nonpolitical resources, subordinate groups will consider commercial activity more rewarding, at least in the short to medium run, than a battle with the superordinate group for status within the political arena.

This brings us to questions raised in the first chapter of this book: What factors encourage peaceful coexistence in potentially unstable multiethnic states, and how do these factors influence post-communist development? The Kyrgyz, Kazakh, and Latvian cases indicate that power dispersion is a key factor in ensuring stability in multiethnic states and that at least at first this dispersion need not involve *political* power. As long as an ethnic minority occupies a satisfactory position vis-à-vis the ethnic majority of the state in question through profitable economic activity, it may peacefully coexist with the politically dominant group.

Appendix
Methods

Likely Permanent Resident Interview Questions

Nationality, Gender, Age, Level of Education, Occupation

- Place of birth; if not in this country, then when did you move to this country?
- What languages do you speak? What language do you speak at home?
- Have you ever visited an organization that represents the interests of local Russians? If yes, did this organization assist you? If no, have you heard of such organizations? Why haven't you visited one of these organizations?
- How have conditions changed for Russians since the collapse of the Soviet Union?
- In your opinion, does the current government represent the interests of local Russians?
- Do you think that Russians need to organize in order to protect their interests here? If yes, which interests need to be protected?
- It does not seem that Russians are inclined to engage in mass mobilization to protect their interests; in your opinion, why is this the case?
- What do you think of the current status of the Russian language?
- Do you think that Russians are oppressed? If so, which rights?
- What are you most afraid of in terms of the future of the Russian population?
- Have you ever considered migrating from this country?
- Which factors influence your decision to remain in this country?
- What needs to change for the Russian population to be satisfied with local conditions?

Likely Permanent Resident Sample Parameters

The Kyrgyz Sample (generated between September 1999 and February 2000)

Total Number of Respondents: 50

Women   25 (50%)   Men   25 (50%)

Age Range

23–30:	7 (14%)	51–60:	4 (8%)
31–40:	15 (30%)	61–69:	4 (8%)
41–50:	20 (40%)		

Level of Education

Higher   35 (70%)   High school   7 (14%)
Vocational   8 (16%)

Present Occupation

Teacher	9	Personnel	1
Professor	3	Secretary	2
Librarian	1	Inspector	1
Doctor	2	Driver	2
Geologist	2	Cabinet maker	1
Engineer	5	Janitor	1
Lawyer	1	Student	1
Business	5	Unemployed	6
Administration	3	Pensioner	4

Place of Birth

Kyrgyzstan	27 (54%)	Uzbekistan	5 (10%)
Russia	12 (24%)	Kazakhstan	4 (8%)
Belarus	1 (2%)	Turkmenistan	1 (2%)

Languages Spoken

Russian	22 (44%)
Russian and a foreign language, but not Kyrgyz	18 (36%)
Russian and a bit of Kyrgyz	10 (20%)

The Kazakh Sample (generated between March 2000 and August 2000)

Total Number of Respondents: 50

Women   25 (50%)   Men   25 (50%)

Age Range

24–30:   7 (14%)   51–60:   12 (24%)
31–40:   9 (18%)   61–69:   5 (10%)
41–50:   15 (30%)   70–75:   2 (4%)

Level of Education

Higher   41 (82%)   High school   4 (8%)
Vocational   5 (10%)

Present Occupation

Teacher	2	Administration	3
Professor	4	Secretary	1
Engineer	3	Landscaper	1
Aviation	1	Unemployed	4
Accountant	4	Pensioner	7
Business	16	Stay-at-home mom	1
Journalist	2		

Place of Birth

Kazakhstan	30 (60%)	Uzbekistan	1 (2%)
Russia	15 (30%)	Kyrgyzstan	1 (2%)
Belarus	1 (2%)	Tajikistan	1 (2%)
Ukraine	1 (2%)		

Languages Spoken

Russian   20 (40%)
Russian and a foreign language, but not Kyrgyz   22 (44%)
Russian and a bit of Kyrgyz   8 (16%)

The Latvian Sample (generated between September 2000 and December 2000)

Total Number of Respondents: 40

Women   20 (50%)   Men   20 (50%)

Age Range

28–30:	3 (7.5%)	51–60:	10 (25%)
31–40:	6 (15%)	61–65:	2 (5%)
41–50:	19 (47.5%)		

Level of Education

Higher	26 (65%)	High school	3 (8%)
Vocational	11 (27%)		

Present Occupation

Teacher	5	Cook	1
Professor	1	Hairdresser	1
Researcher	1	Construction	1
Engineer	5	Security guard	1
Business	14	Building manager	1
Journalist	2	Music editor	1
Mailman	1	Unemployed	3
Caretaker	1	Stay-at-home mom	1

Place of Birth

Latvia	26 (65%)	Kyrgyzstan	1 (2.5%)
Russia	10 (25%)	Kazakhstan	1 (2.5%)
Ukraine	1 (2.5%)	Azerbaijan	1 (2.5%)

Languages Spoken

Russian	0
Russian and a foreign language, but not Latvian	1 (2.5%)
Russian and some Latvian	39 (97.5%)

Official Category of Latvian Language Proficiency

Beginner	3 (9%)	Advanced	14 (40%)
Intermediate	18 (51%)		

Unofficial Category of Latvian Language Proficiency (perceived level of language proficiency for Russians without certification)

Beginner	1 (20%)	Advanced	1 (20%)
Intermediate	3 (60%)		

Potential Migrant Interview Questions

Nationality, Gender, Age, Level of Education, Occupation

- Place of birth; if not in this country, then when did you move to this country?
- What languages do you speak? What language do you speak at home?
- When did you begin to think about the possibility of migration?
- When did you finally decide to migrate?
- Have you ever visited an organization that represents the interests of local Russians? If yes, did this organization assist you? If no, have you heard of such organizations? Why haven't you visited one of these organizations?
- How have conditions changed for Russians since the collapse of the Soviet Union?
- In your opinion does the current government represent the interests of local Russians?
- Which factors have influenced your decision to migrate from this country?
- Are there any organizations that assist you with migration procedures? If yes, have you visited that organization yet?
- What do you think of the current status of the Russian language?
- What steps have you already taken in order to migrate?
- Do you have relatives and/or friends in Russia? If so, can they assist you upon arrival?
- You've decided to move to Russia. Why did you choose Russia?
- What kind of life do you expect in Russia?
- What needs to change in order for you to remain in this country?

Potential Migrant Sample Parameters

The Kyrgyz Sample (generated between September 1999 and February 2000)

Total Number of Respondents: 115

Women   57 (50%)   Men   58 (50%)

Age Range

17–20:	6 (5%)	51–60:	14 (12%)
21–30:	19 (16.5%)	61–69:	8 (7%)
31–40:	34 (29.5%)	70–72:	1 (1%)
41–50:	33 (29%)		

Level of Education

Higher   28 (24%)   High school   39 (34%)
Vocational   48 (42%)

Current Employment Status

Employed   60 (52%)   Student   1 (1%)
Unemployed   39 (34%)   Pensioner   10 (9%)
Stay-at-home mom   5 (4%)

Place of Birth

Kyrgyzstan   69 (60%)   Other Soviet republics   21 (18%)
Russia   24 (21%)   Outside Soviet Union   1 (1%)

Languages Spoken

Russian   104 (90%)
Russian and a bit of Kyrgyz   11 (10%)

The Kazakh Sample (generated between March 2000 and August 2000)

Total Number of Respondents: 115

Women   63 (55%)   Men   52 (45%)

Age Range

20–30: 20 (17%)   51–60: 24 (21%)
31–40: 17 (15%)   61–70: 13 (11%)
41–50: 39 (34%)   71–80:   2 (2%)

Level of Education

Higher   45 (39%)   High school   26 (23%)
Vocational   44 (38%)

Current Employment Status

Employed   56 (49%)   Student   1 (1%)
Unemployed   31 (27%)   Pensioner   21 (18%)
Stay-at-home mom   6 (5%)

Place of Birth

| Kazakhstan | 63 (55%) | Other Soviet republics | 12 (10%) |
| Russia | 39 (34%) | Outside Soviet Union | 1 (1%) |

Languages Spoken

| Russian | 101 (88%) |
| Russian and a bit of Kazakh | 14 (12%) |

The Latvian Sample (generated between September 2000 and December 2000)

Total Number of Respondents: 65

| Women | 42 (65%) | Men | 23 (35%) |

Age Range

25–35:	13 (20%)	56–65:	9 (14%)
36–45:	21 (32%)	66–75:	4 (6%)
46–55:	15 (23%)	Over 75:	3 (5%)

Level of Education

| Higher | 27 (41%) | High school | 20 (31%) |
| Vocational | 18 (28%) | | |

Current Employment Status

Employed	25 (38%)	Student	0 (0%)
Unemployed	21 (32%)	Pensioner	16 (25%)
Stay-at-home mom	3 (5%)		

Place of Birth

| Latvia | 9 (14%) | Other Soviet republics | 10 (15%) |
| Russia | 45 (69%) | Outside Soviet Union | 1 (2%) |

Perceived Level of Latvian Language Proficiency

Fluent	5 (8%)	Poor	20 (31%)
Functional	3 (4%)	No proficiency	16 (25%)
Basic	21 (32%)		

Russian Representative Interview Questions

Questions about the Russian Minority

- What issues do Russians in your country confront now that the Soviet Union has collapsed?
- How has the nature of these issues changed over time?
- They say that many Russians have left and are leaving your country. Why do they decide to migrate? What are their motivations?
- Or, they say that few Russians have left and that even fewer are leaving. Why do they decide to stay? What are their motivations?
- What are the potential consequences of Russian migration?
- What position does your organization adopt toward Russian migration?
- How does the language question affect Russians?
- Do Russians in your country face discrimination in the labor market?
- Russians seem to be underrepresented in your government. What are the potential consequences of this?
- How do you characterize the Russian question in your country today?

Questions about the Organization

- When was your organization founded?
- How is your organization funded?
- What does your organization do?
- Who does your organization represent?
- Who can become a member of your organization?
- Why is your organization necessary?
- What were the initial goals of your organization, and how have they evolved over time?
- What are the main goals of your organization today?
- How many members, approximately, does your organization have?
- Why do people join your organization? What do they expect from membership? What are the main differences between your organization and other organizations that represent local Russians?

A representative or representatives from the following organizations were interviewed

Kyrgyzstan

Association of Ethnic Russians
Federal Migration Services of Russia
Public Association of Russians

Russian Cultural Center
Slavic Foundation
Union of Russian Compatriots of Kyrgyzstan (formerly the Association of Ethnic Russians)

Kazakhstan

Public Foundation of Migration (Almaty)
Russian Party (Almaty)
Lad (Almaty, Astana, Ust'-Kamenogorsk)
Russian Community (Almaty, Astana, Ust'-Kamenogorsk)

Latvia

Association of Latvian-Russian Cooperation (Riga)
Center for the Protection of the Russian Language (Riga)
Latvian Association for the Support of Russian-Language Schools (Riga)
OKROL (United Congress of Russian Communities of Latvia [Riga])
Russian Community (Riga, Daugavpils)
Russian Society (Riga)
State Language Center (Riga)
Party of Equal Rights (Riga, Daugavpils)
Party of National Harmony (Riga, Daugavpils)
Russian Party (Riga, Daugavpils)
Socialist Party (Riga, Daugavpils)
Mayer Aleksei Vidovskii (Daugavpils)

Notes

Chapter 1

1. *Borshch* is a classic Russian dish while *besbarmak* is a classic Kazakh dish.
2. Chokan Valikhanov was a nineteenth-century Russian army officer who studied Central Asian history; Abai Kunabaev was a nineteenth-century poet who launched Kazakh as a literary language.
3. The poem is published in Svetlana Nazarova, *Ne ostavliaite na potom. . . .* (Almaty: Stikhotvoreniia, 2005), 20–21.
4. Author's interview, 27 June 2000.
5. Gretchen Helmke and Steven Levitsky, "Informal Institutions and Comparative Politics: A Research Agenda," *Perspectives on Politics* 2, 4 (December 2004): 725.
6. For a complete discussion of these methods, see John McGarry and Brendan O'Leary, "Introduction: The Macro-Political Regulation of Ethnic Conflict," in John McGarry and Brendan O'Leary, eds., *The Politics of Ethnic Conflict Regulation: Case Studies of Protracted Ethnic Conflicts.* (London: Routledge, 1993), 4–37.
7. The titular nation is the nation after which each union republic of the Soviet federation was named. I use the words titular and core interchangeably in reference to the non-Russian group in question.
8. Exit and voice are Albert Hirschman's terms. Albert O. Hirschman, *Exit, Voice, and Loyalty: Responses to Decline in Firms, Organizations, and States* (Cambridge, Mass.: Harvard University Press, 1970).
9. My definition of an opportunity structure differs from the social movement literature definition, which concerns a set of conditions that facilitate political mobilization. For more on this view of political opportunity structures, see Sidney Tarrow, *Power in Movement: Social Movements and Contentious Politics* (Cambridge: Cambridge University Press, 1998).
10. Kathleen Thelen and Sven Steinmo, "Historical Institutionalism in Comparative Politics," in Sven Steinmo, Kathleen Thelen, and Frank Longstreth, eds., *Structuring Politics: Historical Institutionalism in Comparative Analysis* (Cambridge: Cambridge University Press, 1992), 2.
11. Helmke and Levitsky, "Informal Institutions and Comparative Politics," 727.
12. Helmke and Levitsky take seriously Douglass North's point that we need to distinguish informal organizations from informal institutions. North's distinction lies in the difference between the actors (informal organizations) and the rules that govern their behavior (informal institutions). See Douglass C. North,

Institutions, Institutional Change, and Economic Performance (New York: Cambridge University Press, 1990); Helmke and Levitsky, "Informal Institutions and Comparative Politics"; and Gretchen Helmke and Steven Levitsky, eds., *Informal Institutions and Democracy* (Baltimore: Johns Hopkins University Press, 2006), 4–8.

13. Alena V. Ledeneva, *Russia's Economy of Favours: Blat, Networking and Informal Exchange* (Cambridge: Cambridge University Press, 1998), 3.

14. Ibid., 186–87.

15. The following discussion of complementary and competing institutions is based on Helmke and Levitsky's typology of informal institutions, which stems from the interaction of formal and informal institutions and suggests four types of informal institutions: complementary, accommodating, substitutive, and competing. For more on this typology, see Helmke and Levitsky, "Informal Institutions and Comparative Politics."

16. For more on this method, which compares cases that contrast on a series of independent variables, see Adam Przeworski and Henry Teune, *The Logic of Comparative Social Inquiry* (Malabar: Krieger Publishing Company, 1982).

17. King, Keohane, and Verba argue that the best research design "selects observations to ensure variation in the explanatory variable (and any control variables) without regard to the values of the dependent variable." Gary King, Robert O. Keohane, and Sidney Verba, *Designing Social Inquiry: Scientific Inference in Qualitative Research* (Princeton, N.J.: Princeton University Press, 1994), 140.

18. Rogers Brubaker, *Nationalism Reframed: Nationhood and the National Question in the New Europe* (Cambridge: Cambridge University Press, 1996), 41.

19. In 1989 the Latvian SSR population was 52 percent Latvian and 34 percent Russian. See *Results of the 2000 Population and Housing Census in Latvia* (Riga: Central Statistical Bureau of Latvia, 2002), 121. In 1989 the Kyrgyz SSR population was 52 percent Kyrgyz and 21.5 percent Russian. See *Osnovnyye itogi Pervoi natsional'noi perepisi naseleniia Kyrgyzskoi Respubliki 1999 goda* (Bishkek: Natsional'-nyi statisticheskiii komitet Kyrgyzskoi Respubliki, 2000), 26.

20. The appendix contains each set of interview questions.

21. Anatoly M. Khazanov, *After the USSR: Ethnicity, Nationalism, and Politics in the Commonwealth of Independent States* (Madison: University of Wisconsin Press, 1995), 268.

22. Laitin uses the term "Russian-speakers" and Melvin uses the term "Russified settler communities." See David Laitin, *Identity in Formation: The Russian-Speaking Populations in the Near Abroad* (Ithaca, N.Y.: Cornell University Press, 1998), and Neil Melvin, *Russians Beyond Russia: The Politics of National Identity* (London: Royal Institute of International Affairs, 1995).

23. Walker Connor, *Ethnonationalism: The Quest for Understanding* (Princeton, N.J.: Princeton University Press, 1994), 97.

24. *Naselenie Kyrgyzstana, Itogi Pervoi natsional'noi perepisi naseleniia Kyrgyzskoi Respubliki 1999 goda v tablitsakh, Kniga II, chast' pervaia* (Bishkek: Natsional'nyi statisticheskiii komitet Kyrgyzskoi Respubliki, 2000), 72–78. Bishkek is also the capital of Chu Valley, which is one of seven administrative regions or oblasts, and Russians comprise less than 14 percent of every oblast population except Chu Valley, where they comprise 32 percent of the population. Russians constitute 13.2 percent of Issyk-Kul's population, 4 percent of Talas's population, 2.2 percent of Batken's population, 2.1 percent of Jalalabad's population, 1.3 percent of Osh's population, and 0.3 percent of Naryn's population.

25. *Results of the 2000 Population and Housing Census in Latvia*, 124. In each of Latvia's remaining major cities Russians compose less than 40 percent of the

respective population: they constitute 32 percent of Jelgava's population, 37 percent of Jurmala's population, 35 percent of Liepaja's population, and 32 percent of Ventspils's population. Research I conducted in Daugavpils to explore possible regional differences indicates that Russians in Latvia confront similar obstacles and exhibit similar responses to those obstacles regardless of the region in question.

26. *Kratkie itogi perepisi naseleniia 1999 goda v Respublike Kazakhstan* (Almaty: Agentstvo Respubliki Kazakhstan po statistike, 1999), 99–114. Russians make up less than 40 percent of the remaining nine oblasts: they constitute 39.4 percent of Akmola's population, 28.2 percent of Western Kazakhstan's population, 21.8 percent of Almaty's population, 18.1 percent of Zhambyl's population, 16.8 percent of Aktobe's population, 14.8 percent of Mangistau's population, 8.6 percent of Atyrau's population, 8.2 percent of Southern Kazakhstan's population, and 2.9 percent of Kyzlorda's population. I conducted research in Almaty, Astana, and Ust'-Kamenogorsk to assess the Russian minority question in different regions. As was the case in Latvia, I found that Russians in Kazakhstan confront similar obstacles and exhibit similar responses to those obstacles regardless of the region in question.

27. Although the fate of migrants from former Soviet republics who now reside in Russia is beyond the scope of this analysis, Hilary Pilkington has interviewed actual migrants from Central Asia and the Caucasus. See Pilkington, *Migration, Displacement and Identity in Post-Soviet Russia* (London: Routledge 1998).

28. I interviewed 110 potential migrants in Bishkek, 110 in Almaty, and 65 in Riga; 50 likely permanent residents of Bishkek, 50 of Almaty, and 40 of Riga; and numerous representatives of Russians in Bishkek, Almaty, and Riga.

29. The appendix contains potential migrant and likely permanent resident sample parameters.

30. To the best of my knowledge this organization no longer exists.

31. In a discussion regarding participant observation of criminals, John Irwin recommends relying on referrals to build a network of contacts. See Irwin, "Participant Observation of Criminals," in Jack Douglas, ed., *Research on Deviance* (New York: Random House, 1972), 117–37.

32. For example, Bhavna Dave argues that moderate nationalization drove Russian-speakers from Kazakhstan while a harsher form of nationalization caused Russian-speakers in Latvia to organize politically. According to Dave, "This is because the awareness of being 'less than equal' citizens is mitigated by the promise of equality and economic betterment connected to the integration of the Baltic states within a European framework." See Dave, *Kazakhstan: Ethnicity, Language, and Power* (London: Routledge, 2007), 103.

Chapter 2

1. Karl W. Deutsch singles out social mobilization or the development of markets, industries, literacy, and mass communication as a decisive factor in national integration. See Deutsch, *Nationalism and Social Communication: An Inquiry into the Foundations of Nationality* (Cambridge, Mass.: MIT Press, 1953). The literature on nation-building was heavily influenced by Deutsch's work on nation-building as a process of territorial-cultural integration achieved via standardization and social mobilization.

2. This is Carl J. Friedrich's conceptualization of nation-building. See Fried-

rich, "Nation-Building?" in Karl W. Deutsch and William J. Foltz, eds., *Nation-Building* (New York: Atherton Press, 1963), 32. Stein Rokkan has a similar view of nation-building. His model of state formation and nation-building consists of four phases: the first covers initial state-building processes that occur at the elite level of society; the second covers the inclusion of the masses into the system, which is based on recently generated widespread feelings of identity with the political system; the third covers the active participation of the masses in the system; the fourth covers the expansion of the state's administrative apparatus into society. See Rokkan, "Dimensions of State Formation and Nation-Building: A Possible Paradigm for Research on Variations Within Europe," in Charles Tilly, ed., *The Formation of National States in Western Europe* (Princeton, N.J.: Princeton University Press, 1975), 562–600.

3. Connor, *Ethnonationalism*, 29–66.

4. Ibid., 56.

5. Brubaker, *Nationalism Reframed*, 9.

6. Ibid.

7. Ibid., 174.

8. The exception is the signal Russia sent that it was ready—*diplomatically, militarily, and economically*—to support Moldova's Transnistrian population, which is 23 percent Russian. For more on the Transnistrian secession war, see Melvin, *Russians Beyond Russia*; Charles King, *Post-Soviet Moldova: A Borderland in Transition* (Iasi: Center for Romanian Studies, 1997); Pal Kolsto and Andrei Malgin, "The Transnistrian Republic: A Case of Politicized Regionalism," *Nationalities Papers* 26, 1 (1998): 103–27; Charles King, *The Moldovans: Romania, Russia, and the Politics of Culture* (Stanford, Calif.: Hoover Institution Press, 2000).

9. Brubaker, *Nationalism Reframed*, 178.

10. John N. Hazard, "Managing Nationalism: State, Law and the National Question in the USSR," in Alexander J. Motyl, ed., *Thinking Theoretically About Soviet Nationalities* (New York: Columbia University Press, 1992), 96.

11. Russification ensured that Russians were generally monolingual, while members of other nationalities were generally bilingual.

12. Brubaker, *Nationalism Reframed*, 63. Italics mine.

13. Laitin, *Identity in Formation*.

14. Melvin, *Russians Beyond Russia*, 127.

15. Jeff Chinn and Robert Kaiser, *Russians as the New Minority* (Boulder, Colo.: Westview Press, 1996).

16. Dave, *Kazakhstan*, 119.

17. Ibid., 126.

18. Hirschman, *Exit, Voice, and Loyalty*.

19. Thelen and Steinmo, "Historical Institutionalism in Comparative Politics."

20. Ira Katznelson and Barry R. Weingast, "Intersection Between Historical and Rational Choice Institutionalism," in Ira Katznelson and Barry R. Weingast, eds., *Preferences and Situations: Points of Intersection Between Historical and Rational Choice Institutionalism* (New York: Russell Sage Foundation, 2005), 1–24.

21. Jack Knight, *Institutions and Social Conflict* (Cambridge: Cambridge University Press, 1992).

22. Kathleen Thelen, "How Institutions Evolve: Insights from Comparative Historical Analysis," in James Mahoney and Dietrich Reuschemeyer, eds., *Comparative Historical Analysis in the Social Sciences* (Cambridge: Cambridge University Press, 2003), 212.

23. Scholars who adopt one of many possible historical approaches to the study of post-communist transformation include Edward Schatz, *Modern Clan Politics: The Power of "Blood" in Kazakhstan and Beyond* (Seattle: University of Washington Press, 2004); Marc Morje Howard, *The Weakness of Civil Society in Post-Communist Europe* (Cambridge: Cambridge University Press, 2003); Beverly Crawford and Arend Lijphart, eds., *Liberalization and Leninist Legacies: Comparative Perspectives on Democratic Transitions* (Berkeley: University of California Press, 1997); Stephen E. Hanson, "The Leninist Legacy and Institutional Change," *Comparative Political Studies* 28, 2 (1995): 306–14; Grzegorz Ekiert and Jan Kubik, *Rebellious Civil Society* (Ann Arbor: University of Michigan Press, 1999); Ken Jowitt, *New World Order: The Leninist Extinction* (Berkeley: University of California Press, 1992); Juan Linz and Alfred Stepan, *Problems of Democratic Transition and Consolidation: Southern Europe, South America, and Post-Communist Europe* (Baltimore: Johns Hopkins University Press, 1996); Valerie Bunce, *Subversive Institutions: The Design and the Destruction of Socialism and the State* (Cambridge: Cambridge University Press, 1999); David Stark and Laszlo Bruszt, *Postsocialist Pathways: Transforming Politics and Property in East Central Europe* (Cambridge: Cambridge University Press, 1998); Gerald A. McDermott, *Embedded Politics: Industrial Networks and Institutional Change in Postcommunism* (Ann Arbor: University of Michigan Press, 2002); and Ronald Grigor Suny, *The Revenge of the Past: Nationalism, Revolution, and the Collapse of the Soviet Union* (Stanford, Calif.: Stanford University Press, 1993).

24. Grzegorz Ekiert and Stephen E. Hanson, *Capitalism and Democracy in Central and Eastern Europe: Assessing the Legacy of Communist Rule* (Cambridge: Cambridge University Press, 2003).

25. See Grzegorz Ekiert and Stephen E. Hanson, "Time, Space, and Institutional Change in Central and Eastern Europe," in Ekiert and Hanson, *Capitalism and Democracy in Central and Eastern Europe*, 15–48.

Chapter 3

1. The 1916 rebellion was sparked by a decree that ordered the mobilization of Central Asian men for noncombatant military service, despite the fact that Central Asians were traditionally exempt from military service of any kind. Fueled by brewing resentment, Kyrgyz and Kazakh forces killed over two thousand Russians and Cossacks. According to Richard Pipes, the revolt was "the most violent expression of popular dissatisfaction in the history of Russia between the revolutions of 1905 and 1917." Pipes, *The Formation of the Soviet Union* (Cambridge: Cambridge University Press, 1997), 83.

2. Teresa Rakowska-Harmstone, "The Dialectics of Nationalism in the USSR," *Problems of Post-Communism* 23, 3 (May/June 1974): 10.

3. Gail Warshofsky Lapidus, "Ethnonationalism and Political Stability: The Soviet Case," *World Politics* 36, 4 (July 1984): 566.

4. Philip G. Roeder, "Soviet Federalism and Ethnic Mobilization," *World Politics* 43 (January 1991): 199.

5. Brubaker, *Nationalism Reframed*, 45.

6. For more on the development and nature of the Soviet federation, see Victor Zaslavsky, "Success and Collapse: Traditional Soviet Nationality Policy," in Ian Bremmer and Ray Taras, eds., *Nations and Politics in the Soviet Successor States* (Cambridge: Cambridge University Press, 1993), 29–42; Graham Smith, "Nationalities Policy from Lenin to Gorbachev," in Graham Smith, ed., *The*

Nationalities Question in the Soviet Union (London: Longman Group, 1990), 1–20; and Karen Dawisha and Bruce Parrott, *Russia and the New States of Eurasia* (Cambridge: Cambridge University Press, 1994).

7. For a comprehensive analysis of this process, see Francine Hirsch, "Toward an Empire of Nations: Border-Making and the Formation of Soviet National Identities," *Russian Review* 59 (April 2000): 201–26; and Francine Hirsch, *Empire of Nations: Ethnographic Knowledge and the Making of the Soviet Union* (Ithaca, N.Y.: Cornell University Press, 2005).

8. Walker Connor, "Soviet Policies Toward the Non-Russian Peoples in Theoretic and Historic Perspective: What Gorbachev Inherited," in Alexander J. Motyl, ed., *The Post-Soviet Nations: Perspectives on the Demise of the USSR* (New York: Columbia University Press, 1992), 30.

9. Dawisha and Parrott, *Russia and the New States of Eurasia*, 9.

10. Connor, "Soviet Policies Toward the Non-Russian Peoples in Theoretic and Historic Perspective," 31.

11. Richard E. Ericson, "Soviet Economic Structure and the National Question," in Alexander J. Motyl, ed., *The Post-Soviet Nations: Perspectives on the Demise of the USSR* (New York: Columbia University Press, 1992), 242. The need for regional economic equality was acknowledged regularly in official statements prior to 1972. Gertrude E. Schroeder, "Nationalities and the Soviet Economy," in Lubomyr Hajda and Mark Beissinger, eds., *The Nationalities Factor in Soviet Politics and Society* (Boulder, Colo.: Westview Press, 1990).

12. Ronald Grigor Suny, "Nationalist and Ethnic Unrest in the Soviet Union," *World Policy Journal* 6 (1988–89): 506–7.

13. Zvi Gitelman, "Development and Ethnicity in the Soviet Union," in Alexander J. Motyl, ed., *The Post-Soviet Nations: Perspectives on the Demise of the USSR* (New York: Columbia University Press, 1992), 225.

14. Smith, "Nationalities Policy from Lenin to Gorbachev," 8.

15. Khrushchev introduced this formula in 1961 at the Twenty-Second Congress of the Communist Party of the Soviet Union. Teresa Rakowska-Harmstone, "Minority Nationalism Today: An Overview," in Robert Conquest, ed., *The Last Empire: Nationality and the Soviet Future* (Stanford, Calif.: Hoover Institution Press, 1986), 237.

16. Mark R. Beissinger, *Nationalist Mobilization and the Collapse of the Soviet State* (Cambridge: Cambridge University Press, 2002), 53.

17. Schroeder, "Nationalities and the Soviet Economy," 43.

18. Connor, "Soviet Policies Toward the Non-Russian Peoples in Theoretic and Historic Perspective," 44–45.

19. The first secretaries of the Uzbek and Tajik parties passed away prior to the purge, but Gorbachev replaced their counterparts in the Kyrgyz, Kazakh, and Turkmen republics with individuals he perceived as dedicated to socialism but simultaneously open to reform.

20. Beissinger, *Nationalist Mobilization and the Collapse of the Soviet State*, 57.

21. William Fierman, "The Soviet 'Transformation' of Central Asia," in William Fierman, ed., *Soviet Central Asia: The Failed Transformation* (Boulder, Colo.: Westview Press, 1991), 11.

22. Shirin Akiner, "Social and Political Reorganization in Central Asia: Transition from Pre-Colonial to Post-Colonial Society," in Touraj Atabaki and John O'Kane, eds., *Post-Soviet Central Asia* (New York: St. Martin's Press, 1998), 13.

23. Olivier Roy, *The New Central Asia: The Creation of Nations* (New York: New York University Press, 2000), 78.

24. Eugene Huskey, "Kyrgyzstan: The Politics of Demographic and Economic Frustration," in Ian Bremmer and Ray Taras, eds., *Nations and Politics in the Soviet Successor States* (Cambridge: Cambridge University Press, 1993), 402.

25. For excellent accounts of the *hujum* in the Uzbek republic, see Douglas Northrop, *Veiled Empire: Gender and Power in Stalinist Central Asia* (Ithaca, N.Y.: Cornell University Press, 2004); and Marianne Kamp, *The New Woman in Uzbekistan: Islam, Modernity, and Unveiling Under Communism* (Seattle: University of Washington Press, 2006).

26. Dawisha and Parrott, *Russia and the New States of Eurasia*, 111.

27. Eric McGlinchey, "Autocrats, Islamists, and the Rise of Radicalism in Central Asia," *Current History* 104, 684 (October 2005): 336.

28. Yaacov Ro'i, "The Secularization of Islam and the USSR's Muslim Areas," in Yaacov Ro'i, ed., *Muslim Eurasia: Conflicting Legacies* (London: Frank Cass and Company, 1995), 5–16.

29. Pauline Jones Luong, *Institutional Change and Political Continuity in Post-Soviet Central Asia* (Cambridge: Cambridge University Press, 2002), 72–73.

30. Ibid., 72.

31. Mark Saroyan, "Islamic Clergy and Community in the Soviet Union," in Edward W. Walker, ed., *Minorities, Mullahs, and Modernity: Reshaping Community in the Former Soviet Union* (Berkeley: International and Area Studies, University of California, 1997), 44–45.

32. Roy, *The New Central Asia*, 150.

33. Ghoncheh Tazmini, "The Islamic Revival in Central Asia: A Potent Force or a Misconception?" *Central Asian Survey* 20, 1 (2001): 63–83.

34. For more on Gorbachev's decision to adopt a comparatively lenient policy toward religion, see Mehrdad Haghayeghi, *Islam and Politics in Central Asia* (New York: St. Martin's Press, 1995).

35. Adeeb Khalid, *Islam after Communism: Religion and Politics in Central Asia* (Berkeley: University of California Press, 2007), 119.

36. For more on parallel Islam, see Khazanov, *After the USSR*; and Martha Brill Olcott, "Islam and Fundamentalism in Independent Central Asia," in Yaacov Ro'i, ed., *Muslim Eurasia: Conflicting Legacies* (London: Frank Cass and Company, 1995), 21–37.

37. Khalid, *Islam after Communism*, 102.

38. Roy, *The New Central Asia*, 152.

39. Bolshevik leaders referred to the Kazakhs as Kyrgyz and to the Kyrgyz as Kara-Kyrgyz.

40. Beatrice F. Manz, "Historical Background," in Beatrice F. Manz, ed., *Central Asia in Historical Perspective* (Boulder, Colo.: Westview Press, 1994), 13.

41. Pipes, *The Formation of the Soviet Union*, 83.

42. Martha Brill Olcott, "Kazakhstan: Pushing for Eurasia," in Ian Bremmer and Ray Taras, eds., *New States, New Politics: Building the Post-Soviet Nations* (Cambridge: Cambridge University Press, 1997), 550.

43. Gregory J. Massell, *The Surrogate Proletariat: Moslem Women and Revolutionary Strategies in Soviet Central Asia, 1919–1929* (Princeton, N.J.: Princeton University Press, 1974), 73.

44. Ibid., 61.

45. Ian Murray Matley, "Industrialization," in Edward Allworth, ed., *Central Asia: 130 Years of Russian Dominance, A Historical Overview* (Durham, N.C.: Duke University Press, 1994), 331.

46. Michael Rywkin, *Moscow's Lost Empire* (New York: M. E. Sharpe, 1994), 89.

47. Robert A. Lewis, "The Mixing of Russians and Soviet Nationalities and Its Demographic Impact," in Edward Allworth, ed., *Soviet Nationality Problems* (New York: Columbia University Press, 1971), 159–60.

48. In the official definition, a *kulak*, or moneymaking farm, had five features: (1) hires wage labor for employment, (2) maintains an industrial undertaking such as a butter-making system, (3) hires out high-tech agricultural machinery, (4) hires out premises for rent, and (5) engages in commercial activity or earns income not deriving from work. However, Moscow granted local authorities permission to alter the definition to suit local conditions. This enhanced the random nature of the *kulak* classification system so that "it was possible for zealous and 'vigilant' executants to find kulaks wherever they chose to look." For an in-depth analysis of Soviet collectivization, see Moshe Lewin, *Russian Peasants and Soviet Power: A Study of Collectivization* (Evanston, Ill.: Northwestern University Press, 1968), 491.

49. Ronald Grigor Suny, *The Soviet Experiment: Russia, the USSR, and the Successor States* (New York: Oxford University Press, 1998), 226.

50. Anatoly M. Khazanov, "Underdevelopment and Ethnic Relations in Central Asia," in Beatrice F. Manz, ed., *Central Asia in Historical Perspective* (Boulder, Colo.: Westview Press, 1994), 145.

51. Nancy Lubin, "Ethnic and Demographic Trends," in William Fierman, ed., *Soviet Central Asia: The Failed Transformation* (Boulder, Colo.: Westview Press, 1991), 48.

52. Fierman, "The Soviet 'Transformation' of Central Asia," 20. According to Akiner, the urban populations of Kyrgyzstan and Kazakhstan consisted of Russians (over 50 percent of each population), the titular nationality (17 percent of each population), and others. Akiner, "Social and Political Reorganization in Central Asia," 15.

53. Roman Levita and Mikhail Loiberg, "The Empire and the Russians," in Vladimir Shlapentokh, Munir Sendich, and Emil Payin, eds., *The New Russian Diaspora: Russian Minorities in the Former Soviet Republics* (Armonk, N.Y.: M. E. Sharpe, 1994), 15.

54. Paul Kolstoe, *Russians in the Former Soviet Republics* (Bloomington: Indiana University Press, 1995), 49.

55. Martha Brill Olcott, *The Kazakhs* (Stanford, Calif.: Hoover Institution Press, 1997), 224.

56. Michael Rywkin, *Moscow's Muslim Challenge* (Armonk, N.Y.: M. E. Sharpe, 1990), 61.

57. Walter C. Clemens Jr., *Baltic Independence and Russian Empire* (New York: St. Martin's Press, 1991), 57.

58. Though Russia had acquired all Latvian territories with the final partition of Poland, German nobles continued to hold positions of influence because Russia needed local administrators to manage the region.

59. Anatol Lieven, *The Baltic Revolution: Estonia, Latvia, Lithuania and the Path to Independence* (New Haven, Conn.: Yale University Press, 1993), 182.

60. Latvians and Estonians are Protestant; Lithuanians are Catholic.

61. An indication of this is the fact that during the most intense tsarist Russification period (1885–95), the volume of Latvian-language writing in belles lettres or practical work did not decrease. Andrejs Plakans, *The Latvians: A Short History* (Stanford, Calif.: Hoover Institution Press, 1995), 101.

62. Graham Smith, "Latvians," in Graham Smith, ed., *The Nationalities Question in the Soviet Union* (London: Longman Group, 1990), 56.

63. Plakans, *The Latvians*, 108.

64. Ibid., 113. In the latter half of the nineteenth century, Germans occupied the most important political and economic positions while most Latvians were peasants. Nils Muiznieks, "Latvia: Origins, Evolution, and Triumph," in Ian Bremmer and Ray Taras, eds., *Nations and Politics in the Soviet Successor States* (Cambridge: Cambridge University Press, 1993), 183.

65. Chinn and Kaiser, *Russians as the New Minority*, 111.

66. Nils Muiznieks, "Latvia: Restoring a State, Rebuilding a Nation," in Ian Bremmer and Ray Taras, eds., *New States, New Politics: Building the Post-Soviet Nation* (Cambridge: Cambridge University Press, 1997), 378. The party consisted of a mere five thousand members at the time.

67. Romuald J. Misiunas and Rein Taagepera, *The Baltic States: Years of Dependence, 1940–1980* (Berkeley: University of California Press, 1983), 78.

68. Muiznieks, "Latvia: Origins, Evolution, and Triumph," 185.

69. Misiunas and Taagepera, *The Baltic States*, 111.

70. Plakans, *The Latvians*, 156.

71. Smith, "Latvians," 58.

72. Misiunas and Taagepera, *The Baltic States*, 361.

73. Smith, "Latvians," 61.

74. Only 240 of 1,500 schools in Latvia were bilingual in 1967. Misiunas and Taagepera, *The Baltic States*, 189.

75. Muiznieks, "Latvia: Origins, Evolution, and Triumph," 188.

76. Lieven, *The Baltic Revolution*, 187.

77. Kolstoe, *Russians in the Former Soviet Republics*, 66–67.

78. Robert J. Kaiser, "Ethnic Demography and Interstate Relations in Central Asia," in Roman Szporluk, ed., *National Identity and Ethnicity in Russia and the New States of Eurasia* (Armonk, N.Y.: M. E. Sharpe, 1994), 245.

79. Igor Zevelev, *Russia and Its New Diasporas* (Washington, D.C.: United States Institute of Peace Press, 2001), 109.

80. Martha Brill Olcott, "Central Asia: The Reformers Challenge a Traditional Society," in Lubomyr Hajda and Mark Beissinger, eds., *The Nationalities Factor in Soviet Politics and Society* (Boulder, Colo.: Westview Press, 1990), 262.

81. Fierman, "The Soviet 'Transformation' of Central Asia," 35. Although Fierman's statistics for proportional increases do not cover Kazakhs, there is no reason to assume that Kazakh statistics differ significantly from the following statistics: Uzbeks (from 9 to 24 percent), Tajiks (from 8 to 21 percent), Kyrgyz (from 9 to 26 percent), and Turkmen (from 11 to 25 percent).

82. Robert J. Kaiser, "Social Mobilization in Soviet Central Asia," in Robert A. Lewis, ed., *Geographic Perspectives on Soviet Central Asia* (London: Routledge, 1992), 275.

83. Since the end of World War II, Slavic settlers had dominated the scientific labor force. The Soviet definition of a scientific worker was broad enough to cover individuals working at mid and upper levels in the state and party apparatuses and therefore included scientific, technical, and political cadres. Steven L. Burg, "Central Asian Political Participation and Soviet Political Development," in Yaacov Ro'i, ed., *The USSR and the Muslim World: Issues in Domestic and Foreign Policy* (London: George Allen and Unwin, 1984), 42–43.

84. Michael Rywkin, "National Symbiosis: Vitality, Religion, Identity, Allegiance," in Yaacov Ro'i, ed., *The USSR and the Muslim World: Issues in Domestic and Foreign Policy* (London: George Allen and Unwin, 1984), 6.

85. Gitelman, "Development and Ethnicity in the Soviet Union," 226.

86. Chinn and Kaiser, *Russians as the New Minority*, 221.

87. Fierman, "The Soviet 'Transformation' of Central Asia," 25.

88. Nancy Lubin, *Labour and Nationality in Soviet Central Asia: An Uneasy Compromise* (Princeton, N.J.: Princeton University Press, 1984), 78.

89. Khazanov, *After the USSR*, 263.

90. Between 1940 when Stalin annexed the Baltics and 1941 when Hitler invaded Latvia, a brief but brutal period of Soviet rule marked by the deportation of over fifteen thousand people devastated Latvians. Many Latvians welcomed the German occupation as liberation from the Soviets. At least one hundred thousand Latvians abandoned their homeland when a second Soviet occupation appeared imminent, and many joined German forces or fought guerrilla warfare in the forests to resist the occupation. For more on this time period, see Muiznieks, "Latvia: Origins, Evolution, and Triumph," and Muiznieks, "Latvia: Restoring a State, Rebuilding a Nation." For an excellent anthropological account of how Latvians remember the Soviet occupation, see Vieda Skultans, *The Testimony of Lives: Narrative and Memory in Post-Soviet Latvia* (London: Routledge, 1998).

91. Lieven, *The Baltic Revolution*, 183; Plakans, *The Latvians*, 154.

92. Lieven, *The Baltic Revolution*, 184.

93. Rasma Karklins, *Ethnopolitics and Transition to Democracy: The Collapse of the USSR and Latvia* (Washington, D.C.: Woodrow Wilson Center Press, 1994), 123.

94. Graham Smith, "The Ethnic Democracy Thesis and the Citizenship Question in Estonia and Latvia," *Nationalities Papers* 24, 2 (1996): 203.

95. Romuald J. Misiunas, "The Baltic Republics: Stagnation and Strivings for Sovereignty," in Lubomyr Hajda and Mark Beissinger, eds., *The Nationalities Factor in Soviet Politics and Society* (Boulder, Colo.: Westview Press, 1990), 204–27; Irena Saleniece and Sergei Kuznetsovs, "Nationality Policy, Education and the Russian Question in Latvia Since 1918," in Christopher Williams and Thanasis D. Sfikas, eds., *Ethnicity and Nationalism in Russia, the CIS and the Baltic States* (Hants: Ashgate Publishing Company, 1999), 236–63; John Ginkel, "Identity Construction in Latvia's 'Singing Revolution': Why Inter-Ethnic Conflict Failed to Occur," *Nationalities Papers* 30, 3 (2002): 418.

96. Muiznieks, "Latvia: restoring a state, rebuilding a nation," 379.

97. Eric Rudenshiold, "Ethnic Dimensions in Contemporary Latvian Politics: Focusing Forces for Change," *Soviet Studies* 44, 4 (1992): 610.

98. Lieven, *The Baltic Revolution*, 187.

99. *Itogi perepisi naseleniia 1989 goda po Latvii: Statisticheskii sbornik* (Riga: Goskomstat Latviiskoi Respubliki, 1989), 117–19.

100. Richard Shryock, "Indigenous Economic Managers," in Edward Allworth, ed., *Nationality Group Survival in Multi-Ethnic States: Shifting Support Patterns in the Soviet Baltic Region* (New York: Praeger, 1977), 109.

101. Judith Fleming, "Political Leaders," in Edward Allworth, ed., *Nationality Group Survival in Multi-Ethnic States: Shifting Support Patterns in the Soviet Baltic Region* (New York: Praeger, 1977), 132.

102. Plakans, *The Latvians*, 154.

103. Ibid., 160.

104. The remaining 4 percent of state and party positions were occupied by Lithuanians and "others." *Itogi perepisi naseleniia 1989 goda po Latvii*, 117–19.

105. Misiunas and Taagepera, *The Baltic States*, 197.

106. Ibid., 162.

107. Muiznieks, "Latvia: Origins, Evolution, and Triumph," 196.

108. Juris Dreifelds, *Latvia in Transition* (Cambridge: Cambridge University Press, 1996), 72.

109. Although Latvia's language law was not passed until 1989, the Supreme Soviet declared Latvian the republic's state language and legalized the republic's independence-era national flag on 29 September 1988.

110. Kolstoe, *Russians in the Former Soviet Republics*, 116.

111. *Referendum in the Soviet Union: A Compendium of Reports on the March 17, 1991 Referendum on the Future of the USSR* (Washington, D.C.: Commission on Security and Cooperation in Europe, 1991), 3.

112. Muiznieks, "Latvia: Origins, Evolution, and Triumph," 199. Voters were asked the following question: Do you support the democratic and independent statehood of the Republic of Latvia? Of eligible voters, almost 90 percent (87.5) participated in the referendum. *Referendum in the Soviet Union*, 7.

113. Manz, "Historical Background," 20.

114. Khazanov, *After the USSR*, 141.

115. *Referendum in the Soviet Union*, 34.

116. For a detailed account of the collapse of the Soviet Union and the formation of the Commonwealth of Independent States, see Beissinger, *Nationalist Mobilization and the Collapse of the Soviet State*.

117. Rasma Karklins, *Ethnic Relations in the USSR: The Perspective from Below* (Winchester: Allen and Unwin, 1986).

Chapter 4

1. For more on Russia's foreign policy toward Central Asia, see Lena Jonson, "Russia and Central Asia," in Roy Allison and Lena Jonson, eds., *Central Asian Security: The New International Context* (London: Royal Institute of International Affairs, 2001), 95–126.

2. Dmitri Trenin, "Russia and Central Asia," in Eugene Rumer, Dmitri Trenin, and Huasheng Zhao, *Central Asia: Views from Washington, Moscow, and Beijing* (New York: M. E. Sharpe, 2007), 75–136.

3. Roman Mogilevsky and Rafkat Hasanov, "Economic Growth in Kyrgyzstan," in Gur Ofer and Richard Pomfret, eds., *The Economic Prospects of the CIS: Sources of Long Term Growth* (Cheltenham, UK: Edward Elgar Publishing Limited, 2004), 229.

4. *Enhancing the Prospects for Growth and Trade of the Kyrgyz Republic* (Washington, D.C.: World Bank, 2005), 73.

5. Stanislav Zhukov, "Foreign Trade and Investment," in Boris Rumer, ed., *Central Asia and the New Global Economy* (New York: M. E. Sharpe, 2000), 177.

6. Martin C. Spechler, "The Economies of Central Asia: A Survey," *Comparative Economic Studies* 50 (2008): 37.

7. Graham Smith, "Transnational Politics and the Politics of the Russian Diaspora," *Ethnic and Racial Studies* 22, 3 (3 May 1999): 509.

8. Dreifelds, *Latvia in Transition*, 144.

9. All of the export/import data are from the *Statistical Yearbook of Latvia 2004* (Riga: Central Statistical Bureau of Latvia, 2004), 190.

10. Robert A. Dahl, *Democracy and Its Critics* (New Haven, Conn.: Yale University Press, 1989), 119.

11. The constitution and the laws on citizenship prohibit dual citizenship.

12. *Zakon o grazhdanstve Kyrgyzskoi Respubliki* (26 October 1990), Articles 1 and 2.

13. *Zakon o grazhdanstve Kyrgyzskoi Respubliki* (18 December 1993), Article 1.

14. Article 4 establishes the equality of citizenship regardless of how it is acquired.

15. *Postanovlenie Verkhovnoga Soveta Latviiskoi Respubliki, o vosstanovlenii prav grazhdan Latviiskoi Respubliki i osnovnykh usloviiakh naturalizatsii* (15 September 1991), preamble.

16. A noncitizen is a permanent resident of Latvia who is a citizen of the former USSR, an entity that no longer exists. *Zakon o statuse grazhdan byvshego SSR, ne imeiushchikh grazhdanstva Latvii ili drugogo gosudarstva* (25 April 1995). Approximately 19,236 permanent residents of Latvia have Russian citizenship. *Results of the 2000 Population and Housing Census in Latvia*, 138.

17. People eligible for citizenship through registration include individuals who contribute in a unique way to society, individuals and their descendants who have legally resided in Latvia since 17 June 1940, and individuals and their descendants who can claim citizenship of the first Latvian Republic and who have mastered the Latvian language.

18. This policy does expand the definition of a citizen to include Latvians and Livonians (an indigenous Finno-Ugric people also known as Livs) who registered before March 1996, women and their descendants who according to the 1919 law on citizenship lost Latvian citizenship, and individuals who either completed a full course of study in a school with Latvian as the language of instruction or received basic or specialized education in a Latvian school. Most contemporary Russian residents did not reside in Latvia in 1919 and were educated in their native language because there was no incentive to be educated in Latvian during the Soviet era.

19. *Zakon o grazhdanstve* (22 July 1994), Article 11.

20. Certain individuals are exempt from testing including individuals who were educated in a Latvian-language school, pensioners who legally came to Latvia and have resided in Latvia since the occupation, individuals who were citizens of Lithuania or Estonia before the occupation and have resided in Latvia for at least five years, and invalids with vision, hearing, or speech difficulties (ibid., Article 21).

21. A. Elkin, "G. Ulmanis: 'Na grazhdanstve ne ostanovimcia,'" *CM*, 15 October 1999, 3.

22. It should be noted that the individuals most likely to support the amendments—noncitizens—could not vote because of their legal status. Ina Oshkaia, "Narod Latvii vybiraet demokratiiu," *Respublika*, 5 October 1998, 1.

23. *Izmeneniia v zakone o grazhdanstve* (1998). Certain groups may be considered earlier than this, including Latvians and Livonians being repatriated to Latvia, individuals who on 17 June 1940 were citizens of Lithuania or Estonia and have resided in Latvia for at least five years, and individuals who on 1 September 1939 were citizens of Poland and have resided in Latvia for at least five years. The final group, individuals married for at least ten years to a citizen who has resided in Latvia for at least five years, is not restrictive.

24. Article 3. Minor-age children, however, were able to acquire citizenship simultaneously with parents undergoing naturalization.

25. The Latvian Human Rights Committee has compiled a list of fifty-seven restrictions placed on noncitizens. The list can be obtained from the Latvian Human Rights Committee, 102-a Dzirnavu Street, Riga. See http://www.minelres.lv/ or call (371) 728–9473. Alternatively, a list of seventy legal differences is published in Miroslavs Mitrofanovs, Aleksandrs Gamelejevs, Vik-

tors Buzajevs, Aleksejs Dimitrovs, and Tatjana Zdanoka, eds., *The Last Prisoners of the Cold War: The Stateless People of Latvia in Their Own Words* (Riga: Avert-R Ltd., 2006).

26. Marja Nissinen, *Latvia's Transition to a Market Economy: Political Determinants of Economic Reform Policy* (London: Macmillan Press, 1999).

27. V. Buzayev, G. Kotov, and L. Raihman, *Comment on the List of Differences Between the Rights of Latvian Citizens and Non-Citizens* (Riga: Latvian Human Rights Committee, 1999), 3.

28. The following individuals are eligible for a 3 Lat fee: members of poor families or poor persons living separately; unemployed persons registered with the State Employment Service; members of families in which there are three or more minor-age children; persons receiving old-age and long-term service pensions; disabled persons of category II and III; and pupils, students, and full-time students of education establishments certified by the state. Politically repressed persons, disabled persons of category I, orphans and children who are not under their parents' charge, and persons sheltered by social care institutions are exempt from payment. Regulation No. 234 of the Cabinet of Ministers, Riga, 5 June 2001, http://www.np.gov.lv/.

29. These July 2005 data are generated by Latvia's Board for Citizenship and Migration Affairs and posted on the Naturalization Board of the Republic of Latvia's Web site: http://www.np.gov.lv/.

30. A. Eliukeiova Kokshetay, "Russkii iazyk dolzhen byt gosudarstvennym," *Lad* 2, 126 (2005).

31. *Naselenie Kyrgyzstana, Itogi Pervoi natsional'noi perepisi naseleniia Kyrgyzskoi Respubliki 1999,* 116–17.

32. Ibid., 116.

33. *Zakon o gosudarstvennom iazyke Kirgizskoi SSR* (23 September 1989), Article 8.

34. Ibid., Article 11.

35. Ibid., introduction, Articles 1 and 4.

36. The Kyrgyz constitution was adopted in 1993 and amended in 1996, 1998, 2003, and 2006. Following a referendum it was amended again in 2007. Article 5 of each constitution contains stipulations regarding language.

37. *Konstitutsiia Kyrgyzskoi Respubliki,* Article 43 or 44 depending on the particular constitution consulted.

38. *Ukaz prezidenta Kyrgyzskoi Respubliki o merakh po regulirovaniiu migratsionnykh protsessov v Kyrgyzskoi Respubliki* (14 June 1994).

39. *Pravitel'stvo Kyrgyzskoi Respubliki Postanovlenie, o realizatsii ukaza prezidenta Kyrgyzskoi Respubliki A. Akaeva "o merakh po regulirovaniiu migratsionnogo protsessa v Kyrgyzskoi Respublike"* (1 September 1994), Point 2.

40. N. Kosmarskaia, "Khotiat li Russkie v Rossiiu?" in A. R. Viatkina, N. P. Kosmarskoi, and C. A. Panarina, eds., *V dvizhenii dobrovol'nom i vynuzhdennom* (Moskva: Natlis Press, 1999), 180–214.

41. V. Kozlinskii, "Dooronbeka Sadyrbaeva prigovorili k smerti," *Vechernii Bishkek,* 6 January 1998, 2.

42. Author's interview, 14 March 2000. The National Commission for the State Language was established on 20 January 1998 by Presidential Decree Number 21.

43. *Pravitel'stvo Kyrgyzskoi Respubliki Postanovlenie, o voprosakh dal'neishego razvitiia gosudarstvennogo iazika Kyrgyzskoi Respubliki* (7 April 1999), Point 3.

44. *Zakon Respubliki Kyrgyzstan o gosudarstvennoi sluzhbe* (30 November 1999), Article 12.

45. Speech by Askar Akayev, "Eto vybor epokhi," *Slovo Kyrgyzstana,* 27 April 2000, 6.

46. *Zakon Kyrgyzskoi Respubliki ob ofitsial'nom iazyke Kyrgyzskoi Respubliki* (25 May 2000), Article 1.

47. Ibid., Article 5.

48. Ibid., Articles 2, 3, 13.

49. *Zakon o gosudarstvennom iazyke Kirgizskoi SSR* (23 September 1989), Article 21.

50. *Zakon Respubliki Kyrgyzstan ob obrazovanii* (December 1992 and November 1997), Article 5. Kyrgyzstan's 1992 law on education was amended in 1997, but in the process of revision nothing changed in respect to the language of instruction issue. The Kyrgyz constitution does not address this issue.

51. In an unpublished article a representative of the Slavic Foundation claims that there are 143 schools with Russian instruction and more than 300 schools providing Russian and Kyrgyz instruction. Furthermore, he asserts that while in the immediate aftermath of the Soviet Union's collapse there was an attempt to liquidate Russian schools, now there is a growth in such schools. See V. V. Vishnevskii, "Russkii iazyk kak factor politicheskoi stabil'nosti i mezhnatsional'nogo obshcheniia v Kirgizskoi Resublike," October 2004.

52. *Zakon Kyrgyzskoi Respubliki o gosudarstvennom iazyke Kyrgyzskoi Respubliki* (12 February 2004), Article 18.

53. *Programma razvitiia gosudarstvennogo iazyka Kyrgyzskoi Respubliki na 2000–2010 gody* (20 September 2000).

54. *Zakon Kyrgyzskoi Respubliki o gosudarstvennom iazyke Kyrgyzskoi Respubliki* (12 February 2004), Article 2.

55. Ibid., Articles 8, 9, 14.

56. Ibid., Article 1.

57. *Zakon Latviiskoi Sovetskoi Sotsialisticheskoi Respubliki o iazykakh* (5 May 1989), preamble.

58. *Results of the 2000 Population and Housing Census in Latvia,* 147.

59. *Zakon Latviiskoi Respubliki o iazykakh* (31 March 1992), Article 8.

60. The 1989 language law ensures the development of cultures other than Latvian in their native languages. *Zakon Latviiskoi Sovetskoi Sotsialisticheskoi Respubliki o iazykakh* (5 May 1989), Article 15.

61. *Zakon Latviiskoi Respubliki o iazykakh* (31 March 1992), Articles 4, 7, 8, 9.

62. Author's interview with the director of the State Language Center, 22 November 2000.

63. Latvia lacked constitutional status until 1998, when amendments confirmed Latvian as the state language. Though the amended constitution does not mention Russian, Amendment 114 does recall the 1989 stipulation regarding the development of cultures other than Latvian in their native languages. The amendment states that "individuals belonging to a national minority have the right to the preservation and development of their language, and ethnic and cultural distinctive quality." Although this is a concession to minorities, one year later elites adopted legislation that unambiguously solidified a rigid linguistic regime. Constitutional amendments are published in *Diena,* 4 November 1998, 1.

64. *Zakon o gosudarstvennom iazyke* (21 December 1999), Article 1.

65. Latvian is the required language of all state and municipal agencies, courts and matters related to the judicial system, other public organizations and enterprises, private organizations and enterprises, and matters related to self-employed individuals when their activities affect the public interest.

66. In 1992 a Council of Ministers Resolution was adopted that established a system of language testing based on three levels of proficiency. Only individuals who received an education in Latvian were exempt from testing. Employees in almost all professions, including janitors, were required to take the exam. As of 1994, individuals were required to pay a fee for the language test. See Aina Antane and Boris Tsilevich, "Nation-Building and Ethnic Integration in Latvia," in Pal Kolsto, ed., *Nation-Building and Ethnic Integration of Post-Soviet Societies: An Investigation of Latvia and Kazakhstan* (Boulder, Colo.: Westview Press, 1999), 114–16.

67. The first and second constitutions were passed in 1992 and 1998 respectively, while the third version was adopted in accordance with a referendum in 2007. *Diena,* 4 November 1998, 1, Article 112. Although some articles of the constitution specify "every citizen" versus "everyone," Article 112 does not.

68. *Zakon Latviiskoi Sovetskoi Sotsialisticheskoi Respubliki o iazykakh* (5 May 1989), Articles 11, 12.

69. *Zakon ob obrazovanii* (19 June 1991), Article 5.

70. Ibid.

71. *Zakon Latviiskoi Respubliki o iazykakh* (31 March 1992), Article 11.

72. Ibid., Article 12.

73. *Zakon ob obrazovanii* (17 November 1998), Article 9.

74. *Zakon ob obshchem obrazovanii* (10 June 1998), Article 38.

75. *Zakon ob obrazovanii* (17 November 1998), Article 9.

76. *Zakon ob obrazovanii* (17 November 1998, *c izmeneniuami vnecennymi po sostoianiiu 5 Fevralia 2004 goda)*, Article 9.

77. *Integratsiia obshchestva v Latvii: kontseptsiia gosudarstvennoi programmy* (Riga: Upravlenie Naturalizatsii Latiiskoi Respubliki, 1999), 31. For more on the program, see the Latvian Embassy's Web site: http://www.latvia-usa.org/insoc.html.

78. Ibid.

79. Author's interview, 17 November 2000.

80. Brubaker, *Nationalism Reframed,* 92.

81. Author's interview, 3 January 2000.

82. Author's interview, 3 November 2000.

83. Valentin Kistanov, "Natsional'nost' stala professiei," *Chas,* 21 May 2004, 7.

84. Kosmarskaia, "Khotiat li Russkie v Rossiiu?" 194.

85. The percentage in Riga is lower because a considerable portion of respondents (58 percent) identifies formal nationalization policies, which are not relevant in Kyrgyzstan.

86. Author's interview, 14 January 2000.

87. Author's interview, 7 November 2000.

88. Author's interview, 18 January 2000.

89. Author's interview, 20 October 2000.

90. Author's interview, 20 January 2000.

91. V. V. Vishnevskii, "Migratsiia naseleniiz Kirgizii: prichiny i sledstviia," *Res Publica,* 3–9 November 1998, p. 3.

92. Author's interview, 2 February 2000.

93. Author's interview, 1 February 2000.

94. Author's interview, 31 October 2000.

95. Connor, *Ethnonationalism,* 196.

96. The rector of the Kyrgyz-Russian Slavic University, which is funded by

Russia, is Russian. Author's interview with a representative of the Slavic Foundation, 21 October 1999.

97. Author's interview with a representative of the Slavic Foundation, 25 July 2005.

98. Author's interview with a former vice president of the Union of Russian Compatriots, 2 December 1999. The Union of Russian Compatriots was called the Association of Ethnic Russians until 2003.

99. Author's interview with the chairman of the Union of Russian Compatriots, 25 July 2005.

100. Author's interview with a representative of the Public Association of Russians, 21 July 2005.

101. Author's interview with a representative of the Party of National Harmony, 11 July 2005.

102. Author's interview with the president of the Association of Latvian-Russian Cooperation, 5 October 2000.

103. Author's interview with the president of Russian Society, 4 October 2000.

104. David J. Smith, Artis Pabriks, Aldis Purs, and Thomas Lane, *The Baltic States: Estonia, Latvia, and Lithuania* (London: Routledge, 2002), 49.

105. The remaining 4 percent of state and party positions were occupied by Lithuanians and "others." *Itogi perepisi naseleniia 1989 goda po Latvii*, 117–19.

106. Scholars who have made this argument provide scant supportive evidence. See, for example, Mark A. Jubulis, *Nationalism and Democratic Transition: The Politics of Citizenship and Language in Post-Soviet Latvia* (Lanham, Md.: University Press of America, 2001); Nissinen, *Latvia's Transition to a Market Economy*; and Melvin, *Russians Beyond Russia*.

107. Author's interviews with an independent journalist who specializes in tracking Latvia's rich and famous, 5 July 2005, and with a former minister for Special Assignments for Society Integration Affairs under the Cabinet of Ministers of the Republic of Latvia, 6 July 2005.

108. Author's interview with a former minister for Special Assignments for Society Integration Affairs, 6 July 2005.

109. Artis Pabriks and Aldis Purs, *Latvia: The Challenges of Change* (London: Routledge, 2001), 92.

110. Author's interviews with representatives of Latvia's Association for the Support of Russian-Language Schools (29 June 2005); the Socialist Party (7 July 2005); the Party of National Harmony (11 July 2005); another representative of the Party of National Harmony (15 July 2005); and a former minister for Special Assignments for Society Integration Affairs (6 July 2005).

111. Author's interview, 30 June 2005.

112. Nissinen, *Latvia's Transition to a Market Economy*, 105.

113. Author's interview, 5 July 2005.

114. Nils Muiznieks, "Latvia's Changing System of Ethnic Stratification," unpublished paper presented at the conference "Democracy and Ethnopolitics," Riga, 9–11 March 1994.

115. Aadne Aasland, "Citizenship Status and Social Exclusion," *Journal of Baltic Studies* 33, 1 (Spring 2002): 61.

116. Valentinas Mite, "Latvia: Russian Speakers Hold Their Own on the Business Front," *Radio Free Europe/Radio Liberty*, 17 May 2002, 2.

117. Author's interview, 29 June 2005.

118. Author's interview, 1 July 2005.

119. *Society Integration and Business: The Ethnic Dimension* (Riga: Baltic Institute of Social Sciences, Latvian Academy of Sciences Institute of Economics, 2004), 37.

120. The experts I refer to here include a representative of the Socialist Party (author's interview, 7 July 2005), two representatives of the Party of National Harmony (author's interviews, 11 July 2005 and 15 July 2005), and a representative of the Russian Party (author's interview, 8 July 2005).

121. Lieven, *The Baltic Revolution*, xxviii.

122. Helen M. Morris, "The Non-citizens of the EU," in David J. Smith, ed., *The Baltic States and Their Region: New Europe or Old?* (Amsterdam: Rodopi, 2005), 255.

123. Pal Kolsto, *Political Construction Sites: Nation-Building in Russia and the Post-Soviet States* (Boulder, Colo.: Westview Press, 2000), 120.

124. Graham Smith, "When Nations Challenge and Nations Rule: Estonia and Latvia as Ethnic Democracies," *International Politics* 33 (March 1996): 37.

125. Igor' Vatolin, "Russkaia obshchina: kakoi ei byt'?" *Chas*, 8 May 2004, 2. Many individuals, including the aforementioned former minister for Special Assignments for Society Integration Affairs and representatives of Latvia's Association for the Support of Russian-Language Schools and OKROL, claim that Russian businessmen back OKROL.

126. Author's interview with a representative of the Party of National Harmony, 1 November 2000.

127. Antane and Tsilevich, "Nation-Building and Ethnic Integration in Latvia," 151.

128. Karklins, *Ethnopolitics and Transition to Democracy*, 132.

129. Author's interviews with an independent journalist who tracks the country's rich and famous (5 July 2005); a representative of the Party of National Harmony (11 July 2005); and a former minister for Special Assignments for Society Integration Affairs (6 July 2005).

130. Richard Rose, "New Baltic Barometer IV: A Survey Study," *Studies in Public Policy* 338 (Glasgow: University of Strathclyde, 2000), 5.

131. Richard Rose, "New Baltic Barometer VI: A Post-Enlargement Survey," *Studies in Public Policy* 338 (Glasgow: University of Strathclyde, 2005), 39.

132. Zevelev, *Russia and Its New Diasporas*, 126.

133. Author's interview, 27 October 2000.

134. Artis Pabriks, *Occupational Representation and Ethnic Discrimination in Latvia* (Riga: Soros Foundation, 2002), 42–43.

135. *Society Integration and Business*, 8.

136. Author's interview with a representative of the Socialist Party, 6 October 2000.

137. Author's interview with a representative of the Association of Latvian-Russian Cooperation, 5 October 2000.

138. Author's interview with a representative of the Association for the Support of Russian-Language Schools, 29 June 2005.

139. Author's interview with a representative of the Party of National Harmony, 11 July 2005.

140. *Society Integration and Business*, 13.

141. Pabriks, *Occupational Representation and Ethnic Discrimination in Latvia*, 43.

142. Author's interview with a spokesman for OKROL, 6 July 2005.

143. Author's interview, 1 July 2005.

144. *Partiia Ravnopravie: kratko o programme, strukture, istorii* (Riga: Editorial Commission of the Party, 2000).

145. Elina Chuianova, "Vmeste my budem sil'nee," *Chas,* 2 September 2004, 2.

146. For biographical details, see Al'fred Rubiks, *Trebuiu priznat' nevinovnym!* (Moscow: Mezhdunarodnye otnosheniia, 2001).

147. *Programma Sotsialisticheskoi partii Latvii* (15 January 1994), 10–11.

148. Author's interview, 7 July 2005.

149. Chinn and Kaiser, *Russians as the New Minority,* 220–21.

150. Ibid., 220.

151. Ibid., 78.

152. Robert Kaiser, *The Geography of Nationalism in Russia and the USSR* (Princeton, N.J.: Princeton University Press, 1994), 349.

153. A clan is an informal social institution based on ties of kinship (or fictitious kinship) that provides political, social, and economic opportunities to its members. See Kathleen Collins, "The Political Role of Clans in Central Asia," *Comparative Politics* 35, 2 (January 2003): 173.

154. Kathleen Collins, "Clans, Pacts, and Politics in Central Asia," *Journal of Democracy* 13, 3 (July 2002): 142.

155. Ibid., 148.

156. *Kyrgyzskaia gosudarstvennost' Statistika vekov* (Bishkek: Natsional'nyi statisticheskii komitet Kyrgyzskoii Respubliki, 2003), 175.

157. V. Khaug, "Demograficheskie tendentsii, formirovanie natsii i mezhetnicheskie otnosheniia v Kyrgyzstane," in Z. Kudabaev, M. Giio, and M. Denisenko, eds., *Naselenie Kyrgyzstana* (Bishkek: Natsional'nyi statisticheskii komitet Kyrgyzskoii Respubliki, 2004), 142.

158. Schatz, *Modern Clan Politics,* 95.

159. Author's interview, 25 January 2000.

160. Author's interview, 25 July 2005.

161. Author's interview, 12 January 2000.

162. Author's interview, 25 July 2005.

163. Author's interview, 25 July 2005.

164. Author's interview, 21 July 2005.

165. Author's interview, 21 January 2000.

166. *Konstitutsiia Kyrgyzskoi Respubliki,* Article 8.

167. Author's interview, 25 July 2005.

168. Author's interview, 25 July 2005.

169. Author's interview, 21 July 2005.

Chapter 5

1. Author's interview, 3 January 2000.

2. Author's interview, 30 October 2000.

3. Author's interview, 22 December 1999.

4. Author's interview with a representative of the Socialist Party, 6 October 2000.

5. Author's interview, 23 October 2000.

6. Personal interview, 10 November 2000.

7. Author's interview, 7 November 2000.

8. These data are generated by Latvia's Board for Citizenship and Migration

Affairs and posted on the Naturalization Board of the Republic of Latvia's Web site: http://www.np.gov.lv/.

9. Author's interview with a representative of Russian Society, 4 October 2000.

10. Author's interview, 20 November 2000.

11. Author's interview, 30 October 2000.

12. The wage data are from the *Statistical Yearbook of Latvia 2004*, 58.

13. The fee reduction is part of the *Regulation on the State Duty Payable for Submission of a Naturalization Application*, Regulation No. 234 of the Cabinet of Ministers (Riga, 5 June 2001). The wage data are from the *Statistical Yearbook of Latvia 2004*, 58.

14. Andrei Mamykin, "Naturalizatsiia—eto ne strashno: Kak ia stal grazhdaninom Latvii," *Chas*, 23 August 2000, 5.

15. Author's interview, 17 October 2000.

16. Author's interview with a representative of the Association for the Support of Russian-Language Schools, 18 October 2000.

17. Author's interview, 30 October 2000.

18. Robert J. Kaiser, "Nationalizing the Work Force: Ethnic Restratification in the Newly Independent States," *Post-Soviet Geography* 36, 2 (1995): 105.

19. Author's interview, 21 January 2000.

20. Author's interview, 17 November 2000.

21. However, the ban on dual citizenship does vex Russians who reside in Kyrgyzstan but work in Russia because labor migrants confront bureaucratic hurdles that would be eliminated if Kyrgyzstan permitted dual citizenship. Author's interview with the president of the Slavic Foundation (21 December 1999) and with a former director of the Federal Migration Services of Russia in Kyrgyzstan (26 January 2000).

22. The most likely explanation for this surprisingly low figure is that naturalization, although offensive to most Russians, is nevertheless a solution to the citizenship dilemma.

23. Author's interview, 18 October 2000.

24. V. M. Ploskikh and V. A. Voropaeva, "Kyrgyzsko-rossiiskie otnosheniia: K probleme migratsionnkh protsessov," in *Vneshniaia migratsiia russkoiazychnogo naseleniia Kyrgyzstana: Problemy i posledstviia* (Bishkek: Ilim, 2000), 47.

25. Author's interview with a former director of the Federal Migration Services of Russia, 26 January 2000.

26. Author's interview, 24 December 1999.

27. In March 2005 President Akayev fled Kyrgyzstan in the wake of mass demonstrations. Parliamentary elections in February sparked protests in the south, where opposition forces seized control of various government buildings. Easy victory encouraged the opposition to take the protests to the capital, where they joined demonstrators who demanded new parliamentary elections as well as Akayev's resignation. Akayev resigned on 4 April and Bakiyev won presidential elections that were held on 10 July.

28. Author's interview, 6 November 2000.

29. Author's interview with a representative of Russian Society, 4 October 2000.

30. Author's interview with a representative of the Party of National Harmony, 1 November 2000.

31. Author's interview, 7 November 2000.

32. Representatives of Kyrgyzstan's Russian minority population agree that

there are plenty of Russian-language schools in Bishkek, where Russians are most heavily concentrated.

33. V. Korchagina, "Valerii Vishnevskii: Ia—ne 'natsmen'shinstvo.' Ia Russkii," *Vechernyi Bishkek*, 15 June 1994, 2.

34. This estimate is based on the fact that 52.4 percent of the country's population in 1989 was Kyrgyz, while 59.7 percent of the country's population in 1995 was Kyrgyz. See *Statisticheskii ezhegodnik Kyrgyzskoi Respubliki 1995 chast' 1* (Bishkek: Natsional'nyi statisticheskii komitet Kyrgyzskoii Respubliki, 1996), 20.

35. Author's interview, 3 January 2000.

36. Author's interview, 5 January 2000.

37. Author's interview, 2 February 2000.

38. Author's interview, 7 December 1999.

39. Respondents who did consider the economy problematic specified the need for industrial development, increased salaries and pensions, job creation, and a higher standard of living.

Chapter 6

1. Pilkington, *Migration, Displacement and Identity in Post-Soviet Russia*, 126.

2. See http://www.freedomhouse.org/template.cfm?page=15.

3. Igor Kustov, "Problema iazyka: Reaktsiia—migratsiia," *Res Publica*, 18 February 1997, 3–4.

4. K. Isaev and G. Gorborukova, "Migratsiia: Problemy i perspectivy," *Ekho Nauki* 2–3 (1997): 125.

5. Author's interview with a former director of the Federal Migration Services of Russia, 26 January 2000.

6. A. O. Orusbaev, "Sud'ba russkogo iazyka v Kirgizii," in G. N. Khlypenko, ed., *Russkie v Kyrgyzstane: Nauchno-issledovatel'skie stat'i i materealy* (Bishkek: NII Regional'nogo slavianovedeniia KRSU, 2002), 163.

7. G. V. Kumskov, "Vozdeistvie migratsii russkoizychnovo naseleniia na sotsial'no-ekonomicheskuiu sferu Kyrgyzstana," in *Vneshniaia migratsiia russkoiazychnogo naseleniia Kyrgyzstana: Problemy i posledstviia* (Bishkek: Ilim, 2000), 87.

8. L. IU. Nemeshina, "Russkii faktor v Kyrgyzstane," in G. N. Khlypenko, ed., *Russkie v Kyrgyzstane: Nauchno-issledovatel'skie stat'i i materealy* (Bishkek: NII Regional'nogo Slavianovedeniia KRSU, 2002), 118.

9. *Ukaz prezidenta Kyrgyzskoi Respubliki o merakh po regulirovaniiu migratsionnykh protsessov v Kyrgyzskoi Respubliki* (14 June 1994).

10. *Osnovnye itogi Pervoi natsional'noi perepisi naseleniia Kyrgyskoi Respubliki*, 26.

11. The 1970–75 life expectancy at birth rate differs from the 1995–2000 life expectancy at birth rate by four and a half years in Kyrgyzstan. See *Human Development Report 2000* (New York: United Nations Development Programme, 2000), 187.

12. L. M. Torgasheva, "Vliianie migratsionnykh protsessov na demograficheskuiu situatsiiu v Kyrgyskoi Respublike," in *Vneshniaia migratsiia russkoiazychnogo naseleniia Kyrgyzstana: Problemy i posledstviia* (Bishkek: Ilim, 2000), 61.

13. Author's interview, 6 December 1999.

14. Author's interview, 15 November 1999.

15. There are 177 possible rankings. Human development indices take into account three dimensions: (1) a long and healthy life, (2) knowledge, and (3) a decent standard of living. See *Human Development Report 2005* (New York: United Nations Development Programme, 2005).

16. Ibid., 250.

17. Ibid.

18. Ibid., 285.

19. Author's interview, 6 December 1999.

20. Pilkington, *Migration, Displacement and Identity in Post-Soviet Russia*, 178.

21. Author's interview, 23 November 1999.

22. Although Russia's oligarchs invest abroad in order to avoid financial repercussions of falling out of favor with the president and/or his prime minister, the Medvedev-Putin administration does seek to redirect domestic investment.

23. Kathleen Braden, "Kyrgyzstan," in Philip R. Pryde, ed., *Environmental Resources and Constraints in the Former Soviet Republics* (Boulder, Colo.: Westview Press, 1995), 311.

24. *Enhancing the Prospects for Growth and Trade of the Kyrgyz Republic*, 15.

25. In 1990, 32,893 Russians left and in 1991, 32,032 Russians left. These data were provided by the Natsional'ny statisticheskii komitet Kyrgyzskoi Respubliki.

26. *Osnovnye itogi Pervoi natsional'noi perepisin naseleniia Kyrgyzskoi Respubliki*, 26.

27. Valery Tishkov, "'Don't Kill Me, I'm a Kyrgyz!': An Anthropological Analysis of Violence in the Osh Ethnic Conflict," *Journal of Peace Research* 32, 2 (1995): 134.

28. Valery Tishkov claims that 120 Uzbeks, 50 Kyrgyz, and 1 Russian were killed, while Gene Huskey claims that about 230 people were killed. See ibid., 134–35; and Huskey, "Kyrgyzstan," 406.

29. *Kyrgyzstan: Obshchaia otsenka sostoianiia strany* (Bishkek: Tsentr sotsial'-nykh i ekonomicheskikh issledovanii, 1999), 31.

30. Aleksandr Iurasov, "Etnorossiiane v Kyrgyzstane: Novye tendentsii i perspectivy v razvitii," *Informatsionno-Analiticheskaia Gazeta*, no. 1 (March 1998): 3.

31. Aleksei Sukhov, "Russkie v Kyrgyzstane: Uezzhat' ili ostavat'cy?" *Lad* 6, 130 (2005): 6.

32. V. I. Ostapchuk, "Migratsionnaia i demograficheskaia situatsiia v Kyrgyzstane," in *Vneshniaia migratsiia russkoiazychnogo naseleniia Kyrgyzstana: Problemy i posledstviia* (Bishkek: Ilim, 2000), 41. Residents are periodically deprived of natural gas because Kyrgyzstan has accrued a substantial debt to Uzbekistan since the disintegration of all-union economic ties, and suppliers cease gas deliveries to chastise the Kyrgyz government for its inability and/or unwillingness to pay its bills.

33. Ibid., 38.

34. Artem Petrov, "Russkie uezzhaiut," *Delo No.*, 19 January 2000, 2.

35. Artem Petrov, "Nuzhny li bol'shoi Rossii Russkie iz malen'kogo Kyrgyzstana?" *Delo No.*, 10 November 1999, 8.

36. Author's interview, 2 December 1999.

37. V. Akchurin, "Ukrotit' beg," *Slovo Kyrgyzstana*, 14 May 2004, 9.

38. T. Seiitbekov, "Ne pokidaute dom nash obshchii!" *Slovo Kyrgyzstana*, 5 March 2004, 6.

39. L. V. Ostapenko, "Voprosy trudovoi zaniatosti," in S. S. Savoskul, A. I. Ginzburg, M. N. Gulboglo, and V. A. Tishkov, *Russkie v novom zarybezh'e: Kyrgyziia* (Moskva: Mezhdistsiplinarnyi akademicheskii tsentr sotsial'nykh nauk, 1995), 92.

40. John Anderson, *Kyrgyzstan: Central Asia's Island of Democracy?* (Amsterdam: Harwood Academic Publishers, 1999), 67.

41. Author's interview with a former director of the Federal Migration Services of Russia in Kyrgyzstan, 26 January 2000.

42. Author's interview, 22 November 1999.

43. Author's interview, 15 November 1999.

44. Askar Akayev, "Brat'ia na vse vremena," in A. I. Ivanov, ed., *Rossiiane v Kyrgyzstane* (Bishkek: Literaturnyi Kyrgyzstan, 1999), 10.

45. Petrov, "Russkie uezzhaiut."

46. Tamara Slashcheva, "Velika Rossia, da otstupat' nekuda," *Res Publika*, 22 August 1995, 3.

47. Author's interview, 18 November 1999.

48. "Russkii vopros," *Vechernii Bishkek*, 19 April 2005, 2.

49. Sukhov, "Russkie v Kyrgyzstane."

50. See "Kyrgyzstan: After the Revolution," Asia Report No. 97 (International Crisis Group, 4 May 2005), 16.

51. Aleksandr Tuzov, "Chemodan, vokzal, Rossiia?" *Vechernii Bishkek*, 15 April 2005, 5.

52. Author's interview with the chairman of the Ministry of Internal Affairs Department of Migration in the Kyrgyz Republic, 25 July 2005.

53. Author's interview, 6 December 1999.

54. G. V. Kumskov, *Zakonomernosti i osobennosti razvitiia migratsionnykh protsessov Kyrgyzstana na sovremennom etape* (Bishkek: Ilim, 2002), 77.

55. *Results of the 2000 Population and Housing Census in Latvia*, 121.

56. The 1970–75 life expectancy at birth rate differs from the 1995–2000 life expectancy at birth rate by less than two years. See *Human Development Report 2000*, 187.

57. In 1989 there were 905,515 permanent Russian residents of Latvia. *Results of the 2000 Population and Housing Census in Latvia*, 121.

58. Aleksandr Vasil'ev, "Tikhii iskhod," *Chas*, 8 May 1999, 4.

59. Author's interview, 23 November 2000.

60. Russian potential migrants in Riga completed a written survey that contained the following age categories: 25–35, 36–45, 46–55, 56–65, 66–75, older than 75. The survey was conducted between September and December 2000 but individual questionnaires were not dated.

61. Author's interview with a representative of the Center for the Preservation of the Russian Language, 25 October 2000.

62. Author's interview with a cochairman of OKROL, 6 July 2005.

63. Pilkington, *Migration, Displacement and Identity in Post-Soviet Russia*, 125.

64. According to the same data, on average 10 percent of migrants choose the second most popular migration destination, which, depending on the year in question, has been Ukraine, Germany, or the United States. *Statistical Yearbook of Latvia 2004*, 44.

65. *Human Development Report 2005*, 250.

66. Ibid., 285.

67. Ibid., back cover.

68. *Statistical Yearbook of Latvia 2004*, 128.

69. Juris Dreifelds, "Latvia," in Philip R. Pryde, ed., *Environmental Resources and Constraints in the Former Soviet Republics* (Boulder, Colo.: Westview Press, 1995), 113–17.

70. *Human Development Report 2005*, 280.

71. Author's interview, 4 July 2005.

72. Author's interview with a representative of the Party of National Harmony, 11 July 2005.

73. Klara Hallik, "Nationalising Policies and Integration Challenges," in Marju Lauristin and Mati Heidmets, eds., *The Challenge of the Russian Minority: Emerging Multicultural Democracy in Estonia* (Tartu: Tartu University Press, 2002), 65–88.

74. Kolsto, *Political Construction Sites*, 120.

75. James Hughes, "'Exit' in Deeply Divided Societies: Regimes of Discrimination in Estonia and Latvia and the Potential for Russophone Migration," *Journal of Common Market Studies* 43, 4 (2005): 754.

76. Ibid., 751.

77. Ibid.

78. Tarrow, *Power in Movement*, 2.

79. David A. Snow and Robert D. Benford, "Master Frames and Cycles of Protest," in Aldon Morris and Carol McClurg Mueller, eds., *Frontiers in Social Movement Theory* (New Haven, Conn.: Yale University Press, 1992), 137.

80. Ibid. Italics mine.

81. William A. Gamson, *Talking Politics* (Cambridge: Cambridge University Press, 1992), 7.

82. Ibid., 32.

83. Author's interview, 21 January 2000.

84. Gamson, *Talking Politics*, 32.

85. Author's interview, 17 October 2000.

86. Ron Aminzade and Doug McAdam, "Emotions and Contentious Politics," in Ronald R. Aminzade, Jack A. Goldstone, Doug McAdam, Elizabeth J. Perry, William H. Sewell, Jr., Sidney Tarrow, and Charles Tilly, eds., *Silence and Voice in the Study of Contentious Politics* (Cambridge: Cambridge University Press, 2001), 17.

87. Ibid.

88. Milton J. Esman, "Perspectives on Ethnic Conflict in Industrialized Societies," in Milton J. Esman, ed., *Ethnic Conflict in the Western World* (Ithaca, N.Y.: Cornell University Press, 1977), 378.

89. Aminzade and McAdam, "Emotions and Contentious Politics," 36.

90. Ibid., 44–45.

91. See Ronald Aminzade et al., *Silence and Voice in the Study of Contentious Politics* (Cambridge: Cambridge University Press, 2001).

92. *Ustav Russkoi Obshchiny Latvii* (Riga, 1992), section 1.1; and *Ustav Russkogo Obshchestva v Latvii* (Riga, 1996), section 1.1.

93. *Ustav Russkoi Obshchiny Latvii* (Riga, 1992), section 1.4; *Ustav Russkogo Obshchestva v Latvii* (Riga, 1996), section 13.

94. Author's interview with a representative of Russian Community, 10 October 2000.

95. Ibid.

96. Ibid.

97. Author's interview with a spokesperson for Russian Society, 4 October 2000.

98. Ibid.

99. *Ustav obshchestvennoi organizatsii Latviiskaia assotsiatsiia v podderzhku shkol c obucheniem na russkom iazyke* (Riga, 1996), section 2.1.

100. Author's interview with the president of the Association for the Support of Russian-Language Schools, 18 October 2000.

101. Ibid.

102. Ibid. According to the association, one subject is taught in Latvian while

the next is taught in Russian. In other words, the state's program simply alters language from class to class.

103. Author's interview with the president of the Association for the Support of Russian-Language Schools, 29 June 2005.

104. Author's interview with a representative of the Center for the Preservation of the Russian Language, 25 October 2000.

105. Ibid.

106. Ibid.

107. Ibid.

108. Approximately 19,236 permanent residents of Latvia have Russian citizenship. *Results of the 2000 Population and Housing Census in Latvia*, 138.

109. Author's interview with a leading representative of the Association of Latvian-Russian Cooperation, 5 October 2000.

110. Ibid.

111. Ibid.

112. Latvia is a multiparty parliamentary democracy with a list proportional representation electoral system. The country consists of five electoral districts, and candidates for election must be a member of a political alliance or on a party list. Electoral law forbids noncitizens from running for local or national office, so Russians in parliament either received citizenship automatically in 1991 or chose to naturalize. Parties representing Russians that manage to surpass the 5 percent electoral threshold do so because of votes they receive in heavily Russian electoral districts, such as Riga and Latgale. For more on Latvia's electoral system, see Pal Kolsto, ed., *Nation-Building and Ethnic Integration in Post-Soviet Societies: An Investigation of Latvia and Kazakhstan* (Boulder, Colo.: Westview Press, 1999).

113. The most recent legislative elections were in October 2006. For Human Rights in a United Latvia garnered 6 percent of the vote and won six seats.

114. Author's interview, 20 October 2000.

115. *Programma "Russkoi Partii" Latvii na vybory v Rizhskuiu Gorodskuiu Dumu 9 marta 1997 goda.*

116. Author's interview with a spokesperson for the Russian Party, 20 October 2000.

117. Ibid.

118. Ibid.

119. Author's interview, 7 July 2005.

120. Author's interview, 6 October 2000.

121. Ibid.

122. Ibid.

123. *Politicheskoe programmnoe zaiavlenie Sotsialisticheskoi partii Latvii* (30 October 1999), 16.

124. Author's interview, 6 October 2000.

125. *Partiia Ravnopravie: Kratko o programme, strukture, istorii* (Riga: Editorial Commission of the Party, 2000), 25, italics mine.

126. Author's interview with a leading representative of the Equal Rights Party, 3 October 2000.

127. Ibid.

128. Ibid.

129. *Programma partii Narodnogo Soglasiia* (Riga, 1997), 5.

130. Author's interview with a spokesperson for the Party of National Harmony, 1 November 2000.

131. Ibid.

132. Ibid.

133. Ibid.

134. Ibid.

135. Author's interview with the same spokesperson for the Party of National Harmony, 11 July 2005.

136. Leonid Fedoseev, "Chego khotiat russkie Latvii?" *Chas*, 6 March 2004, 1.

137. Viacheslav Ivanov, "V Rige moratoria ne budet," *Chas*, 26 May 2004, 4.

138. Ibid.

139. Iakov G. Pliner, *Sozvezdie problem obrazovaniia* (Riga: Latviiskii institut pravovykh issledovanii, 1998), 18.

40. "Takaia reforma nam ne nuzhna!" *Chas*, 29 January 2004, 3.

141. Author's interview with a leading representative of OKROL, 6 July 2005.

142. Vadim Radionov, "Repshe: 'Vsekh za reshetku!'" *Chas*, 12 May 2004, 1–2.

143. Elina Chuianova, "O Latviia, pechalen tvoi udel!" *Chas*, 12 February 2004, 2.

144. "V piketakh—i star i mlad," *Chas*, 16 April 2004, 1.

145. Igor' Vatolin, "Protesty naractaiut—pravitel'stvu khot' by khny," *Chas*, 16 April 2004, 4.

146. Because its sole purpose was to organize protests against education policy, Headquarters became obsolete once the policy went into effect.

147. "My ne raby!" *Chas*, 26 January 2004, 1–2.

148. Pliner is quoted in Igor' Vatolin, "Nas obmanuli: Vperedi—'pustye shkoly,'" *Chas*, 23 January 2004, 2.

149. "Pervyi den' evropy," *Chas*, 3 May 2004, 1.

150. Elina Chuianova, "Daugava razdelila obshchestvo," *Chas*, 3 May 2004, 2.

151. Kira Savchenko, "Strasbur uznal nashikh," *Chas*, 22 July 2004, 1.

152. Viacheslav Ivanov, "Pochemu my reshili golodat'," *Chas*, 23 August 2004, 2; Viacheslav Ivanov, "Golodaite—vlastiam vse ravno," *Chas*, 14 September 2004, 1.

153. Chuianova, "Vmeste my budem sil'nee," *Chas*, 2 September 2004, 2.

154. Author's interview with a representative of the Party of National Harmony, 11 July 2005.

155. Author's interview with an OKROL activist who participated in the hunger strike, 30 June 2005.

156. V. Vishnevskii, "Vybrannyi mekhanizm golosovaniia—neuvazhenie k narody," *Res Publica*, 2 November 1998, 2.

157. Author's interview with a representative of the Slavic Foundation, 21 October 1999.

158. Author's interview with a representative of the Slavic Foundation, 25 July 2005.

159. Author's interview with a representative of the Slavic Foundation, 21 December 1999.

160. The assembly's presidium consists of representatives from sixty institutions including the Association of the Georgians, the Association of the Jews, the Fund to Support Small and Medium Businesses Under the President, and the Center of Economic and Social Reform Under the Ministry of Finance. For a list of organizations represented in the assembly's presidium, see *Spisok chlenov soveta Assamblei Naroda Kyrgyzstana*, 27 October 1998.

161. Author's interview with a representative of the Slavic Foundation, 21 December 1999.

162. See the university's Web site for more information: http://www .krsu.edu.kg/Rus/Hi.htm.

163. Author's interview with the chairman of the Union of Russian Compatriots, 25 July 2005.

164. Slashcheva, "Velika Rossia, da otstupat' nekuda."

165. Author's interview with a representative of the Union of Russian Compatriots, 25 July 2005.

166. *Ustav respublikanskoi assotsiatsii Etnicheskikh Rossiian Kyrgyzskoi Respubliki "Soglasie"* (Bishkek, 1994), section 2.2.

167. Author's interview with a former vice president of the Union of Russian Compatriots, 2 December 1999.

168. Kathryn H. Anderson and Stephen P. Heyneman, "Education and Social Policy in Central Asia: The Next Stage of Transition," *Social Policy and Administration* 39, 4 (August 2005): 368.

169. Ibid., 375.

170. Petrov, "Russkie uezzhaiut."

171. The Public Association of Russians was founded in 2003, and the Harmony Russian Cultural Center was founded in 2005.

172. Author's interview with a representative of the Public Association of Russians, 21 July 2005.

173. Ibid.

174. Author's interview with the president of the Russian Cultural Center, 8 July 2005.

Chapter 7

1. Esman, *Ethnic Politics*, 229–30.

2. Kolsto, *Nation-Building and Ethnic Integration in Post-Soviet Societies*, 6.

3. Ibid., 42. And even though he identifies Kazakhstan and Latvia as bipolar states, Kolsto reminds us that in his view Kazakhstan is "strongly" bipolar and Latvia is "moderately" bipolar.

4. Brubaker, *Nationalism Reframed*.

5. See Smith, "When Nations Challenge and Nations Rule"; Graham Smith and Andrew Wilson, "Rethinking Russia's Post-Soviet Diaspora: The Potential for Political Mobilization in Eastern Ukraine and North-east Estonia," *Europe-Asia Studies* 49, 5 (1997): 845–64; Pal Kolsto and Boris Tsilevich, "Patterns of Nation Building and Political Integration in a Bifurcated State: Ethnic Aspects of Parliamentary Elections in Latvia," *East European Politics and Societies* 11, 2 (Spring 1997): 366–91; Anton Steen, "Ethnic Relations, Elites and Democracy in the Baltic States," *Journal of Communist Studies and Transition Politics* 16, 4 (December 2000): 68–87; Smith et al., *The Baltic States*; and Sammy Smooha, "The Model of Ethnic Democracy: Israel as a Jewish and Democratic State," *Nations and Nationalism* 8, 4 (2002): 475–503.

6. Sammy Smooha, "Minority Status in an Ethnic Democracy: The Status of the Arab Minority in Israel," *Ethnic and Racial Studies* 13, 3 (July 1990): 391.

7. Sammy Smooha, "Types of Democracy and Modes of Conflict Management in Ethnically Divided Societies," *Nations and Nationalism* 8, 4 (2002): 428.

8. See Aadne Aasland, "The Russian Population in Latvia: An Integrated Minority?" *Journal of Communist Studies and Transition Politics* 10, 2 (June 1994):

233–60; Laitin, *Identity in Formation*; Kolsto, *Nation-Building and Ethnic Integration in Post-Soviet Societies*.

9. Arend Lijphart, *Democracy in Plural Societies: A Comparative Exploration* (New Haven, Conn.: Yale University Press, 1977), 25.

10. Ian Lustick, "Stability in Deeply Divided Societies: Consociationalism versus Control," *World Politics* 31, 3 (April 1979): 327–28.

11. Ibid.

12. Michele E. Commercio, "Systems of Partial Control: Ethnic Dynamics in Post-Soviet Estonia and Latvia," *Studies in Comparative International Development* 43, 1 (January 2008): 81–100.

13. Uzbeks are also a sizable minority: they accounted for 12.9 percent of Kyrgyzstan's population in 1989 and 13.8 percent in 1999. *Osnovnye itogi Pervoi natsional'noi perepisi naseleniia Kyrgyskoi Respubliki*, 26.

14. Author's interview, 12 January 2000.

15. Cyril Lin, "Private Sector Development in the Kyrgyz Republic: Issues and Options," report prepared for the Asian Development Bank (21 January 2007), 15, accessed on 4 November 2008 via the Asian Development Bank Web site, http://www.adb.org/.

16. Mogilevsky and Hasanov, "Economic Growth in Kyrgyzstan," 243.

17. Spechler, "The Economies of Central Asia: A Survey," 36.

18. For a detailed discussion of the Estonian ethnic system, which is also characterized by partial control, see Commercio, "Systems of Partial Control."

19. In 1993 Latvia's Way garnered 32 percent of the vote and acquired 36 of 100 seats.

20. Miroslavs Mitrofanovs, Aleksandrs Gamelejevs, Viktors Buzajevs, Aleksejs Dimitrovs, and Tatjana Zdanoka, eds., *The Last Prisoners of the Cold War: The Stateless People of Latvia in Their Own Words* (Riga: Avert-R Ltd., 2006), 3.

21. Steen, "Ethnic Relations, Elites and Democracy in the Baltic States," 74.

22. Kolsto, *Political Construction Sites*, 114.

23. Steen, "Ethnic Relations, Elites and Democracy in the Baltic States," 74.

24. Respondents were asked, "Which of the following best describes your employer? Is it: state budgetary organization, state-owned enterprise, privatized enterprise, mixed state-private, new private enterprise, foreign-owned enterprise/joint venture, or other?" See Rose, "New Baltic Barometer VI," 39.

25. See Michele E. Commercio, "Exiles in the Near Abroad: The Russian Minorities in Latvia and Kyrgyzstan," *Problems of Post-Communism* 51, 6 (November/December 2004): 23–32; Zevelev, *Russia and Its New Diasporas*; and Smith, "When Nations Challenge and Nations Rule."

26. These individuals were either self-employed or worked for privatized firms, new private enterprises, or foreign-owned firms. See Rose, "New Baltic Barometer IV," 5.

27. The 2004 survey categories changed slightly. Here the private sector refers to a privatized enterprise, a private enterprise that was established after 1990, or a foreign-owned enterprise. See Rose, "New Baltic Barometer VI," 39.

28. Smith et al., *The Baltic States*.

29. *Statistical Yearbook of Latvia 2004*, 14, 52.

30. Morris, "The Non-citizens of the EU," 255.

31. *Society Integration and Business*, 83.

32. Pabriks, *Occupational Representation and Ethnic Discrimination in Latvia*, 42–43.

33. Smooha, "The Model of Ethnic Democracy," 478.

34. Ian Bremmer, "Nazarbaev and the North: State-building and Ethnic Relations in Kazakhstan," *Ethnic and Racial Studies* 17, 4 (October 1994): 621.

35. Elena Brusilovskaia, "Poligon dlia demokratii," *Argumenti i Fakti*, no. 4 (January 2000): 3.

36. Kolsto, *Political Construction Sites*, 131.

37. Natsuko Oka, "Nationalities Policy in Kazakhstan: Interviewing Political and Cultural Elites," in *The Nationalities Question in Post-Soviet Kazakhstan* (Chiba: Institute of Developing Economies, 2002), 112.

38. "Problemy pereselentsev—problemy gosudarstva," *Kazakhstanskaia Pravda*, 27 May 1998, 1. Approximately one-third of the world's Kazakhs reside beyond Kazakhstan's borders. Altynshash Dzhaganovu, chairman of the Agency for Migration and Demography, interview in *Kazakhstanskaia Pravda*, 16 January 2003, 3.

39. Approximately five hundred thousand Kazakhs abandoned their homeland in response to the 1916 uprising, Bolshevik revolution, civil war, widespread famine, forced collectivization, and de-nomadization. Anatoly M. Khazanov, "Ethnic Problems of Contemporary Kazakhstan," *Central Asian Survey* 14, 2 (1995): 246.

40. In 1993 the quota was 10,000 families, in 1994 it was 7,000 families, in 1995 it was 5,000 families, in 1996 it was 4,000 families, in 1997 it was 2,180 families, and in 1998 it was 3,000 families. The 1993–96 figures are from Erlan Karin and Andrei Chebatarev, "The Policy of Kazakhization in State and Government Institutions in Kazakhstan," in *The Nationalities Question in Post-Soviet Kazakhstan* (Chiba: Institute of Developing Economies, 2002), 95. The 1997 and 1998 figures are from presidential decrees issued in 1997 and 1998, respectively. *Ukaz prezidenta Respubliki Kazakhstan o kvote immigratsii na 1997 god* (27 March 1997), and *Ukaz prezidenta Respubliki Kazakhstan o kvote immigratsii na 1998 god* (3 April 1997).

41. Elena Iur'evna Sadovskaia, "Vneshniaia migratsiia v Respublike Kazakhstan v 1990-e gody: Prichiny, posledstviia, prognoz," *Tsentral'naia Aziia iKul'tura Mira*, no. 1 (1998): 57.

42. *Postonovlenie kabineta ministrov Respubliki Kazakhstan o merakh po realizatsii postonovleniia Verkhovhogo Soveta Respubliki Kazakhstan "o vvedenii v deistvie zakona Respubliki Kazakhstan 'ob immigratsii'"* (15 December 1992), *Polozhenie o departmente po migratsii naseleniia*, point 4.

43. *Postonovlenie kabineta ministrov Respubliki Kazakhstan ob utverzhdenii poriadka sozdaniia immigratsionnogo zemel'nogo fonda* (2 August 1994), point 2.

44. *Ukaz prezidenta Respubliki Kazakhstan ob osnovnykh napravleniiakh migratsionnoi politiki do 2000 goda* (19 March 1997).

45. *Zakon Respubliki Kazakhstan o migratsii naseleniia* (13 December 1997), Article 29.

46. Despite generous state assistance, returning Kazakhs confront numerous problems. Many are unable to secure homes or jobs because they do not speak Russian or Kazakh: in 1998, 4,700 families who had returned to Kazakhstan lacked housing, and 54 percent of the migrants that year were unable to find a job. Zautbek Turisbekov, chairman of the Agency for Migration and Demography, interview in *Argumenty i Fakty*, no. 46 (November 1998): 3. In addition, many *oralmans* lack Kazakh citizenship even though the law on citizenship grants them the right to obtain Kazakh citizenship. The process required for migrant Kazakhs to obtain citizenship is complex: time and language skills are necessary to process the eighteen required documents. Often migrant Kazakhs give up

prior citizenship because many countries, such as Mongolia, do not permit dual citizenship; they come to Kazakhstan without citizenship and reside there without citizenship for at least two years. These migrants have trouble finding work and are denied unemployment benefits because they are not citizens. Some migrants from Mongolia are then forced to return to their country of origin. Dzhganova interview. For more on the situation of *oralmans*, see Tulegen Izdibaev, "Zakon o migratsii v Kazakhstane fakticheski ne ispolnizetsia," *Panorama*, 24 December 1999, 4; and Antynshash Dzhaganova, "Vernost' otchei zemle," *Kazakhstanskaia Pravda*, 23 October 1999, 2.

47. These are registered *oralmans*. The total number of *oralmans* is higher but unknown. Martha Brill Olcott, *Kazakhstan: Unfulfilled Promise* (Washington, D.C.: Carnegie Endowment for International Peace, 2002), 176. One source claims that between 1991 and 1997 about 38,000 Kazakh families, or 164,000 Kazakhs, returned to Kazakhstan. "Problemy preselentsev—problemy gosudarstva."

48. The 2004 quota was ten thousand families, and the 2005 quota was fifteen thousand families. Meiram Baigazin, "Migratsionnaia situatsiia v Kazakhstane," *Tsentral'naia Aziia i Kavkaz* 5, 35 (2004): 195–96.

49. Nurbulat Masanov, "Perceptions of Ethnic and All-National Identity in Kazakhstan," in *The Nationalities Question in Post-Soviet Kazakhstan* (Chiba: Institute of Developing Economies, 2002), 56.

50. Taras Kuzio, "History, Memory and Nation-Building in the Post-Soviet Colonial Space," *Nationalities Papers* 30, 2 (2002): 258.

51. Masanov, "Perceptions of Ethnic and All-National Identity in Kazakhstan," 56.

52. See Ian Bremmer and Cory Welt, "Kazakhstan's Quandary," *Journal of Democracy* 6, 3 (July 1995): 139–54; Michele E. Commercio, "The 'Pugachev Rebellion' in the Context of Post-Soviet Nationalization," *Nationalities Papers* 32, 1 (March 2004): 87–113; and Schatz, *Modern Clan Politics*.

53. Kuzio, "History, Memory and Nation Building in the Post-Soviet Colonial Space," 258.

54. Henry R. Huttenbach, "Whither Kazakhstan? Changing Capitals: From Almaty to Aqmola/Astana," *Nationalities Papers* 26, 3 (1998): 584.

55. Richard L. Wolfel, "North to Astana: Nationalistic Motives for the Movement of the Kazakh(stani) Capital," *Nationalities Papers* 30, 3 (2002): 497–98.

56. Edward Schatz, "What Capital Cities Say About State and Nation Building," *Nationalism and Ethnic Politics* 9 (2004): 129.

57. Ibid., 122–23.

58. Edward Schatz, "Framing Strategies and Non-Conflict in Multi-Ethnic Kazakhstan," *Nationalism and Ethnic Politics* 6, 2 (Summer 2000): 79.

59. Sally N. Cummings, "Legitimation and Identification in Kazakhstan," *Nationalism and Ethnic Politics* 12 (2006): 184.

60. Ibid.

61. Dave, *Kazakhstan: Ethnicity, Language, and Power*, 101.

62. I. Erofeeva, "Regional'nyi aspekt slavianskoi migratsii iz Kazakhstana," in A. R. Viatkina, N. P. Kosmarskoi, and C. A. Panarina, eds., *V dvizhenii dobrovol'nom i vynuzhdennom* (Moscow: Natalis Press, 1999), 173.

63. Author's interview, 20 August 2000.

64. Author's interview, 7 July 2000.

65. Author's interview with a leading representative of Lad, 2 August 2005.

66. Ia. P. Belousov, "Russkie v Kazakhstane: Problemy i perspectivy," in V. D.

Kurganskaya, ed., *Problemy sotsial'noi stabil'nosti v polietnicheskom obshchestve* (Almaty: Center for Liberal Arts Research, 2001), 203.

67. The press referred to the alleged coup attempt as the "Pugachev Rebellion" because the leader of the Ust'-Kamenogorsk group calls himself Pugachev. For more on the incident, see Commercio, "The 'Pugachev Rebellion' in the Context of Post-Soviet Kazakh Nationalization."

68. Robert Kaiser and Jeff Chinn, "Russian-Kazakh Relations in Kazakhstan," *Post-Soviet Geography* 36, 5 (1996): 267.

69. *Kazakhstan v tsifrakh 2004* (Almaty: Agentstvo Respubliki Kazakhstan po statistike, 2004), 117.

70. Ibid., 54.

71. *Kratkii statisticheskii ezhegodnik Kazakhstana 2004* (Almaty: Agentstvo Respubliki Kazakhstan po statistike, 2004), 15.

72. Spechler, "The Economics of Central Asia: A Survey," 33.

73. World Bank Data accessed on 13 March 2009: http://web.worldbank.-org/WBSITE/EXTERNAL/COUNTRIES/ECAEXT/EXTECAR EGTOPPRV SECDE V/0,,contentMDK:20508461~pagePK:34004173~piPK:34003707~theS itePK:570955, 00.html.

74. Spechler, "The Economies of Central Asia: A Survey," 33.

75. *Kazakhstan v tsifrakh 2004*, 155.

76. For a cautious interpretation of the applicability of Dutch Disease arguments to Kazakhstan, see Yelena Kalyuzhnova, James Pemberton, and Bulat Mukhamediyev, "Natural Resources and Economic Growth in Kazakhstan," in Gur Ofer and Richard Pomfret, eds., *The Economic Prospects of the CIS: Sources of Long Term Growth* (Cheltenham, UK: Edward Elgar Publishing Limited, 2004), 249–67.

77. Valentina Dmitrievna Kurganskaia, *Pravosoznanie etnicheskikh grupp Kazakhstana: Sotsiokul'turnyi kontekst formirovaniia* (Almaty: Tsentr gumanitarnykh issledovanii, 2004), 166.

78. Olcott, *The Kazakhs*, 243.

79. Ibid., 244.

80. N. Loginova, "Sotsial'no-psikhologicheskaia adaptatsiia Russkikh v suverennom Kazakhstane," *Mysl'*, no. 7 (1995): 40.

81. Olcott, *Kazakhstan*, 174.

82. *Kazakhstan v tsifrakh 2004*, 31.

83. Author's interview with a representative of Lad, 2 August 2005; author's interview with a representative of Russian Society, 3 August 2005.

84. Author's interview with the founder of Kazakhstan's Russian Party, 2 August 2005. The Russian Party survived for less than a year. Shortly after it was registered in April 2002, the government passed a law on political parties forbidding the creation of parties on the basis of "professional, racial, national, ethnic, and religious affiliation" and establishing new registration guidelines. A party must have no less than fifty thousand members, branches in all oblasts as well as Almaty and Astana, and no less than seven hundred members in each branch. See *Zakon Respubliki Kazakhstan o politicheskuk partiiax* (15 July 2002), Articles 5, 10. According to its founder, the Russian Party met these requirements and tried to re-register under a new name (the Party of Compatriots), but the authorities refused to register the party.

85. Author's interview with a former president of Kazakhstan's Political Science Association, 1 August 2005.

86. Author's interview, 20 April 2000.

87. Schatz, *Modern Clan Politics*, 91.
88. Author's interview, 23 May 2000.
89. Author's interview, 30 May 2000.
90. The European Bank for Reconstruction and Development 2005 report on the Kyrgyz Republic is posted on http://www.ebrd.com/.
91. Pilkington, *Migration, Displacement and Identity in Post-Soviet Russia*, 144–45.
92. Ibid., 5.
93. Russia's first citizenship law, passed in 1992 and amended in 1995, was liberal: anyone who held USSR citizenship on 6 February 1992 and was a resident of any former republic prior to that date could obtain Russian citizenship if they applied by February 1995 and had not taken citizenship of another country. Various amendments extended this deadline. The 2002 legislation included new requirements that apply to migrants from former Soviet republics such as a five-year residency period, a job, and proficiency in Russian. The 2003 policy abrogated certain restrictions for migrants from former republics who were officially registered in Russia, while the 2006 policy permits these individuals to obtain Russian citizenship without meeting the requirements mentioned above.
94. For a comprehensive summary of these approaches to nationalism, see John Breuilly, *Nationalism and the State* (Manchester: Manchester University Press, 1982), 18–35.
95. Ibid., 1–2.
96. Alexander J. Motyl, "The Modernity of Nationalism: Nations, States and Nation-States in the Contemporary World," *Journal of International Affairs* 45, 2 (Winter 1992): 313.

Bibliography

English-Language Sources

Aasland, Aadne. 1994. "The Russian Population in Latvia: An Integrated Minority?" *Journal of Communist Studies and Transition Politics* 10, 2 (June): 233–60.
———. 2002. "Citizenship Status and Social Exclusion." *Journal of Baltic Studies* 33, 1 (Spring): 57–77.
Akiner, Shirin. 1998. "Social and Political Reorganization in Central Asia: Transition from Pre-Colonial to Post-Colonial Society." In Touraj Atabaki and John O'Kane, eds., *Post-Soviet Central Asia*. New York: St. Martin's Press, 1–34.
Allison, Roy, and Lena Jonson, eds. 2001. *Central Asian Security: The New International Context*. London: Royal Institute of International Affairs.
Allworth, Edward, ed. 1994. *Central Asia: 130 Years of Russian Dominance, A Historical Overview*. Durham, N.C.: Duke University Press.
Aminzade, Ronald, et al. 2001. *Silence and Voice in the Study of Contentious Politics*. Cambridge: Cambridge University Press.
Aminzade, Ron, and Doug McAdam. 2001. "Emotions and Contentious Politics." In Ronald R. Aminzade, Jack A. Goldstone, Doug McAdam, Elizabeth J. Perry, William H. Sewell, Jr., Sidney Tarrow, and Charles Tilly, eds., *Silence and Voice in the Study of Contentious Politics*. Cambridge: Cambridge University Press, 14–50.
Anderson, John. 1999. *Kyrgyzstan: Central Asia's Island of Democracy?* Amsterdam: Harwood Academic Publishers.
Anderson, Kathryn H., and Stephen P. Heyneman. 2005. "Education and Social Policy in Central Asia: The Next Stage of Transition." *Social Policy and Administration* 39, 4 (August): 361–80.
Antane, Aina, and Boris Tsilevich. 1999. "Nation-Building and Ethnic Integration in Latvia." In Pal Kolsto, ed., *Nation-Building and Ethnic Integration in Post-Soviet Societies: An Investigation of Latvia and Kazakstan*. Boulder, Colo.: Westview Press, 63–152.
Beissinger, Mark R. 2002. *Nationalist Mobilization and the Collapse of the Soviet State*. Cambridge: Cambridge University Press.
Braden, Kathleen. 1995. "Kyrgyzstan." In Philip R. Pryde, ed., *Environmental Resources and Constraints in the Former Soviet Republics*. Boulder, Colo.: Westview Press, 307–23.
Bremmer, Ian. 1994. "Nazarbaev and the North: State-building and Ethnic Relations in Kazakhstan." *Ethnic and Racial Studies* 17, 4 (October): 619–35.
Bremmer, Ian, and Cory Welt. 1995. "Kazakhstan's Quandary." *Journal of Democracy* 6, 3 (July): 139–54.

Breuilly, John. 1982. *Nationalism and the State.* Manchester: Manchester University Press.

Brubaker, Rogers. 1996. *Nationalism Reframed: Nationhood and the National Question in the New Europe.* Cambridge: Cambridge University Press.

Bunce, Valerie. 1999. *Subversive Institutions: The Design and the Destruction of Socialism and the State.* Cambridge: Cambridge University Press.

Burg, Steven L. 1984. "Central Asian Political Participation and Soviet Political Development." In Yaacov Ro'i, ed., *The USSR and the Muslim World: Issues in Domestic and Foreign Policy.* London: George Allen and Unwin, 40–62.

Buzayev, V., G. Kotov, and L. Raihman. 1999. *Comment on the List of Differences Between the Rights of Latvian Citizens and Non-Citizens.* Riga: Latvian Human Rights Committee.

Chinn, Jeff, and Robert Kaiser. 1996. *Russians as the New Minority.* Boulder, Colo.: Westview Press.

Clemens, Walter C. Jr. 1991. *Baltic Independence and Russian Empire.* New York: St. Martin's Press.

Collins, Kathleen. 2002. "Clans, Pacts, and Politics in Central Asia." *Journal of Democracy* 13, 3 (July): 137–52.

———. 2003. "The Political Role of Clans in Central Asia." *Comparative Politics* 35, 2 (January): 171–90.

Commercio, Michele E. 2004. "Exiles in the Near Abroad: The Russian Minorities in Latvia and Kyrgyzstan." *Problems of Post-Communism* 51, 6 (November/December): 23–32.

———. 2004. "The 'Pugachev Rebellion' in the Context of Post-Soviet Nationalization." *Nationalities Papers* 32, 1 (March): 87–113.

———. 2008. "Systems of Partial Control: Ethnic Dynamics in Post-Soviet Estonia and Latvia." *Studies in Comparative International Development* 43, 1 (January): 81–100.

Connor, Walker. 1972. "Nation-Building or Nation-Destroying." *World Politics* 24 (April): 319–55.

———. 1992. "Soviet Policies Toward the Non-Russian Peoples in Theoretic and Historic Perspective: What Gorbachev Inherited." In Alexander J. Motyl, ed., *The Post-Soviet Nations: Perspectives on the Demise of the USSR.* New York: Columbia University Press, 30–49.

———. 1994. *Ethnonationalism: The Quest for Understanding.* Princeton, N.J.: Princeton University Press.

Crawford, Beverly, and Arend Lijphart, eds. 1997. *Liberalization and Leninist Legacies: Comparative Perspectives on Democratic Transitions.* Berkeley: University of California Press.

Cummings, Sally N. 2006. "Legitimation and Identification in Kazakhstan." *Nationalism and Ethnic Politics* 12: 177–204.

Dahl, Robert A. 1989. *Democracy and Its Critics.* New Haven, Conn.: Yale University Press.

Dave, Bhavna. 2007. *Kazakhstan: Ethnicity, Language, and Power.* London: Routledge.

Dawisha, Karen, and Bruce Parrott. 1994. *Russia and the New States of Eurasia.* Cambridge: Cambridge University Press.

Demographic Statistics in the Baltic Countries. 1996. Tallin, Riga, Vilnius: Statistical Office of Estonia, Central Statistical Bureau of Latvia, Lithuanian Department of Statistics.

Demographic Yearbook of Latvia. 2000. Riga: Central Statistical Bureau of Latvia.

Deutsch, Karl W. 1953. *Nationalism and Social Communication: An Inquiry into the Foundations of Nationality.* Cambridge, Mass.: MIT Press.

Dreifelds, Juris. 1995. "Latvia." In Philip R. Pryde, ed., *Environmental Resources and Constraints in the Former Soviet Republics.* Boulder, Colo.: Westview Press, 109–23.

——. 1996. *Latvia in Transition.* Cambridge: Cambridge University Press.

Ekiert, Grzegorz, and Stephen E. Hanson. 2003. *Capitalism and Democracy in Central and Eastern Europe: Assessing the Legacy of Communist Rule.* Cambridge: Cambridge University Press.

——. 2003. "Time, Space, and Institutional Change in Central and Eastern Europe." In Grzegorz Ekiert and Stephen E. Hanson, eds., *Capitalism and Democracy in Central and Eastern Europe: Assessing the Legacy of Communist Rule.* Cambridge: Cambridge University Press, 15–48.

Ekiert, Grzegorz, and Jan Kubik. 1999. *Rebellious Civil Society.* Ann Arbor: University of Michigan Press.

Enhancing the Prospects for Growth and Trade of the Kyrgyz Republic. 2005. Washington, D.C.: World Bank.

Ericson, Richard E. 1992. "Soviet Economic Structure and the National Question." In Alexander J. Motyl, ed., *The Post-Soviet Nations: Perspectives on the Demise of the USSR.* New York: Columbia University Press, 240–71.

Esman, Milton J. 1977. "Perspectives on Ethnic Conflict in Industrialized Societies." In Milton J. Esman, ed., *Ethnic Conflict in the Western World.* Ithaca, N.Y.: Cornell University Press.

——. 1994. *Ethnic Politics.* Ithaca, N.Y.: Cornell University Press.

Feldman, Gregory. 2003. "The European-ness of Estonia's Ethnic Integration Policy: Nation, Culture, and Security in an Applicant State." *Cambridge Review of International Affairs* 16, 2 (July): 223–38.

Fierman, William. 1991. "The Soviet 'Transformation' of Central Asia." In William Fierman, ed., *Soviet Central Asia: The Failed Transformation.* Boulder, Colo.: Westview Press, 11–35.

Fleming, Judith. 1977. "Political Leaders." In Edward Allworth, ed., *Nationality Group Survival in Multi-Ethnic States: Shifting Support Patterns in the Soviet Baltic Region.* New York: Praeger, 123–47.

Friedrich, Carl J. 1963. "Nation-Building?" In Karl W. Deutsch and William J. Foltz, eds., *Nation-Building.* New York: Atherton Press, 27–32.

Gamson, William A. 1992. *Talking Politics.* Cambridge: Cambridge University Press.

Ginkel, John. 2002. "Identity Construction in Latvia's 'Singing Revolution': Why Inter-Ethnic Conflict Failed to Occur." *Nationalities Papers* 30, 3: 403–33.

Gitelman, Zvi. 1992. "Development and Ethnicity in the Soviet Union." In Alexander J. Motyl, ed., *The Post-Soviet Nations: Perspectives on the Demise of the USSR.* New York: Columbia University Press, 220–39.

Haghayeghi, Mehrdad. 1995. *Islam and Politics in Central Asia.* New York: St. Martin's Press.

Hallik, Klara. 2002. "Nationalising Policies and Integration Challenges." In Marju Lauristin and Mati Heidmets, eds., *The Challenge of the Russian Minority: Emerging Multicultural Democracy in Estonia.* Tartu: Tartu University Press, 65–88.

Hanson, Stephen E. 1995. "The Leninist Legacy and Institutional Change." *Comparative Political Studies* 28, 2: 306–14.

Hazard, John N. 1992. "Managing Nationalism: State, Law and the National

Question in the USSR." In Alexander J. Motyl, ed., *Thinking Theoretically About Soviet Nationalities*. New York: Columbia University Press, 96–140.

Helmke, Gretchen, and Steven Levitsky. 2004. "Informal Institutions and Comparative Politics: A Research Agenda." *Perspectives on Politics* 2, 4 (December): 725–40.

———, eds. 2006. *Informal Institutions and Democracy*. Baltimore: Johns Hopkins University Press.

Hirsch, Francine. 2000. "Toward an Empire of Nations: Border-Making and the Formation of Soviet National Identities." *Russian Review* 59 (April): 201–26.

———. 2005. *Empire of Nations: Ethnographic Knowledge and the Making of the Soviet Union*. Ithaca, N.Y.: Cornell University Press.

Hirschman, Albert O. 1970. *Exit, Voice, and Loyalty: Responses to Decline in Firms, Organizations, and States*. Cambridge, Mass.: Harvard University Press.

Howard, Marc Morje. 2003. *The Weakness of Civil Society in Post-Communist Europe*. Cambridge: Cambridge University Press.

Hughes, James. 2005. "'Exit' in Deeply Divided Societies: Regimes of Discrimination in Estonia and Latvia and the Potential for Russophone Migration." *Journal of Common Market Studies* 43, 4: 739–62.

Human Development Report 2000. 2000. New York: United Nations Development Programme.

Human Development Report 2005. 2005. New York: United Nations Development Programme.

Huskey, Eugene. 1993. "Kyrgyzstan: The Politics of Demographic and Economic Frustration." In Ian Bremmer and Ray Taras, eds., *Nations and Politics in the Soviet Successor States*. Cambridge: Cambridge University Press, 398–418.

Huttenbach, Henry R. 1998. "Whither Kazakhstan? Changing Capitals: From Almaty to Aqmola/Astana." *Nationalities Papers* 26, 3: 581–87.

Irwin, John. 1972. "Participant Observation of Criminals." In Jack Douglas, ed., *Research on Deviance*. New York: Random House, 117–37.

Jowitt, Ken. 1992. "New World Order: The Leninist Extinction." Berkeley: University of California Press.

Jubulis, Mark A. 2001. *Nationalism and Democratic Transition: The Politics of Citizenship and Language in Post-Soviet Latvia*. Lanham, Md.: University Press of America.

Kaiser, Robert J. 1992. "Social Mobilization in Soviet Central Asia." In Robert A. Lewis, ed., *Geographic Perspectives on Soviet Central Asia*. London: Routledge, 251–78.

———. 1994. "Ethnic Demography and Interstate Relations in Central Asia." In Roman Szporluk, ed., *National Identity and Ethnicity in Russia and the New States of Eurasia*. Armonk, N.Y.: M. E. Sharpe, 230–65.

———. 1994. *The Geography of Nationalism in Russia and the USSR*. Princeton, N.J.: Princeton University Press.

———. 1995. "Nationalizing the Work Force: Ethnic Restratification in the Newly Independent States." *Post-Soviet Geography* 36, 2: 87–111.

Kaiser, Robert, and Jeff Chinn. 1996. "Russian-Kazakh Relations in Kazakhstan." *Post-Soviet Geography* 36, 5: 257–73.

Kalyuzhnova, Yelena, James Pemberton, and Bulat Mukhamediyev. 2004. "Natural Resources and Economic Growth in Kazakhstan." In Gur Ofer and Richard Pomfret, eds., *The Economic Prospects of the CIS: Sources of Long Term Growth*. Cheltenham, UK: Edward Elgar Publishing Limited, 249–67.

Kamp, Marianne. 2006. *The New Woman in Uzbekistan: Islam, Modernity, and Unveiling Under Communism*. Seattle: University of Washington Press.

Karin, Erlan, and Andrei Chebatarev. 2002. "The Policy of Kazakhization in State and Government Institutions in Kazakhstan." In *The Nationalities Question in Post-Soviet Kazakhstan*. Chiba: Institute of Developing Economies, 69–108.

Karklins, Rasma. 1986. *Ethnic Relations in the USSR: The Perspective from Below*. Winchester: Allen and Unwin.

———. 1994. *Ethnopolitics and Transition to Democracy: The Collapse of the USSR and Latvia*. Washington, D.C.: Woodrow Wilson Center Press.

Katznelson, Ira, and Barry R. Weingast, eds. 2005. *Preferences and Situations: Points of Intersection Between Historical and Rational Choice Institutionalism*. New York: Russell Sage Foundation.

Khalid, Adeeb. 2007. *Islam after Communism: Religion and Politics in Central Asia*. Berkeley: University of California Press.

Khazanov, Anatoly M. 1994. "Underdevelopment and Ethnic Relations in Central Asia." In Beatrice F. Manz, ed., *Central Asia in Historical Perspective*. Boulder, Colo.: Westview Press, 144–63.

———. 1995. *After the USSR: Ethnicity, Nationalism, and Politics in the Commonwealth of Independent States*. Madison: University of Wisconsin Press.

———. 1995. "Ethnic Problems of Contemporary Kazakhstan." *Central Asian Survey* 14, 2: 243–64.

King, Charles. 1997. *Post-Soviet Moldova: A Borderland in Transition*. Iasi: Center for Romanian Studies.

———. 2000. *The Moldovans: Romania, Russia, and the Politics of Culture*. Stanford, Calif.: Hoover Institution Press.

King, Gary, Robert O. Keohane, and Sidney Verba. 1994. *Designing Social Inquiry: Scientific Inference in Qualitative Research*. Princeton, N.J.: Princeton University Press.

Knight, Jack. 1992. *Institutions and Social Conflict*. Cambridge: Cambridge University Press.

Kolsto, Pal, ed. 1999. *Nation-Building and Ethnic Integration in Post-Soviet Societies: An Investigation of Latvia and Kazakhstan*. Boulder, Colo.: Westview Press.

———. 2000. *Political Construction Sites: Nation-Building in Russia and the Post-Soviet States*. Boulder, Colo.: Westview Press.

Kolsto, Pal, and Andrei Malgin. 1998. "The Transnistrian Republic: A Case of Politicized Regionalism." *Nationalities Papers* 26, 1: 103–27.

Kolsto, Pal, and Boris Tsilevich. 1997. "Patterns of Nation Building and Political Integration in a Bifurcated State: Ethnic Aspects of Parliamentary Elections in Latvia." *East European Politics and Societies* 11, 2 (Spring): 366–91.

Kolstoe, Paul. 1995. *Russians in the Former Soviet Republics*. Bloomington: Indiana University Press.

Kuzio, Taras. 2002. "History, Memory and Nation Building in the Post-Soviet Colonial Space." *Nationalities Papers* 30, 2: 241–64.

Kyrgyzstan: After the Revolution. 2005. Asia Report No. 97. International Crisis Group. 4 May. 1–22.

Laitin, David. 1998. *Identity in Formation: The Russian-Speaking Populations in the Near Abroad*. Ithaca, N.Y.: Cornell University Press.

Lapidus, Gail Warshofsky. 1984. "Ethnonationalism and Political Stability: The Soviet Case." *World Politics* 36, 4 (July): 555–80.

Ledeneva, Alena V. 1998. *Russia's Economy of Favours: Blat, Networking and Informal Exchange*. Cambridge: Cambridge University Press.

Levita, Roman, and Mikhail Loiberg. 1994. "The Empire and the Russians." In

Vladimir Shlapentokh, Munir Sendich, and Emil Payin, eds., *The New Russian Diaspora: Russian Minorities in the Former Soviet Republics.* Armonk, N.Y.: M. E. Sharpe, 3–20.

Lewin, Moshe. 1968. *Russian Peasants and Soviet Power: A Study of Collectivization.* Evanston, Ill.: Northwestern University Press.

Lewis, Robert A. 1971. "The Mixing of Russians and Soviet Nationalities and Its Demographic Impact." In Edward Allworth, ed., *Soviet Nationality Problems.* New York: Columbia University Press, 117–67.

Lieven, Anatol. 1993. *The Baltic Revolution: Estonia, Latvia, Lithuania and the Path to Independence.* New Haven, Conn.: Yale University Press.

Lijphart, Arend. 1977. *Democracy in Plural Societies: A Comparative Exploration.* New Haven, Conn.: Yale University Press.

Lin, Cyril. 2007. "Private Sector Development in the Kyrgyz Republic: Issues and Options." Report prepared for the Asian Development Bank (21 January 2007), 1–101. Accessed on 4 November 2008 via the Asian Development Bank Web site: http://www.adb.org.

Linz, Juan, and Alfred Stepan. 1996. *Problems of Democratic Transition and Consolidation: Southern Europe, South America, and Post-Communist Europe.* Baltimore: Johns Hopkins University Press.

Lubin, Nancy. 1984. *Labour and Nationality in Soviet Central Asia: An Uneasy Compromise.* Princeton, N.J.: Princeton University Press.

———. 1991. "Ethnic and Demographic Trends." In William Fierman, ed., *Soviet Central Asia: The Failed Transformation.* Boulder, Colo.: Westview Press, 36–61.

Luong, Pauline Jones. 2002. *Institutional Change and Political Continuity in Post-Soviet Central Asia.* Cambridge: Cambridge University Press.

Lustick, Ian. 1979. "Stability in Deeply Divided Societies: Consociationalism versus Control." *World Politics* 31, 3 (April): 325–44.

Manz, Beatrice F. 1994. "Historical Background." In Beatrice F. Manz, ed., *Central Asia in Historical Perspective.* Boulder, Colo.: Westview Press, 4–22.

Masanov, Nurbulat. 2002. "Perceptions of Ethnic and All-National Identity in Kazakhstan." In *The Nationalities Question in Post-Soviet Kazakhstan.* Chiba: Institute of Developing Economies, 1–68.

Massell, Gregory J. 1974. *The Surrogate Proletariat: Moslem Women and Revolutionary Strategies in Soviet Central Asia, 1919–1929.* Princeton, N.J.: Princeton University Press.

Matley, Ian Murray. 1994. "Industrialization." In Edward Allworth, ed., *Central Asia: 130 Years of Russian Dominance, A Historical Overview.* Durham, N.C.: Duke University Press, 309–48.

McDermott, Gerald A. 2002. *Embedded Politics: Industrial Networks and Institutional Change in Postcommunism.* Ann Arbor: University of Michigan Press.

McGarry, John, and Brendan O'Leary, eds. 1993. *The Politics of Ethnic Conflict Regulation: Case Studies of Protracted Ethnic Conflicts.* London: Routledge.

McGlinchey, Eric. 2005. "Autocrats, Islamists, and the Rise of Radicalism in Central Asia." *Current History* 104, 684 (October): 336–42.

Melvin, Neil. 1995. *Russians Beyond Russia: The Politics of National Identity.* London: Royal Institute of International Affairs.

Misiunas, Romuald J. 1990. "The Baltic Republics: Stagnation and Strivings for Sovereignty." In Lubomyr Hajda and Mark Beisisinger, eds., *The Nationalities Factor in Soviet Politics and Society.* Boulder, Colo.: Westview Press, 204–27.

Misiunas, Romuald J., and Rein Taagepera. 1983. *The Baltic States: Years of Dependence, 1940–1980.* Berkeley: University of California Press.

Mite, Valentinas. 2002. "Latvia: Russian Speakers Hold Their Own on the Business Front." *Radio Free Europe/Radio Liberty* 17 (May): 2.

Mitrofanovs, Miroslavs, Aleksandrs Gamelejevs, Viktors Buzajevs, Aleksejs Dimitrovs, and Tatjana Zdanoka, eds. 2006. *The Last Prisoners of the Cold War: The Stateless People of Latvia in Their Own Words.* Riga: Avert-R Ltd.

Mogilevsky, Roman, and Rafkat Hasanov. 2004. "Economic Growth in Kyrgyzstan." In Gur Ofer and Richard Pomfret, eds., *The Economic Prospects of the CIS: Sources of Long Term Growth.* Cheltenham, UK: Edward Elgar Publishing Limited, 224–48.

Morris, Helen M. 2005. "The Non-citizens of the EU." In David J. Smith, ed., *The Baltic States and Their Region: New Europe or Old?* Amsterdam: Rodopi, 251–73.

Motyl, Alexander J. 1992. "The Modernity of Nationalism: Nations, States and Nation-States in the Contemporary World." *Journal of International Affairs* 45, 2 (Winter): 307–23.

Muiznieks, Nils. 1993. "Latvia: Origins, Evolution, and Triumph." In Ian Bremmer and Ray Taras, eds., *Nations and Politics in the Soviet Successor States.* Cambridge: Cambridge University Press, 182–205.

———. 1994. "Latvia's Changing System of Ethnic Stratification." Paper presented at the conference "Democracy and Ethnopolitics." Riga, 9–11 March.

———. 1997. "Latvia: Restoring a State, Rebuilding a Nation." In Ian Bremmer and Ray Taras, eds., *New States, New Politics: Building the Post-Soviet Nation.* Cambridge: Cambridge University Press, 376–403.

Nissinen, Marja. 1999. *Latvia's Transition to a Market Economy: Political Determinants of Economic Reform Policy.* London: MacMillan Press.

North, Douglass C. 1990. *Institutions, Institutional Change, and Economic Performance.* New York: Cambridge University Press.

Northrop, Douglas. 2004. *Veiled Empire: Gender and Power in Stalinist Central Asia.* Ithaca, N.Y.: Cornell University Press.

Oka, Natsuko. 2002. "Nationalities Policy in Kazakhstan: Interviewing Political and Cultural Elites." In *The Nationalities Question in Post-Soviet Kazakhstan.* Chiba: Institute of Developing Economies, 109–57.

Olcott, Martha Brill. 1995. "Islam and Fundamentalism in Independent Central Asia." In Yaacov Ro'i, ed., *Muslim Eurasia: Conflicting Legacies.* London: Frank Cass and Company, 21–37.

———. 1990. "Central Asia: The Reformers Challenge a Traditional Society." In Lubomyr Hajda and Mark Beissinger, eds., *The Nationalities Factor in Soviet Politics and Society.* Boulder, Colo.: Westview Press, 253–80.

———. 1997. *The Kazakhs.* Stanford, Calif.: Hoover Institution Press.

———. 1997. "Kazakhstan: Pushing for Eurasia." In Ian Bremmer and Ray Taras, eds., *New States, New Politics: Building the Post-Soviet Nations.* Cambridge: Cambridge University Press, 547–70.

———. 2002. *Kazakhstan: Unfulfilled Promise.* Washington, D.C.: Carnegie Endowment for International Peace.

Pabriks, Artis. 2002. *Occupational Representation and Ethnic Discrimination in Latvia.* Riga: Soros Foundation.

Pabriks, Artis, and Aldis Purs. 2001. *Latvia: The Challenges of Change.* London: Routledge.

Park, Andrus. 1994. "Ethnicity and Independence: The Case of Estonia in Comparative Perspective. *Europe-Asia Studies* 46, 1: 69–87.

Pilkington, Hilary. 1998. *Migration, Displacement and Identity in Post-Soviet Russia.* London: Routledge.

Pipes, Richard. 1997. *The Formation of the Soviet Union.* Cambridge: Cambridge University Press.

Plakans, Andrejs. 1995. *The Latvians: A Short History.* Stanford, Calif.: Hoover Institution Press.

Poppe, Edwin, and Louk Hagendoorn. 2003. "Titular Identification of Russians in Former Soviet Republics." *Europe-Asia Studies* 55, 5: 771–87.

Przeworski, Adam, and Henry Teune. 1982. *The Logic of Comparative Social Inquiry.* Malabar: Krieger Publishing Company.

Rakowska-Harmstone, Teresa. 1974. "The Dialectics of Nationalism in the USSR." *Problems of Post-Communism* 23, 3 (May/June): 1–22.

———. 1986. "Minority Nationalism Today: An Overview." In Robert Conquest, ed., *The Last Empire: Nationality and the Soviet Future.* Stanford, Calif.: Hoover Institution Press, 235–64.

Referendum in the Soviet Union: A Compendium of Reports on the March 17, 1991 Referendum on the Future of the USSR. 1991. Washington, D.C.: Commission on Security and Cooperation in Europe.

Results of the 2000 Population and Housing Census in Latvia. 2002. Riga: Central Statistical Bureau of Latvia.

Roeder, Philip G. 1991. "Soviet Federalism and Ethnic Mobilization." *World Politics* 43 (January): 196–232.

Ro'i, Yaacov. 1995. "The Secularization of Islam and the USSR's Muslim Areas." In Yaacov Ro'i, ed., *Muslim Eurasia: Conflicting Legacies.* London: Frank Cass and Company, 5–16.

Rokkan, Stein. 1975. "Dimensions of State Formation and Nation-Building: A Possible Paradigm for Research on Variations Within Europe." In Charles Tilly, ed., *The Formation of National States in Western Europe.* Princeton, N.J.: Princeton University Press, 562–600.

Rose, Richard. 2000. "New Baltic Barometer IV: A Survey Study." *Studies in Public Policy* 338. Glasgow: University of Strathclyde.

———. 2005. "New Baltic Barometer VI: A Post-Enlargement Study." *Studies in Public Policy* 338. Glasgow: University of Strathclyde.

Roy, Olivier. 2000. *The New Central Asia: The Creation of Nations.* New York: New York University Press.

Rudenshiold, Eric. 1992. "Ethnic Dimensions in Contemporary Latvian Politics: Focusing Forces for Change." *Soviet Studies* 44, 4: 609–39.

Rumer, Boris, ed. 2000. *Central Asia and the New Global Economy.* New York: M. E. Sharpe.

Rumer, Eugene, Dmitri Trenin, and Huasheng Zhao. 2007. *Central Asia: Views from Washington, Moscow, and Beijing.* New York: M. E. Sharpe.

Rywkin, Michael. 1984. "National Symbiosis: Vitality, Religion, Identity, Allegiance." In Yaacov Ro'i, ed., *The USSR and the Muslim World: Issues in Domestic and Foreign Policy.* London: George Allen and Unwin, 3–15.

———. 1990. *Moscow's Muslim Challenge.* Armonk, N.Y.: M. E. Sharpe.

———. 1994. *Moscow's Lost Empire.* New York: M. E. Sharpe.

Saleniece, Irena, and Sergei Kuznetsovs. 1999. "Nationality Policy, Education and the Russian Question in Latvia Since 1918." In Christopher Williams and Thanasis D. Sfikas, eds., *Ethnicity and Nationalism in Russia, the CIS and the Baltic States.* Hants: Ashgate Publishing Company, 236–63.

Saroyan, Mark. 1997. "Islamic Clergy and Community in the Soviet Union." In Edward W. Walker, ed., *Minorities, Mullahs, and Modernity: Reshaping Community in the Former Soviet Union.* Berkeley: International and Area Studies, University of California, 43–56.

Schatz, Edward. 2000. "Framing Strategies and Non-Conflict in Multi-Ethnic Kazakhstan." *Nationalism and Ethnic Politics* 6, 2 (Summer): 71–94.

———. 2004. *Modern Clan Politics: The Power of "Blood" in Kazakhstan and Beyond.* Seattle: University of Washington Press.

———. 2004. "What Capital Cities Say About State and Nation Building." *Nationalism and Ethnic Politics* 9: 111–40.

Schroeder, Gertrude E. 1990. "Nationalities and the Soviet Economy." In Lubomyr Hajda and Mark Beissinger, eds., *The Nationalities Factor in Soviet Politics and Society.* Boulder, Colo.: Westview Press, 43–71.

Shryock, Richard. 1977. "Indigenous Economic Managers." In Edward Allworth, ed., *Nationality Group Survival in Multi-Ethnic States: Shifting Support Patterns in the Soviet Baltic Region.* New York: Praeger, 83–122.

Skultans, Vieda. 1998. *The Testimony of Lives: Narrative and Memory in Post-Soviet Latvia.* London: Routledge.

Smith, David J., Artis Pabriks, Aldis Purs, and Thomas Lane. 2002. *The Baltic States: Estonia, Latvia, and Lithuania.* London: Routledge.

Smith, Graham. 1990. "Latvians." In Graham Smith, ed., *The Nationalities Question in the Soviet Union.* London: Longman Group, 54–71.

———. 1990. "Nationalities Policy from Lenin to Gorbachev." In Graham Smith, ed., *The Nationalities Question in the Soviet Union.* London: Longman Group, 1–20.

———. 1996. "The Ethnic Democracy Thesis and the Citizenship Question in Estonia and Latvia." *Nationalities Papers* 24, 2: 199–216.

———. 1996. "When Nations Challenge and Nations Rule: Estonia and Latvia as Ethnic Democracies." *International Politics* 33 (March): 27–43.

———. 1999. "Transnational Politics and the Politics of the Russian Diaspora." *Ethnic and Racial Studies* 22, 3 (3 May): 500–523.

Smith, Graham, and Andrew Wilson. 1997. "Rethinking Russia's Post-Soviet Diaspora: The Potential for Political Mobilization in Eastern Ukraine and North-east Estonia." *Europe-Asia Studies* 49, 5: 845–64.

Smooha, Sammy. 1990. "Minority Status in an Ethnic Democracy: The Status of the Arab Minority in Israel." *Ethnic and Racial Studies* 13, 3 (July): 389–413.

———. 2002. "The Model of Ethnic Democracy: Israel as a Jewish and Democratic State." *Nations and Nationalism* 8, 4: 475–503.

———. 2002. "Types of Democracy and Modes of Conflict Management in Ethnically Divided Societies." *Nations and Nationalism* 8, 4: 423–31.

Snow, David A., and Robert D. Benford. 1992. "Master Frames and Cycles of Protest." In Aldon Morris and Carol McClurg Mueller, eds., *Frontiers in Social Movement Theory.* New Haven, Conn.: Yale University Press.

Society Integration and Business: The Ethnic Dimension. 2004. Riga: Baltic Institute of Social Sciences, Latvian Academy of Sciences Institute of Economics.

Spechler, Martin C. 2008. "The Economies of Central Asia: A Survey." *Comparative Economic Studies* 50: 30–52.

Stark, David, and Laszlo Bruszt. 1998. *Postsocialist Pathways: Transforming Politics and Property in East Central Europe.* Cambridge: Cambridge University Press.

Statistical Yearbook of Latvia 2000. 2000. Riga: Central Statistical Bureau of Latvia.

Statistical Yearbook of Latvia 2004. 2004. Riga: Central Statistical Bureau of Latvia.

Steen, Anton. 2000. "Ethnic Relations, Elites and Democracy in the Baltic States." *Journal of Communist Studies and Transition Politics* 16, 4 (December): 68–87.

Suny, Ronald Grigor. 1988–89. "Nationalist and Ethnic Unrest in the Soviet Union." *World Policy Journal* 6: 503–27.

———. 1993. *The Revenge of the Past: Nationalism, Revolution, and the Collapse of the Soviet Union.* Stanford, Calif.: Stanford University Press.

———. 1998. *The Soviet Experiment: Russia, the USSR, and the Successor States.* New York: Oxford University Press.

Tarrow, Sidney. 1998. *Power in Movement: Social Movements and Contentious Politics.* Cambridge: Cambridge University Press.

Tazmini, Ghoncheh. 2001. "The Islamic Revival in Central Asia: A Potent Force or a Misconception?" *Central Asian Survey* 20, 1: 63–83.

Thelen, Kathleen. 2003. "How Institutions Evolve: Insights from Comparative Historical Analysis." In James Mahoney and Dietrich Reuschemeyer, eds., *Comparative Historical Analysis in the Social Sciences.* Cambridge: Cambridge University Press, 208–40.

Thelen, Kathleen, and Sven Steinmo. 1992. "Historical Institutionalism in Comparative Politics." In Sven Steinmo, Kathleen Thelen, and Frank Longstreth, eds., *Structuring Politics: Historical Institutionalism in Comparative Analysis.* Cambridge: Cambridge University Press, 1–32.

Tishkov, Valery. 1995. " 'Don't Kill Me, I'm a Kyrgyz!': An Anthropological Analysis of Violence in the Osh Ethnic Conflict." *Journal of Peace Research* 32, 2: 133–49.

Voormann, Rein, and Jelena Helemae. 2003. "Ethnic Relations in Estonia's Post-Soviet Business Community." *Ethnicities* 3, 4 (December): 509–30.

Wolfel, Richard L. 2002. "North to Astana: Nationalistic Motives for the Movement of the Kazakh(stani) Capital." *Nationalities Papers* 30, 3: 485–506.

World Development Indicators, 2003. 2003. Washington, D.C.: International Bank for Reconstruction and Development/World Bank.

Zaslavsky, Victor. 1993. "Success and Collapse: Traditional Soviet Nationality Policy." In Ian Bremmer and Ray Taras, eds., *Nations and Politics in the Soviet Successor States.* Cambridge: Cambridge University Press, 29–42.

Zevelev, Igor. 2001. *Russia and Its New Diasporas.* Washington, D.C.: United States Institute of Peace Press.

Russian-Language Sources

Books and Chapters in Books

Akaev, Askar. 1999. "Brat'ia na vse vremena." In A. I. Ivanov, ed., *Rossiiane v Kyrgyzstane.* Bishkek: Literaturnyi Kyrgyzstan, 8–14.

Belousov, Ia. P. 2001. "Russkie v Kazakhstane: Problemy i perspectivy." In V. D. Kurganskaya, ed., *Problemy sotsial'noi stabil'nosti v polietnicheskom obshchestve.* Almaty: Center for Liberal Arts Research, 199–206.

Erofeeva, I. 1999. "Regional'nyi aspekt slavianskoi migratsii iz Kazakhstana." In A. R. Viatkina, N. P. Kosmarskoi, and C. A. Panarina, eds., *V dvizhenii dobrovol'-nom i vynuzhdennom.* Moskva: Natalis Press, 154–79.

Khaug, V. 2004. "Demograficheskie tendentsii, formirovanie natsii i mezhetnicheskie otnosheniia v Kyrgyzstane." In Z. Kudabaev, M. Giio, and M. Denisenko, eds., *Naselenie Kyrgyzstana.* Bishkek: Natsional'nyi statisticheskii komitet Kyrgyzskoii Respubliki, 109–57.

Kosmarskaia, N. 1999. "Khotiat li Russkie v Rossiiu?" In A. R. Viatkina, N. P. Kosmarskoi, and C. A. Panarina, eds., *V dvizhenii dobrovol'nom i vynuzhdennom.* Moskva: Natalis Press, 180–214.

Kumskov, G. V. 2000. "Vozdeistvie migratsii russkoizychnovo naseleniia na sotsi-al'no-ekonomicheskuiu sferu Kyrgyzstana." In *Vneshniaia migratsiia russkoia-zychnogo naseleniia Kyrgyzstana: Problemy i posledstviia*. Bishkek: Ilim, 80–88.
————. 2002. *Zakonomernosti i osobennosti razvitiia migratsionnykh protsessov Kyrgyz-stana na sovremennom etape*. Bishkek: Ilim.
Kurganskaia, Valentina Dmitrievna. 2004. *Pravosoznanie etnicheskikh grupp Kazakh-stana: Sotsiokul'turnyi kontekst formirovaniia*. Almaty: Tsentr gumanitarnykh issledovanii.
Nazarova, Svetlana. 2005. *Ne ostavliaite na potom* . . . . Almaty: Stikhotvoreniia.
Nemeshina, L. IU. 2002. "Russkii faktor v Kyrgyzstane." In G. N. Khlypenko, ed., *Russkie v Kyrgyzstane: Nauchno-issledovatel'skie stat'i i materealy*. Bishkek: NII Regional'nogo Slavianovedeniia KRSU, 110–20.
Orusbaev, A. O. 2002. "Sud'ba russkogo iazyka v Kirgizii." In G. N. Khlypenko, ed., *Russkie v Kyrgyzstane: Nauchno-issledovatel'skie stat'i i materealy*. Bishkek: NII Regional'nogo Slavianovedeniia KRSU, 153–65.
Ostapchuk, V. I. 2000. "Migratsionnaia i demograficheskaia situatsiia v Kirgiz-stane." In *Vneshniaia migratsiia russkoiazychnogo naseleniia Kyrgyzstana: Problemy i posledstviia*. Bishkek: Ilim, 35–41.
Ostapenko, L. V. 1995. "Voprosy trudovoi zaniatosti." In S. S. Savoskul, A. I. Ginzburg, M. N. Gulboglo, and V. A. Tishkov, *Russkie v novom zarybezh'e: Kyr-gyziia*. Moskva: Mezhdistsiplinarnyi akademicheskii tsentr sotsial'nykh nauk, 87–143.
Pliner, Iakov G. 1998. *Sozvezdie problem obrazovaniia*. Riga: Latviiskii institut pravo-vykh issledovanii.
Ploskikh, V. M., and V. A. Voropaeva. 2000. "Kyrgyzsko-rossiiskie otnosheniia: K probleme migratsionnkh protsessov." In *Vneshniaia migratsiia russkoiazychnogo naseleniia Kyrgyzstana: Problemy i posledstviia*. Bishkek: Ilim, 42–50.
Rubiks, Al'fred. 2001. *Trebuiu priznat' nevinovnym!* Moscow: Mezhdunarodnye otnosheniia.
Torgasheva, L. M. 2000. "Vliianie migratsionnykh protsessov na demogra-ficheskuiu situatsiiu v Kyrgyskoi Respublike." In *Vneshniaia migratsiia russkoia-zychnogo naseleniia Kyrgyzstana: Problemy i posledstviia*. Bishkek: Ilim, 58–65.

Newspaper and Journal Articles

Akchurin, V. 2004. "Ukrotit' Beg." *Slovo Kyrgyzstana*, 14 May: 9.
Baigazin, Meiram. 2004. "Migratsionnaia situatsiia v Kazakhstane." *Tsentral'naia Aziia i Kavkaz* 5, 35: 195–96.
Brusilovskaia, Elena. 2000. "Poligon dlia demokratii." *Argumenti i Fakti*, no. 4 (January): 1, 3.
Chuianova, Elina. 2004. "O Latviia, pechalen tvoi udel!" *Chas*, 12 February: 2.
————. 2004. "Daugava razdelila obshchestvo." *Chas*, 3 May: 2.
————. 2004. "Vmeste my budem sil'nee." *Chas*, 2 September: 2.
Dzhaganova, Antynshash. 1999. "Vernost' otchei zemle." *Kazakhstanskaia Pravda*, 23 October: 2.
Dzhaganovu, Altynshash. 2003. Interview in *Kazakhstanskaia Pravda*, 16 January: 3.
Elkin, A. 1999. "G. Ulmanis: 'Na grazhdanstve ne ostanovimcia.'" *CM*, 15 Octo-ber: 3.
"Eto vybor epokhi." 2000. *Slovo Kyrygzstana*, 27 April: 1–7.
Fedoseev, Leonid. 2004. "Chego khotiat russkie Latvii?" *Chas*, 6 March: 1.

Isaev, K., and G. Gorborukova. 1997. "Migratsiia: Problemy i perspectivy." *Ekho Nauki*, 2–3: 125.

Iurasov, Aleksandr. 1998. "Etnorossiiane v Kyrgyzstane: Novye tendentsii i perspectivy v razvitii." *Informatsionno-Analiticheskaia Gazeta*, no. 1 (March): 3.

Ivanov, Viacheslav. 2004. "Golodaite—vlastiam vse ravno." *Chas*, 14 September: 1.

———. 2004. "Pochemu my reshili golodat'." *Chas*, 23 August: 2.

———. 2004. "V Rige moratoria ne budet." *Chas*, 26 May: 4.

Izdibaev, Tulegen. 1999. "Zakon o migratsii v Kazakhstane fakticheski ne ispolnizetsia." *Panorama*, 24 December: 4.

Karimov, Daniar. 2004/2005. "Evgenii Kazarinov: Rossiia dolzhna opredelit'-cia." *Vechernii Bishkek*, 29 April: 4.

Kistanov, Valentin. 2004. "Natsional'nost' stala professiei." *Chas*, 21 May: 7.

Kokshetay, Λ. Eliukciova. 2005. "Russkii iazyk dolzhen byt gosudarstvennym." *Lad* 2, 126.

Korchagina, V. 1994. "Valerii Vishnevskii: Ia—ne 'natsmen'shinstvo.' Ia Russkii." *Vechernyi Bishkek*, 15 June: 2.

Kozlinskii, V. 1998. "Dooronbeka Sadyrbaeva prigovorili k smerti." *Vechernii Bishkek*, 6 January: 2.

Kustov, Igor. 1997. "Problema iazyka: Reaktsiia—migratsiia." *Res Publica*, 18 February: 3–4.

Loginova, N. 1995. "Sotsial'no-psikhologicheskaia adaptatsiia Russkikh v suverennom Kazakhstane." *Mysl'*, no. 7: 37–42.

Mamykin, Andrei. 2000. "Naturalizatsiia—eto ne strashno: Kak ia stal grazhdaninom Latvii." *Chas*, 23 August: 5.

"My ne raby!" 2004. *Chas*, 26 January: 1–2.

Oshkaia, Ina. 1998. "Narod Latvii vybiraet demokratiiu." *Respublika*, 5 October: 1.

"Pervyi den' evropy." 2004. *Chas*, 3 May: 1.

Petrov, Artem. 1999. "Nuzhny li bol'shoi Rossii Russkie iz malen'kogo Kyrgyzstana?" *Delo No.*, 10 November: 8.

———. 2000. "Russkie uezzhaiut." *Delo No.*, 19 January: 2.

"Problemy pereselentsev—problemy gosudarstva." 1998. *Kazakhstanskaia Pravda*, 27 May: 1.

Radionov, Vadim. 2004. Repshe: "Vsekh za reshetku!" *Chas*, 12 May: 1–2.

"Russkii vopros." 2005. *Vechernii Bishkek*, 19 April: 2.

Sadovskaia, Elena Iur'evna. 1998. "Vneshniaia migratsiia v Respublike Kazakhstan v 1990-e gody: Prichiny, posledstviia, prognoz." *Tsentral'naia Aziia iKul't-ura Mira*, no. 1: 55–69.

Savchenko, Kira. 2004. "Strasbur uznal nashikh." *Chas*, 22 July: 1.

Seiitbekov, T. 2004. "Ne pokidaute dom nash obshchii!" *Slovo Kyrgyzstana*, 5 March: 6.

Slashcheva, Tamara. 1995. "Velika Rossia, da otstupat' nekuda," *Res Publika*, 22 August: 3.

Sukhov, Aleksei. 2005. "Russkie v Kyrgyzstane: Uezzhat' ili ostavat'cy?" *Lad* 6, 130: 6.

"Takaia reforma nam ne nuzhna!" 2004. *Chas*, 29 January: 3.

Turisbekov, Zautbek. 1998. Interview in *Argumenty i Fakty* 46 (November): 3.

Tuzov, Aleksandr. 2005. "Chemodan, vokzal, Rossiia?" *Vechernii Bishkek*, 15 April: 5.

"V piketakh—i star i mlad." 2004. *Chas*, 16 April: 1.

Vasil'ev, Aleksandr. 1999. "Tikhii iskhod." *Chas*, 8 May: 4.
Vatolin, Igor'. 2004. "Nas obmanuli: Vperedi—'pustye shkoly.'" *Chas*, 23 January: 2.
———. 2004. "Protesty naractaiut—pravitel'stvu khot' by khny." *Chas*, 16 April: 4.
———. 2004. "Russkaia obshchina: Kakoi ei byt'?" *Chas*, 8 May: 2.
Vishnevskii, V. V. 1998. "Migratsiia naseleniiz Kirgizii: Prichiny i sledstviia." *Res Publica*, 3–9 November: 3.
———. 1998. "Vybrannyi mekhanizm golosovaniia—neuvazhenie k narody." *Res Publica*, 2 November: 2.
"Zadacha—pomoch' oralmanam." 2003. *Kazakhstanskaia Pravda*, 16 January: 3.

Legislation (in chronological order)

Zakon Latviiskoi Sovetskoi Sotsialisticheskoi Respubliki o iazykakh. 5 May 1989. In *Verkhovnogo Soveta i Pravitel'stva Latviiskoi Sovetskoi Sotsialisticheskoi Respubliki* 20 (18 May 1989): 510–14.
Zakon o gosudarstvennom iazyke Kirgizskoi SSR. 23 September 1989.
Zakon o grazhdanstve Kyrgyzskoi Respubliki. 26 October 1990.
Zakon ob obrazovanii. 19 June 1991. In *Prava cheloveka: Sbornik zakonodatel'nykh aktov i informativnogo materiala*. Riga: Commission for Human Rights and Public Affairs, 1997, 49–63.
Postanovlenie Verkhovnoga Soveta Latviiskoi Respubliki, o vosstanovlenii prav grazhdan Latviiskoi Respubliki i osnovnykh usloviiakh naturalizatsii. 15 September 1991. In *Vedomosti Verkhovnogo Soveta i Pravitel'stva Latviiskoi Respubliki* 43 (31 October 1991): 2128.
Konstitutsiia Latviiskoi Respubliki. 15 February 1992. In *Prava cheloveka: Sbornik zakonodatel'nykh aktov i informativnogo materiala*. Riga: Commission for Human Rights and Public Affairs, 1997. 9–13.
Zakon Latviiskoi Respubliki o iazykakh. 31 March 1992. In *Verkhovnogo Soveta i Pravitel'stva Latviiskoi Respubliki* 17 (23 April 1992): 938–42.
Postanovlenie kabineta ministrov Respubliki Kazakhstan o merakh po realizatsii postonovleniia Verkhovhogo Soveta Respubliki Kazakhstan "o vvedenii v deistvie zakona Respubliki Kazakhstan 'ob immigratsii.'" 15 December 1992.
Zakon Respubliki Kyrgyzstan ob obrazovanii. December 1992 and November 1997 revised.
Konstitutsiia Respubliki Kazakhstan. 28 January 1993.
Zakon o grazhdanstve Kyrgyzskoi Respubliki. 18 December 1993.
Ukaz prezidenta Kyrgyzskoi Respubliki o merakh po regulirovaniiu migratsionnykh protsessov v Kyrgyzskoi Respublike. 14 June 1994.
Zakon o grazhdanstve. 22 July 1994. In *Prava cheloveka: Sbornik zakonodatel'nykh aktov i informativnogo materiala*. Riga: Commission for Human Rights and Public Affairs, 1997. 25–32.
Postanovlenie kabineta ministrov Respubliki Kazakhstan ob utverzhdenii poriadka sozdaniia immigratsionnogo zemel'nogo fonda. 2 August 1994.
Pravitel'stvo Kyrgyzskoi Respubliki Postanovlenie, o realizatsii ukaza prezidenta Kyrgyzskoi Respubliki A. Akaeva "o merakh po regulirovaniiu migratsionnogo protsessa v Kyrgyzskoi Respublike." 1 September 1994.
Zakon o statuse grazhdan byvshego SSR, ne imeiushchikh grazhdanstva Latvii ili drugogo gosudarstva. 25 April 1995. In *Prava cheloveka: Sbornik zakonodatel'nykh aktov i*

informativnogo materiala. Riga: Commission for Human Rights and Public Affairs, 1997. 33–35.

Ukaz prezidenta Respubliki Kazakhstan ob osnovnykh napravleniiakh migratsionnoi politiki do 2000 goda. 19 March 1997.

Ukaz prezidenta Respubliki Kazakhstan o kvote immigratsii na 1997 god. 27 March 1997.

Ukaz prezidenta Respubliki Kazakhstan o kvote immigratsii na 1998 god. 3 April 1997.

Zakon Respubliki Kazakhstan o migratsii naseleniia. 13 December 1997.

Zakon ob obshchem obrazovanii. 10 June 1998.

Izmeneniia v satverstve Latviiskoi Respubliki. 23 October 1998. In *Diena* (4 November 1998): 1.

Izmeneniia v zakone o grazhdanstve. In *Diena* (4 November 1998): 2.

Zakon ob obrazovanii. 17 November 1998.

Integratsiia obshchestva v Latvii: kontseptsiia gosudarstvennoi programmy. Riga: Upravlenie Naturalizatsii Latviiskoi Respubliki, 1999.

Konstitutsiia Kyrgyzskoi Respubliki. Bishkek: Raritet Info., 1999.

Pravitel'stvo Kyrgyzskoi Respubliki Postanovlenie, o voprosakh dal'neishego razvitiia gosudarstvennogo iazika Kyrgyzskoi Respubliki. 7 April 1999.

Zakon Respubliki Kyrgyzstan o gosudarstvennoi sluzhbe. 30 November 1999.

Zakon o gosudarstvennom iazyke. 21 December 1999. In *Diena* (29 December 1999): 1–2.

Zakon Kyrgyzskoi Respubliki ob ofitsial'nom iazyke Kyrgyzskoi Respubliki. 25 May 2000.

Programma razvitiia gosudarstvennogo iazyka Kyrgyzskoi Respubliki na 2000–2010 gody. 20 September 2000.

Zakon Respubliki Kazakhstan o politicheskuk partiiax. 15 July 2002.

Konstitutsiia Kyrgyzskoi Respubliki. 2003. Bishkek: Raritet Info., 2003.

Zakon ob obrazovanii (17 November 1998, *c izmeneniuami vnecennymi po sostoianiiu 5 Fevralia 2004 goda*).

Konstitutsiia Latviiskoi Respubliki. 2004. Riga: Business Information Bureau, 2004.

Zakon Kyrgyzskoi Respubliki o gosudarstvennom iazyke Kyrgyzskoi Respubliki. 12 February 2004.

Konstitutsiia Kyrgyzskoi Respubliki. 2006. http://www.president.kg/docs/const_2006v/.

Konstitutsiia Kyrgyzskoi Respubliki. 2007. Bishkek: Akademiia, 2008.

Statistics (in chronological order)

Itogi perepisi naseleniia 1989 goda po Latvii: Statisticheskii sbornik. 1989. Riga: Goskomstat Latviiskoi Respubliki.

Statisticheskii ezhegodnik Kyrgyzskoi Respubliki 1995 chast' 1. 1996. Bishkek: Natsional'nyi statisticheskii komitet Kyrgyzskoii Respubliki.

Kratkie itogi perepisi naseleniia 1999 goda v Respublike Kazakhstan. 1999. Almaty: Agentstvo Respubliki Kazakhstan po statistike.

Kyrgyzstan: Obshchaia otsenka sostoianiia strany. 1999. Bishkek: Tsentr sotsial'nykh i ekonomicheskikh issledovanii.

Osnovnye itogi Pervoi natsional'noi perepisi naseleniia Kyrgyzskoi Respubliki 1999 goda. 2000. Bishkek: Natsional'nyi statisticheskii komitet Kyrgyzskoi Respubliki.

Naselenie Kyrgyzstana, Itogi Pervoi natsional'noi perepisi naseleniia Kyrgyzskoi Respubliki 1999 goda v tablitsakh, Kniga II, chast' pervaia. 2000. Bishkek: Natsional'nyi statisticheskii komitet Kyrgyzskoi Respubliki.

Kyrgyzskaia gosudarstvennost' statistika vekov. 2003. Bishkek: Natsional'nyi statisticheskii komitet Kyrgyzskoii Respubliki.
Kazakhstan v tsifrakh 2004. 2004. Almaty: Agentstvo Respubliki Kazakhstan po statistike.
Kratkii statisticheskii ezhegodnik Kazakhstana 2004. 2004. Almaty: Agentstvo Respubliki Kazakhstan po statistike.

Miscellaneous

Partiia Ravnopravie: Kratko o programme, strukture, istorii. 2000. Riga: Editorial Commission of the Party.
Politicheskoe programmnoe zaiavlenie Sotsialisticheskoi partii Latvii. 30 October 1999.
Programma partii Narodnogo Soglasiia. 1997. Riga.
Programma "Russkoi Partii" Latvii na vybory v Rizhskuiu Gorodskuiu Dumu 9 marta 1997 goda.
Programma Sotsialisticheskoi partii Latvii. 15 January 1994.
Spisok chlenov soveta Assamblei Naroda Kyrgyzstana. 27 October 1998.
Ustav obshchestvennoi organizatsii Latviiskaia assotsiatsiia v podderzhku shkol c obucheniem na russkom iazyke. 1996. Riga.
Ustav Respublikanskoi Assotsiatsii Etnicheskikh Rossiian Kyrgyzskoi Respubliki "Soglasie." 1994. Bishkek.
Ustav Russkogo Obshchestva v Latvii. 1996. Riga.
Ustav Russkoi Obshchiny Latvii. 1992. Riga.

Web sites

http://www.adb.org/
http://www.ebrd.com/
http://www.freedomhouse.org/
http://www.legaltext.ee/indexen.htm
http://www.minelres.lv/
http://www.np.gov.lv/
http://www.worldbank.org/

Index

Aasland, Aadne, 78
accommodating nationalization: factors influencing, 21, 49; in Kyrgyzstan, 10, 11, 20, 48, 49, 59–61, 92, 150; perceived ethnic discrimination and, 21
affirmative action policies, 33, 43, 49, 74–75
agriculture: collectivization, 41; in Kazakh SSR, 39; in Kyrgyzstan, 53, 115; Russian labor, 38
Akayev, Askar: accommodating nationalization, 92, 150; campaign to reduce Russian exit, 59, 110, 120; citizenship policies, 53; Kyrgyz staff members, 72; language policies, 59–61, 100–101; regime, 109; resignation, 122, 207 n.27; Slavic University and, 151
all-Union referendum, 47
Almaty: likely permanent residents, 15; potential migrants, 15, 169; Russian population, 14, 91, 165; transfer of capital from, 164
amicable Russian voice, in Kyrgyzstan, 133, 134–36, 149–53
Aminzade, Ron, 137
Andropov, Yuri, 33
antagonistic nationalization: factors influencing, 21, 49; in Latvia, 10, 20, 48, 49, 80, 124–25; perceived ethnic discrimination and, 21; Russian responses, 80, 138–49
Antane, Aina, 80
Assembly of the Peoples of Kyrgyzstan, 150, 151
assimilation: fears of, 101–2, 137, 139; loyalty and, 23
Association for the Support of Russian-Language Schools (Latvia), 78, 82, 97, 140, 146, 147

Association of Ethnic Russians (Kyrgyzstan), 71, 86. *See also* Union of Russian Compatriots
Association of Latvian-Russian Cooperation, 73, 81–82, 140, 141–42
Astana: Russian population, 14; transfer of capital to, 164
authoritarian states, 7, 8, 109, 133

Bakiyev, Kurmanbek, 101, 109, 121, 207 n.27
Baltic republics: German out-migration, 49; industrialization, 40–41, 44; nationalism, 74–75; Russian in-migration, 40–41, 75; Russian minorities, 42, 44–46; Russification policies, 39–41, 45–46; Soviet control, 74–75. *See also* Estonia; Latvia
Berklavs, Eduards, 46
Bishkek Russians: fears for children's future, 120; on ideal post-Soviet society, 104, 105; interviews with, 13; Kyrgyz language skills, 57–58; likely permanent residents, 15; motives for migration, 117–23; perceived ethnic discrimination, 69; perceived rights violations, 98, 100–101, 102–3; perceptions of nationalization practices, 92–93; potential migrants, 14–15, 111; proportion of population, 13–14; Russian-speakers, 57–58; unemployment, 97–98. *See also* Kyrgyzstan, Russian minority; Russian perceptions
blame, sources of: concrete, in Latvia, 136–37, 143, 147; in Kyrgyzstan, 134–36, 150, 153
Braden, Kathleen, 115
Breuilly, John, 176

Islam (*continued*)
lel, 36–37; resurgence in Central Asia,
36; Soviet policies, 33–37

Kaiser, Robert, 22, 167
Karklins, Rasma, 49, 80
Kazakh ethnic system, 162, 168, 175
Kazakh language, 57
Kazakh nationalization: language policy,
57, 165; migration policies, 163; partial
control, 162, 168, 175; personnel policies and practices, 162–63, 165; Russian
perceptions of, 4–5, 154, 165–66; territorial administration policies, 163–64
Kazakh Soviet Socialist Republic (SSR):
agriculture, 39; *korenizatsiya* policies,
168; nomads, 34; Russian minority, 39,
42; Russification policies, 34, 168
Kazakhstan: capital, 164; clan politics, 86,
172; cultural icons, 91; discrimination
against Russians, 91; economic growth,
167; economic restructuring, 167; ethnic relations, 4–5, 163–64; immigration
quotas, 163; Islamic revival, 36; Kyrgyz
migrants in, 118–19; nongovernmental
organizations, 165–66; oil exports, 167;
Pugachev incident, 166–67; returning
Kazakhs (*oralmans*), 163, 216–17 n.46;
Russian exit, 168–71, 172, 175; Russian
middle class, 167–73; Russian population distribution, 14, 191 n.26; trading
partners, 52
KGB. *See* Communist Party, Komsomol,
and KGB in Soviet republics
Khalid, Adeeb, 36
Khrushchev, Nikita, 31–32, 36, 45, 46
Knight, Jack, 24
Kolsto, Pal, 79, 133, 155
Komsomol. *See* Communist Party, Komso-
mol, and KGB in Soviet republics
korenizatsiya (nativization) policies: in
Kazakh SSR, 168; in Kyrgyz SSR, 42,
84–85; in Soviet republics, 27–28, 30–
31, 34, 42, 43, 48–49
Kunabev, Abai, 91
Kuzio, Taras, 164
Kyrgyz citizenship policy, 54–55, 58
Kyrgyz education policy: higher-education
enrollment decisions, 103; languages
used in schools, 34, 61–62; Russian per-
ceptions of, 103; spending, 152

Kyrgyz ethnic system, 157–58, 173–74
Kyrgyzification, 116
Kyrgyz language: modernization, 60; official documents in, 60, 62, 100; promotion of, 60, 62, 115–16; spoken by
Russians, 57–58; as state language, 20,
58–63, 71; use in educational institutions, 34, 61; use under Soviet rule, 34
Kyrgyz language policy, 57–63; compared
to Latvian policy, 20, 67; employment
regulations, 58–59, 60, 71; languages
used in schools, 34, 61–62; perceived
rights violations, 100–101; preservation
of Russian, 20, 59–61, 110; Russian as
language of interethnic communication, 59; Russian as official language, 20,
59–63, 150; Russian perceptions of, 71,
100–101, 121–22
Kyrgyz nationalization: accommodating,
10, 11, 20, 48, 49, 59–61, 92, 150; citizenship policies, 54–55, 58; common home
slogan, 92; economic considerations,
52–53; formal policies, 73–74; informal
practices, 11, 73–74; national security
concerns, 52, 53–54; political hegemony
of elites, 157–58; Russian perceptions
of, 92–93, 99
Kyrgyz Soviet Socialist Republic (SSR): central government policies, 12; citizenship
policies, 53–54; education system, 85;
ethnic division of labor, 53, 98, 108, 110,
119; *korenizatsiya* policy, 42, 84–85; Kyrgyz proportion of population, 12, 42, 53,
85; language law, 58, 59; nomads, 34;
referendum on union, 48; Russian exit
from, 115–16; Russian minority, 12, 25,
39, 42, 53, 84–85; Russification policies,
34; titular dominance of state and party
organs, 25, 84–85; trade, 119
Kyrgyzstan: agriculture, 115; authoritarian
state, 7, 8; clan politics, 85–86, 122, 157;
constitution, 59, 71, 149; corruption,
115, 122–23, 152, 158; economic
growth, 111, 113, 114–15, 173–74; economic restructuring, 53, 85–86; ethnic
conflicts, 115–16; foreign policy, 52;
Freedom House scores, 108; GDP per
capita, 111, 112; human development
indicators, 111; industrial collapse, 104,
119; Islamic revival, 36; Kyrgyz proportion of population, 103; migration of

Kyrgyz, 118–19, 122; Ministry of Foreign Affairs, 92, 118; natural resources, 52; opportunity structures, 84–87; private sector, 86–87, 158; privatization, 85–86; trading partners, 52–53; Tulip Revolution, 8, 122, 133, 157, 207 n.27; unemployment, 104; Uzbek minority, 115–16, 215 n.13

Kyrgyzstan, Russian minority: amicable voice, 133, 134–36, 149–53; economic obstacles, 86–87; lack of political voice, 72; legal rights, 54; linguistic discrimination, 68–72; nongovernmental organizations, 73, 86–87, 134, 149; opportunity structures, 11; political parties, 87; population distribution, 13–14, 190 n.24. *See also* Bishkek Russians; Russian exit from Kyrgyzstan

labor force: agricultural, 38; ethnic division of labor, 53, 98, 108, 110, 119; skilled workers, 38–39, 43, 108, 110, 174; unemployment, 97–98, 104; wages, 96. *See also* personnel policies and practices; public sector employment

labor markets, discrimination in, 9, 66–74

Lad, 165–66, 171

Laitin, David, 22, 23

language policies: distributional consequences, 57; effects on Russian minorities, 20; in former Soviet republics, 19–21; rights violations, 100–101; of Soviet Union, 19, 34. *See also* education, languages used in; Kyrgyz language policy; Latvian language policy

languages: of interethnic communication, 19, 20, 59, 63; Kazakh, 57; official, 19, 20, 59, 60–63, 150; state, 19–20, 58–64, 71, 159; titular, 19–20. *See also* Kyrgyz language; Latvian language; Russian language

Lapidus, Gail, 28

latovichi (Russified Latvians), 40, 46

Latvia: cities, 14; constitution, 65, 202 n.63; economic growth, 104, 128–29, 130, 132; economic restructuring, 123–24, 161; ethnic segregation in businesses, 75, 81–83, 161; EU membership, 53, 54, 56, 133, 134, 147–48; foreign direct investment, 132; foreign policy, 53–54; Freedom House scores, 108; GDP per

capita, 129, 131; human development indicators, 129; independence from Soviet Union, 47; independence in interwar years, 40, 45–46; industrial collapse, 123; natural resources, 129, 132; parliament, 159–60; privatization, 57, 77–78, 161; Soviet annexation, 40, 198 n.90; trading partners, 54; wages, 96; Western orientation, 53–54

Latvia, Russian minority: economic power, 80; fears, 101–2, 137, 139; legal rights, 55–57; linguistic discrimination, 68–70, 82; noncitizens as Negroes, 100, 144; nongovernmental organizations, 11–12, 79–82, 102, 133, 136, 138–42, 147; opportunity structures, 11–12, 76–84, 175; political parties, 11–12, 73, 80, 82–84, 102, 133, 136, 138, 142–45; population distribution, 14, 190–91 n.25; socioeconomic position, 84, 132; views of future, 101–2. *See also* Riga Russians; Russian exit from Latvia

Latvian citizenship policy, 55–57; compared to Kyrgyz policy, 58; government ruling of 1991, 56, 124–25; language requirements, 56, 159; naturalization fees, 57, 96; naturalization procedures, 56, 57, 95–96, 100, 138, 159; opposition, 144; referendum on, 56, 138; restrictions on noncitizens, 56–57, 127; ruling of 1991, 144, 159; Russian perceptions of, 95–96, 100, 105, 124–25, 138, 144

Latvian Communist Party, 40, 41, 45, 46, 83

Latvian education policy: languages used in schools, 61–63, 65–66, 96–97, 101, 126–27, 142–43; law of 1998, 65–66; law of 2004, 146–48; opposition, 144, 146–48; Russian demonstrations against, 80, 137, 146–48; Russian-language schools, 102, 126–27, 140, 142–45, 162; Russian perceptions of, 96–97, 102–3, 105, 136–38

Latvian ethnic system, 158–62, 175

Latvian Human Rights Committee, 127

Latvian language: development of, 64; required use, 63, 202 n.65; as state language, 20, 63–64, 159, 202 n.63; use in Soviet era, 41, 45, 47

Latvian language policy, 63–66; compared to Kyrgyz policy, 20, 67; expanded use of Latvian, 63–64; impact on Russians, 94–97, 101–2, 125–26; languages used in

Acknowledgments

This book is the result of years of work that I would never have accomplished without the help, generosity, and kindness of numerous people. Though there are too many individuals to thank and many individuals whom I will not formally thank out of concern for their safety, I would like to express my sincere gratitude to friends, acquaintances, and colleagues in the United States, Kyrgyzstan, Kazakhstan, and Latvia. Before doing so, however, I would like to acknowledge the generous financial assistance I received from Middlebury College, the Academy for Education Development, the Institute of International Education, the International Research and Exchange Board, the National Science Foundation, and the United States Institute of Peace. Each organization has funded a piece of this project, and I am eternally grateful for that support.

There are a few friends I would like to single out. Steven Cook and Ann Tappert provided, and continue to provide, friendship, encouragement, advice, and intellectual inspiration. In so doing, they both contributed to the evolution of this manuscript, and I thank them for their support. Dawne Deppe and I spent a great deal of valuable time together in Central Asia while she worked for an international development firm and I conducted research. Although we had very different reasons for being in the region, we shared a love for that part of the world.

A plethora of academics contributed to the progression of the manuscript. Thomas Callaghy, Ian Lustick, and Rudra Sil encouraged long-term fieldwork, rigid comparative analysis of multiple cases, and succinct writing. Charles King and James Goldgeier commented on various drafts of the manuscript. Other scholars, including Stephen Hanson, Pauline Jones Luong, Kelly McMann, and Edward Schatz, responded to conference papers I wrote that appear, in some form, in this book. Two anonymous reviewers of this manuscript provided an unusual number of constructive, substantive comments. They obviously put a great deal of effort into their reviews, and I thank them tremendously.

I would also like to thank the wonderful people I worked with at the University of Pennsylvania Press. The acquisitions editor, Peter Agree, and the series editor, Brendan O'Leary, took this project on with enthusiasm. Erica Ginsburg, from the Editing and Production Department, was extremely helpful when it came to the copyediting stage and extremely generous when it came to extending deadlines.

I am grateful to my colleagues—both faculty and staff—at the University of Vermont. They have, since I arrived in 2006, been incredibly supportive of this project. I thank my department for giving me the time, space, and intellectual drive to finish writing this book. I have benefited as well from my colleagues' sound advice.

I cannot thank the hundreds of individuals I interviewed in Kyrgyzstan, Kazakhstan, and Latvia enough. Because of the sensitive nature of our discussions I will not name them. However, I would like to thank them collectively. This book would not exist had it not been for their willingness to discuss their personal views and spend a great deal of time with me. In addition, I am grateful to the librarians who helped me find relevant material and to the women who ran the photocopy machines in the local libraries; their patience and sense of humor got me through long, sometimes frustrating days. Local friends and acquaintances helped me through those long, sometimes frustrating days as well. I had the pleasure of socializing with them often, and I treasure their hospitality, willingness to help me in any way possible, and genuine friendship.

Last, but certainly not least, is my family. My parents not only taught me the priceless value of education but also remained supportive throughout the various stages of this book. In other words, they were there from the beginning to the end. My sister provided support throughout the process, although I am sure she wondered at times why I was so dedicated to studying Russian minority populations in various parts of the world. I always enjoyed staying with her in New York or Connecticut while I attended Association for the Study of Nationalities Conferences, where I presented versions of chapters of this book. Finally, I'd like to thank my husband's aunt, Andrea, a former English teacher, who kindly read through the entire manuscript in search of errors.

I dedicate this book to my husband, Michael David Glod, and our daughter, Nadia Grace Glod. Mike was essential to the completion of this project. His insightful comments, thought-provoking questions, and amazing ability to listen and analyze contributed to its final version. I thank Mike for being my best friend, supporting the project, and reminding me when things got rough that there was a light at the end of the tunnel. Nadia arrived two weeks before her due date, just as I was wrapping up my review of the copyedited version of the manuscript. The joy she brought every day as a beautiful newborn inspired me to finish this project. Thank you, Mike and Nadia.